100 Nature Walks

100 Nature Walks

National Trust

First published in the United Kingdom in 2021 by

National Trust Books
An imprint of HarperCollins Publishers,
1 London Bridge Street
London SE1 9GF www.harpercollins.co.uk

HarperCollins Publishers
Macken House, 39/40 Mayor Street Upper, Dublin 1,
D01 C9W8, Ireland

Text based on *Great British Seasonal Walks*, originally
published by National Trust Books in 2018.

The National Trust is a registered charity, no. 205846

ISBN: 978-1911657-20-0

A CIP catalogue record for this book is available from
the British Library

10 9 8 7 6 5 4

Printed by Replika Press, India

Title page: Wildflowers at Wicken Fen,
Cambridgeshire (walk 31).
Left: View across the Big Pool towards the house at
Dudmaston Estate, Shropshire (walk 41).
Overleaf: Fallow deer at the Crom Estate,
County Fermanagh (walk 86).

If you would like to comment on any aspect of this
book, please contact us at the above address or
national.trust@harpercollins.co.uk

National Trust publications are available at National
Trust shops or online at nationaltrustbooks.co.uk

Contents

North West

North East

Northern Ireland

Scotland

Introduction: 100 Nature Walks

The British coast and countryside in all its natural variety is one of our greatest assets: from the stark, upland landscape of the Brecon Beacons in Powys, to the lush and violet beauty of the Suffolk heathlands; the rugged coastline of Cornwall to the tranquil bays of County Fermanagh; and the snow-capped peaks of the Lake District to the buttercup meadows of Gloucestershire.

The National Trust cares for over 618,000 acres (250,000ha) of land, almost 780 miles (1,255km) of coastline, and more than 300 historic buildings across England, Wales and Northern Ireland. So whether you want to see ancient woodlands, dramatic cliff-tops, picturesque parklands, wild trails or landscaped gardens, you are spoilt for choice when it comes to finding a walk at a National Trust place.

This guide features 100 walks organised by region, so wherever you are, at whatever time of year, you will be able to find the perfect nature walk – be it butterflies on the Isle of Wight, orchids at Calke Abbey or red squirrels at Formby.

100 Nature Walks also showcases walks at properties in Scotland (walks 97–100), with kind permission from the National Trust for Scotland, with routes from four stunning locations.

Above: Bluebells in flower in Leigh Woods, Bristol (walk 7).

About the Walks

For each region, the walks cover a range of points of interest, be they habitat, flora, fauna or conservation, as well as archaeology, architecture or stunning views. Many walks featured celebrate the richness of important UK habitats and the wealth of wildlife they support, including woodland (walks 7, 22 and 95), heathland (walks 11, 34 and 49), coasts (walks 5, 51 and 88) and wetlands (walks 21, 36 and 75). Many of these areas have been designated Sites of Special Scientific Interest and the National Trust works hard to maintain, restore and improve these places for future generations. Other walks focus on birdlife (walks 2, 31 and 71), ancient trees (walks 4, 17 and 59), rare flora (walks 1, 46 and 78), wildflower displays (walks 19, 32 and 66) or much-loved mammals such as deers, otters and red squirrels (walks 12, 50, 80 and 94).

Nearly all the walks are circular, many with cafés and restaurants along the way. General advice about getting to your starting point is provided, along with postcodes for satellite navigation, and although some areas are too remote to make it a viable option, public transport details are available online at www.traveline.org.uk. Also provided are suggestions for local attractions that will help you make the most of your day, such as nearby gardens, castles, country houses and exhibitions, along with information on the all-important availability of toilet facilities.

Many of the walks are suitable for families, with some shorter strolls included, designed specifically with younger children in mind – look out for the family-friendly symbol against appropriate walks

Above: A red squirrel on Brownsea Island, Poole Harbour, Dorset (walk 12).

(see key below). To help you judge which walks might best suit your needs, they are graded according to their level of ease, from easy walks with even paths and few inclines, steps and stiles, through moderate walks with more uneven paths and some steeper climbs, to challenging walks for more adventurous ramblers. Some walks in particular can become very muddy after rain, so look out for the symbol highlighting the need for wellies or walking boots.

Many more walks are available at National Trust places. Visit: www.nationaltrust.org.uk/walking.

Key to walk symbols

- Easy walk
- Moderate walk
- Challenging walk
- Family-friendly walk
- Muddy after rain

Key to map symbols

- ••••• Walk route
- —— Road
- ——— Railway
- **P** Parking
- **WC** Toilets
- **i** Information

- **PH** Public house
- **❚❙** Café/restaurant
- Country house
- Castle
- Museum

Walking Hints and Tips

- Consider taking a mobile phone with you, bearing in mind coverage can be patchy in rural areas.
- If you are walking alone, let someone know where you are and when you expect to return.
- It's advisable to take an Ordnance Survey map with you on country walks to supplement the maps provided.
- Some of the walks take you along small country lanes without pavements. Always walk facing oncoming traffic (except when approaching a right-hand bend, when it is advisable to cross the road for a clear view), keep children and dogs under close control, and wear something light or brightly coloured when visibility is poor (for example at dusk).
- Take special care of children when walking beside water or along cliff-tops.
- Public transport may also change over time, so, if you're thinking of taking a bus or train to your destination, always check timetables and routes online or with a local tourist information centre before setting out.

Follow the Countryside Code

Here's how to respect, protect and enjoy the countryside:

- Always park sensibly, making sure that your vehicle is not blocking access to drives, fields and farm tracks.
- Leave gates as you find them or follow instructions on signs. If walking in a group, make sure the last person knows how to leave the gate.
- In fields where crops are growing, follow the paths wherever possible.
- Don't leave litter and leftover food – it spoils the beauty of the countryside and can be dangerous to wildlife and farm animals, too.
- Avoid damaging, destroying or removing flowers, trees or even rocks: they provide homes for wildlife and add to everyone's enjoyment of the countryside.
- Don't get too close to wild animals or farm animals as they can behave unpredictably.
- Be careful not to drop a match or smouldering cigarette at any time of the year, as this can cause fires.
- Keep dogs under control (see opposite).

Colourful heathland looking towards the sea at Dunwich Heath, Suffolk (walk 34).

50 things to do before you're 11¾

To add to the fun of a family walk, check out '50 things to do before you're 11¾', which encourages kids to discover their wild side and get closer to nature by getting to know a tree, roll down a really big hill, make a home for wildlife or keep a nature diary. To find out more, visit the National Trust website at www.50things.org.uk where children can register for free.

Be dog wise

Please help the National Trust keep the countryside a safe, healthy and enjoyable place for you and your dog, as well as other visitors, wildlife and livestock:

- Always keep your dog in sight and under control, using a lead if requested. (See 'About this walk' feature on individual walks for specific information regarding the control of dogs.)

- Never let your dog chase wildlife or farm animals.

- Observe local notices when you're out and about. There may be restrictions in woodland or on farmland at sensitive times of year, like in spring, during the lambing season, and between the beginning of March and the end of July when ground-nesting birds are on eggs or raising their young.

- Please always pick up after your dog. We ask that if your dog fouls, particularly in car parks, on paths and by picnic spots, you pick up and remove the mess. At some of our sites we've got dedicated dog-mess bins where you can dispose of it.

Above: Wildflowers blooming in the garden at Mount Stewart, County Down (walk 94).
Overleaf: A view across the marram grass and sand dunes at Formby, Merseyside (walk 61).

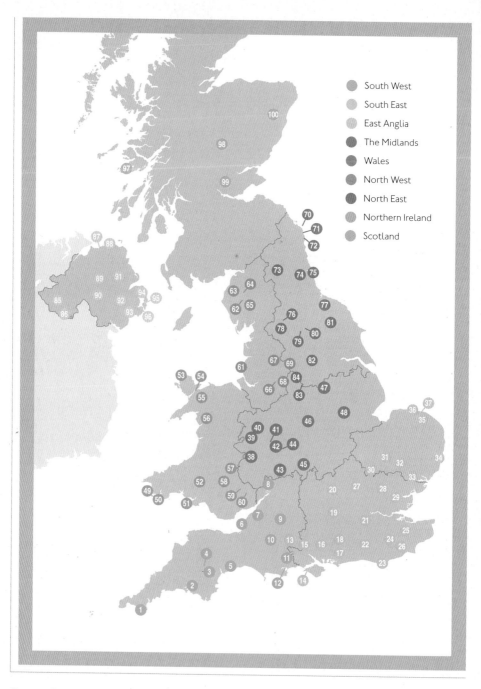

Legend:
- South West
- South East
- East Anglia
- The Midlands
- Wales
- North West
- North East
- Northern Ireland
- Scotland

Opposite: Kynance Cove on the Lizard Peninsula, Cornwall (walk 1).

South West

1. Lizard Rarity Walk

This short walk follows a section of the stunning west coast of the Lizard Peninsula. It takes in breathtaking coastal scenery, traditional agriculture and some of the unique flora and fauna found on The Lizard, including rare clovers and the iconic Cornish chough.

Predannack
Cornwall
TR12 7EZ
01326 222170
lizard@nationaltrust.org.uk

About this walk
Wildflower displays
Unique flora
Wildlife interest
Breathtaking views
Some steep climbs
Dogs welcome; keep under close control near livestock

Distance 1 mile (1.6km)
Time 30–40 mins

Things to see

Above: Upright clover growing at The Lizard.

Rare Flora

The Lizard Peninsula is one of the UK's top sites for rare plants. The remarkable flora is partly due to the unusual geology, including rare serpentine rock and the strange soil conditions it generates, but uncommon species, such as the upright and twin-headed clovers and fringed rupturewort, also grow on the schist and other rock types. The mild winter weather, low summer rainfall and autumn gales also affect the flora that grow there. In early summer these cliffs are swathed in wildflowers: spring squill (and autumn squill in late summer), green winged orchids and the more common thrift and sea campion.

Farming Practices

The wonderful nature conservation and landscape of The Lizard draws thousands of visitors every year, but what the casual visitor may not know is that these wonderful attractions owe everything to farming. If left unmanaged, the coast and the wider Lizard would be overrun with scrub and bramble, which would outcompete the more delicate rare species and make paths impenetrable to the walker. Grazing by tough breeds like Dexter cattle creates the conditions for these species to survive, and the resulting meat is especially tasty as it's slower grown and more naturally fed.

Above: Rugged rocky cliffs near Predannack Head on the South West Coast Path between Mullion and Kynance Cove, Cornwall.

How to Get There

By Train Redruth 20 miles (32.1 km)

By Car From Helston, take A3083 towards The Lizard. After about 5 miles (8km), turn right, opposite Mullion Holiday Park, towards Mullion village. Go through village and follow directions for Mullion Cove. After ½ mile (800m) turn left opposite Mullion Meadows towards Predannack. Stay on road for 1½ miles (2.4km), keeping to left when road forks. Go over cattle grid, across field and downhill. Park in the National Trust car park at the end

OS Map Explorer 103

Start / End Predannack National Trust car park, **OS grid ref: SW 668162**

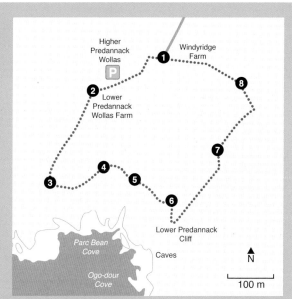

South West

1. Starting from the car park, climb over the stile in the corner. Walk down the narrow green lane for about 110 yards (100m), to the small stream and stepping stones at the bottom. Walk quietly and you may see an adder basking on the path edge or on the rocks near the stream.

2. Take the small wooden stile on your left and follow the path along the edge of the field towards the rock outcrop. As well as lovely views, this outcrop supports some of the unique flora for which The Lizard is famed. Two species of clover (upright and twin-headed) might well be growing under your feet.

3. At the foot of the field in front of you is a small timber and stone stile that leads onto the coast path.

4. Turn left onto the coast path, pausing at the large rock outcrop overlooking Ogo-dour Cove. This is a good spot for watching chough feeding on the short grazed turf. Seals are a common sight, and you might even spot basking sharks in the summer.

5. The coast path drops down into the valley, over a stream, before a steady climb back up the other side.

6. At the top of the hill, a small stone waymarker directs you back towards Predannack Wollas car park. Turn left here, past the clumps of gorse and blackthorn favoured by stonechats and whitethroats in the summer.

7. Climb over the polished serpentine stone stile and walk down the narrow green lane before turning left onto the track.

8. Cross over the small wooden bridge before you return to the car park through the gate ahead.

Make the Most of Your Day
Enjoy the beaches, visit the Wireless Station or take part in one of the events that take place at The Lizard throughout the year.

Food and Facilities
There are cafés at nearby Mullion, and at Lizard Point and Kynance Cove slightly further away; there are toilets in the car parks at those sites. Accommodation is available at the National Trust campsite at Teneriffe Farm.

2. Saltram Boundary Walk

Saltram House
Plymouth
Devon
PL7 1UH
01752 333500
saltram@nationaltrust.org.uk

About this walk
Flower displays
Estuary views
Wildlife interest
Includes a steep section with steps; walking boots recommended especially following wet weather
Dogs welcome on leads
Distance 1 mile (1.6km)
Time 30–40 mins

Saltram's historic parkland is a rare survival of an eighteenth-century estate that provided income for the Parker family and employment for many local people. The park continues to be a working estate today, with much of the land used as permanent pasture for cattle. This pleasant walk follows parkland and woodland, combining views of the Plym estuary and Blaxton saltmarsh along with its varied birdlife, and glorious woodland flower displays in spring and summer.

Things to see

Saltmarsh Birdlife
Behind the seawall at Blaxton is the only saltmarsh habitat on the Plym estuary. It is an important area for birdlife, particularly at high tide, when other feeding grounds are covered by the sea. Migrants using the marsh in spring and autumn include black-tailed and bar-tailed godwits, as well as greenshank, while wintering birds include curlew, redshank and dunlin.

Above: Looking towards Saltram's east front across a bank of daffodils and the East Lawn in April.

Saltram House and Garden
Saltram was home to the Parker family from 1743, when an earlier mansion was remodelled to reflect the family's increasingly prominent position. It's magnificently decorated, with original contents including Chinese wallpapers and an exceptional collection of paintings (several by Sir Joshua Reynolds). It also has a superb country house library and Robert Adam's Neo-classical Saloon. The garden is mostly nineteenth century, with a working eighteenth-century orangery and follies, beautiful shrubberies and imposing specimen trees providing year-round interest.

Above: View over flowers in the garden towards the house.

How to Get There

By Train Plymouth 3½ miles (5.6km)

By Car 3½ miles (5.6km) east of Plymouth city centre. Travelling south (from Exeter): exit from A38 is signed Plymouth City Centre/Plympton/Kingsbridge. At roundabout take centre lane, then third exit for Plympton. Take right-hand lane and follow brown signs. Travelling north (from Liskeard): leave A38 at Plympton exit then follow the instructions above from roundabout

OS Map Landranger 201

Start / End Saltram House car park, **OS grid ref: SX 520556**

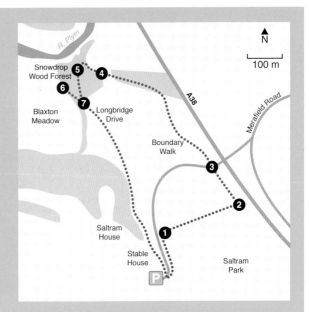

1. From the car park, follow the entrance drive before turning right at the hut. Head up a corridor footpath between fields on rising ground.

2. Turn left at the top of the rise, following the edge of the field; if you are considering a visit in summer you may see South Devon cattle grazing here. View the house and panorama of the Plym on your left.

3. Cross the estate drive; be careful as this is the entrance and exit drive to the estate. Follow the Boundary Walk path down a flight of steps through woodland with the A38 road close by on your right. Before leaving the wood there are some benches with pleasant views towards the estuary.

4. The fenced path crosses pasture fields on leaving the wood, and in front of you is a vista of the Plym Valley, dominated by trees surrounding the river. On the horizon, although obscured by trees, is the Triumphal Arch – a folly erected in 1783 by the Parkers of Saltram.

5. At the drive turn left. This is Longbridge Drive and at this point it is fringed with woodland. In the spring this woodland is carpeted with snowdrops, daffodils and then bluebells.

6. Opposite the Snowdrop Wood Forest School sign, take an optional short deviation down the track to a bench overlooking the saltmarsh, an area known as Blaxton Meadow. It was originally embanked and reclaimed by the Parker family in the 1860s. Since 1986 a restoration scheme has been in operation restoring the land to saltmarsh. The marsh is now a haven for numerous wading birds.

7. Return and carry on along Longbridge Drive, up the steep rise, and back to the car park.

Make the Most of Your Day
The house is full of treasures, stories and intrigue, while the garden has something for everyone, from stunning borders, to a secluded folly, and even croquet. There are also themed family activities throughout the year.

Food and Facilities
Refreshments are available in the Chapel Tea-room and Park Café. Toilets can be found in the stables.

South West

3. A Walk Around Parke

Parke Estate
Bovey Tracey
Newton Abbot
Devon
TQ13 9JQ
01626 834748
parke@nationaltrust.org.uk

About this walk
An insight into country life

Wildlife interest

Can be muddy, especially after wet weather

Dogs welcome; keep under close control near livestock

Distance 1 mile (1.6km)

Time 30–40 mins

This compact estate was once the home of a wealthy local family and probably enabled them to be self sufficient for all their day-to-day needs, with a vegetable garden, fruit garden and orchard, cold house, fishpond, grazing meadows for livestock, beehives for honey, and gardens to wander in for spiritual refreshment. Enjoy all of this and more on this easy circular walk.

Things to see

Above: The house and grounds in spring at Parke, Devon.

Below: Bee on apple blossom at Parke.

Parke Walled Garden
Walled kitchen gardens traditionally supplied a variety of fruit, vegetables and salads for the household. The garden forms part of the remodelled core of the estate dating from the 1820s. Though the estate declined in the late twentieth century, much of the historic layout remains. Clinging to the sides of a valley, the walled garden is a great example of an attempt to impose a conventional layout onto unsuitable terrain; but, despite this, the garden is now re-emerging as a fully working site thanks to the local community.

The Orchard
The extensive orchard surrounding the walled garden on three sides was in use as early as 1841. According to Arthur Stevens, the Parke bailiff between the wars, the apples from the orchard were made into cider, whereas culinary and dessert apples were grown in the walled garden.

The Park at Parke
The landscape you see at Parke today dates from the early nineteenth century, but there are also influences of eighteenth-century principles established by Lancelot 'Capability' Brown, the famous landscape designer of the time. Although there's no evidence to suggest Brown directly influenced Parke, his picturesque style typically included a decorative park with grazing and haymaking. Another familiar Brownian device found at Parke includes trees planted in such a way as to make the landscape appear from within to be surrounded by woodland, as well as providing privacy from the inquisitive eyes of the passer-by.

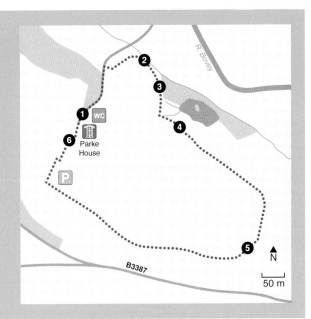

How to Get There

By Train Newton Abbot 6 miles (9.7km); Exeter St David's 16 miles (25.7km)

By Car 2 miles (3.2km) north of A38, Exeter to Plymouth. Take A382 towards Bovey Tracey. At first small roundabout take 2nd exit. At second roundabout take 1st exit. Turn right into Parke Estate and follow signs to car park

OS Map Explorer OL191

Start / End Parke car park, **OS grid ref: SX 805786**

B3387

N

50 m

South West

1. Start by the National Trust ranger's office, which is behind Parke House, below the Walled Garden. Follow the track towards the River Bovey. When you reach the barn and yard on the left, go through the wooden gate on your right into the open parkland. Turn left and walk down between the hedge and the large oak tree to a small leat.

2. Turn right at the leat and follow it for about 65 yards (60m). This man-made waterway (a common feature on Dartmoor) originally powered the wool mill in Bovey Tracey and also fed the estate pond.

3. There should be beehives in front of you. Bear right and follow the ditch that curves around to the left.

4. Cross over a boggy area to get a glimpse of Parke House on your right and the fishpond on your left. The pond is now silted-up and overgrown, providing a great habitat for dragonflies, but would once have supplied protein-rich fish to the House. Continue in a south-westerly direction until you reach the line of Poplar trees and turn right. The field is quite boggy, a good habitat for wildflowers, such as orchids, water-dropworts and sedges.

5. Continue around the parkland in a clockwise direction until you meet the main drive. Follow this and take the left fork towards the car park. Walk carefully though the car park and out of the gate in the far corner down a small lane.

6. On your left you'll see an apple and damson orchard for making cider and preserves. Near the bottom of the lane, look through the wooden door into the walled garden. After you've taken a look, head back to the car park.

Make the Most of Your Day
The walled garden is looked after by National Trust staff and volunteers in partnership with members of the Bovey Tracey Climate Action group; here you can see the fruit, vegetables and cut flowers that have been grown by the team. You can also stop by the orchard. After that, make time to visit the multi-award winning café and restaurant. For those who are feeling more energetic, you can join in the weekly Parkrun that starts on the drive at Parke House.

Food and Facilities
Refreshments are available in the Home Farm Café at Parke. There are public toilets behind Parke House.

4. Teign Gorge Views Walk

Castle Drogo stands high above the ancient woodlands of the Teign Gorge on the edge of Dartmoor, and from the forest in the valley to the borders in the garden, there is a wide variety of flora and fauna. This is a spectacular route that offers some incredible views over Dartmoor while walking amongst gorse and mature oak woodland.

Castle Drogo
Drewsteignton
Near Exeter
Devon
EX6 6PB
01647 433306
castledrogo@nationaltrust.org.uk

About this walk
Incredible views
Ancient woodland
Wildlife interest
Paths are dry and stony, but can be muddy in places
Dogs welcome on leads
Distance 1 mile (1.6km)
Time 40 mins

Things to see

Castle Drogo
The granite walls of Castle Drogo seem to grow out of Dartmoor. Commissioned by Julius Drewe, the castle was designed by Sir Edwin Lutyens, one of the foremost architects of the early twentieth century.

Whiddon Deer Park
Across the deep gorge carved out by the River Teign lies Whiddon Deer Park. Traditionally a symbol of social status, deer parks were used for sport as well as rearing deer and rabbit for the table and providing valued leather and fur.

Above: Mist hanging over the River Teign Gorge at Castle Drogo, Devon.

Below: Autumn on the Castle Drogo estate.

How to Get There

By Car 5 miles (8km) south of A30 Exeter to Okehampton. Take A382 Whiddon Down to Moretonhampstead road and turn off at Sandy Park

OS Map Landranger 191, Explorer 113

Start / End Castle Drogo main car park, **OS grid ref: SX 725902**

Castle Drogo

Piddledown Common

Piddledown Common

Sharp Tor

R. Teign

Whiddon Wood

Whiddon Deer Park

N

100 m

1. From Castle Drogo's main car park, follow the signs for Teign Valley Walks.

2. Turn right and keep following signs for Teign Valley Walks. Walk down through the trees and at the end turn left over the open common. Follow the yellow arrowed route.

3. Continue over the common through a gate and along a path with tall gorse either side, known as Gorse Blossom Walk.

4. Take the right-hand path to descend a short, steep slope onto Hunters Path. Turn right and follow Hunters Path back towards the castle.

5. Stop and admire the view from the crags of Sharp Tor, looking out over Chagford towards Dartmoor. Continue round the hill and take the second flight of steps. (There is no handrail.)

6. At the top of the steps, go through a small gate and bear left up another flight of steps. (There is no handrail.) There is a bench at the top for a quick rest if needed. Continue ahead until you reach the castle drive. Turn left and walk back to the car park.

Make the Most of Your Day

Make time to discover the beautiful Lutyens-designed terraced garden at Castle Drogo with dramatic views of Dartmoor. There's plenty to see, from the rose garden to the quaint Bunty House (Wendy House) complete with its own miniature garden. The rooms inside the castle tell the story of the Drewe Family and the original building of the castle between 1911 and 1930.

Food and Facilities

The café at Castle Drogo showcases local produce, and there is open-air seating and a play area. There are picnic areas and toilets at Drogo and Fingle Bridge.

5. Salcombe Hill to Sidmouth Circular Walk

This spectacular circular walk showcases the Regency town of Sidmouth. Starting with the stunning views across the Sid Valley, part of the Jurassic Coast UNESCO World Heritage Site, the walk takes you down into Sidmouth town through the woods and fields of Salcombe Hill and then upriver through The Byes, Sidmouth's lovely, tranquil riverside park, where you will find a wonderful variety of wildlife.

Salcombe Hill
Sidmouth
Devon
EX10 0NY
01297 680507
southdevon@nationaltrust.org.uk

About this walk
Breathtaking views
Wildflower displays
Wildlife interest

The coastal paths leading down to Sidmouth and path up Soldier's Hill are steep (with steps) and naturally uneven

Dogs welcome but must be kept on a lead on the coast path where cattle grazing signs are displayed

Distance 5 miles (8km)

Time 3 hours

South West

Things to see

Views of the Jurassic Coast
Covering around 95 miles (153km), the Jurassic Coast stretches from Exmouth in East Devon to Studland Bay in Dorset, and spans 185 million years of geological history. Coastal erosion has exposed rock formations that form an almost continuous sequence from the Triassic, Jurassic and Cretaceous periods, providing evidence that over time the area has been desert, shallow tropical sea and marshland.

Opposite: Salcombe Hill Cliff, in Sidmouth, Devon, taken from the beach.

The Byes Riverside Walk
The Byes riverside walk stretches 1¼ miles (2km) between the village of Sidford and the Old Toll House of Sidmouth. The Byes is made up of a series of fields and meadows along the River Sid, which is the smallest river in Devon. It was purchased to encourage wildlife conservation and the footpaths and cycle paths provide free public access for visitors to explore. If you keep your eyes open, you could spot dippers, grey wagtails, kingfishers, tawny owls and even otters playing in and around the fast-flowing river.

Bluebells at Soldier's Hill
Managed by the Woodland Trust, the woods at Soldier's Hill are home to an outstanding display of bluebells during late spring (April to May).

Above left: View west along the Jurassic Coast from Salcombe Hill above Sidmouth, East Devon.

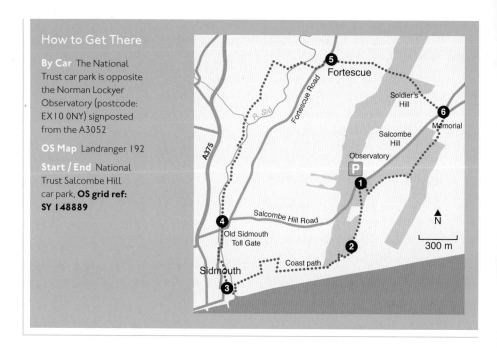

How to Get There

By Car The National Trust car park is opposite the Norman Lockyer Observatory (postcode: EX10 0NY) signposted from the A3052

OS Map Landranger 192

Start / End National Trust Salcombe Hill car park, **OS grid ref: SY 148889**

1. Take the path past the picnic tables and follow the 'Salcombe Hill Cliff and Link to Coast Path' sign. Follow the footpath to the cliff where you can enjoy fantastic views of Sidmouth, High Peak, Ladrum Bay and beyond.

2. As you look from the cliff out to sea, follow the path around to the right and then take the path on the left signposted 'Coast Path Sidmouth ⅔m'. Go down through a small woodland (down a few steps) and across an open field, enjoying the views towards Sidmouth as you walk. Turn right at the end of the field by the 'Coast Path' sign to start following the coast path diversion created in response to recent landslides and erosion to the cliff edge. At the junction, turn left onto Laskeys Lane then continue straight along the footpath next to West Combe House (where Laskeys Lane bears off to the right), which then turns into Cliff Road. At the end of Cliff Road, follow the footpath to the left down the hill and across the temporary bridge constructed over the mouth of the River Sid at the site of the Alma Bridge. After crossing the bridge, turn right and head inland along the left side of The Ham (a small park), which takes you past the decorative seascape mural painted by children from the local area.

3. Continue along the path and at the end of the park, go straight ahead along the National Cycle Network path along Riverside Road. Turn right onto Mill Street by the car park and cross over the footbridge at the ford before continuing along Milford Road. At the junction, cross the road and enter The Byes riverside park to the right of the 'Old Toll House of Sidmouth' and the 'Old Sidmouth Toll Gate'.

4. Follow the footpath upriver along the side of the River Sid, crossing over the third bridge signposted 'Sidford'. Continue walking upriver along the path next to the river towards Sidford through 'Margaret's Meadow and the Gilchrist Field' (which are lovingly cared for by a team of Sid Vale Association volunteers), until you reach an interpretation board at a cycle path junction. Turn right following the 'Fortescue ¼m' sign crossing over a bridge and through some gates, which bring you out onto Fortescue Road. Turn left and follow this quiet road for a short distance before turning right into Griggs Lane (signposted 'Public Footpath to Salcombe Regis').

5. Follow the lane and woodland path up the hill passing through the kissing gate signposted 'Public Footpath Soldier's Hill ¼m'. At the end of the woodland path continue straight across the field and through the kissing gate, which brings you out onto Salcombe Hill Road.

6. Turn right onto the road and then left at the war memorial signposted for cars 'Salcombe Regis ¼m'. Take the path to the right just after the memorial, through the 'SVA Allotment Field Wood' kissing gate and then turn right following the 'Link Path to Salcombe Hill' sign. Follow the path around to the right and then down the steps leading to the left. At the bottom of the steps, follow the path signposted 'Link Path Salcombe Hill' until it stops and then turn left and then right at the 'Public Footpath Salcombe Hill and Car Park' sign. Continue along this footpath until you reach a dirt road next to a barn. Turn right onto the dirt road and follow this back to the National Trust car park where you began your walk.

Make the Most of Your Day
A la Ronde in nearby Exmouth is a quirky, unique and fascinating 16-sided house, full of creative treasures from around the world. The house enjoys a wonderful outlook across the Exe estuary, and outside there are family trails and activities, including garden games.

Food and Facilities
Tea-rooms, pubs, restaurants, banks, a post office and shops can all be found in Sidmouth. Toilets are located at the eastern end of the Esplanade near to the seascape mural and by the town hall in the centre of Sidmouth.

Above: Green-winged orchids at Orcombe Point can be seen from April to May.

6. Brean Down Coastal Walk

Brean
North Somerset
TA8 2RS
01643 862452
breandown@nationaltrust.
org.uk

About this walk
Superb views

Military history

Wildlife interest

Wildflowers

Take care on cliffs

Tide comes in quickly

Steep at first; be aware of
deep mud at high tide

Dogs welcome on leads

Distance 3 miles (4.8km)

Time 1 hour

This magnificent walk takes you along one of the great landmarks of the Somerset coastline. It's a steep climb to the top, but the views out across the Bristol Channel make it well worth the effort. Keep a look out for a great variety of birds, plants and butterflies en route.

Things to see

Vegetation and Wildlife
This large whaleback headland is an extension of the limestone rocks of the Mendip Hills. The vegetation on its steep, rocky, southern slopes and cliffs contrasts with that on the gentler slopes of the north side where the soil is deeper. To preserve the rich variety of vegetation, grass and scrub need to be cut back otherwise they can overwhelm more delicate plants. Cattle, rabbits and feral goats help to mow the turf. Listen out for the loud, sharp call of the stonechat. You may also catch a glimpse of skylark, meadow pipit, linnet and peregrine falcon.

Brean Down Fort
In 1862, 4 acres (1.6ha) were requisitioned at the tip of Brean Down to build up fortifications to protect access to Bristol and Cardiff in fear of the growing strength of France under the rule of Napoleon III. No shots were ever fired in action, but regular drill and gunnery practice was part of the routine. The fort was rearmed at the start of the Second World War.

Above: Trees shaped by the wind on cliff-tops above the beach at Brean Down, Somerset.

Right: Palmerston Fort at Brean Down.

How to Get There

By Train Highbridge
8½ miles (13.7km), and then
by bus

By Car Signposted from
A370 from Weston-super-
Mare to Highbridge, follow
the Burnham and Berrow
coast road; 8 miles (12.9km)
from M5 junction 22

OS Map Landranger 182,
Explorer 153

Start / End Brean Down
Café, **OS grid ref:**
ST 296588

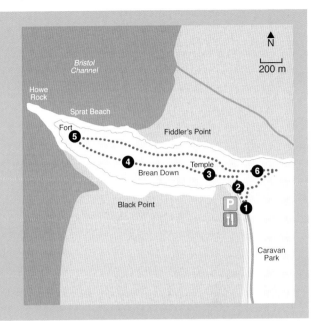

1. Follow the road from the café towards the headland until you reach some fairly steep steps. These will lead you up onto the Down.

2. Once on the Down, take the path to the left, along the southern slopes. In early summer look out for the white flowers of the rare white rock rose which flourishes in the thin limestone soils.

3. Continue along the path until you come to the site of a Romano-Celtic temple. It was built in about AD 340, close to a Bronze Age burial mound. Rock from a quarry on the Down provided some of the stone for the building.

4. Further along the path you will come across the remains of a Celtic field system, a series of small rectangular fields.

5. Continue up towards the fort, which is located on a small hill. Here you can take a closer look at the remains of the fortifications and enjoy spectacular views across the Bristol Channel.

6. From the fort make your way back along the other side of the Down to the site of the Iron Age hill fort. Take a closer look at the banks and ditches before continuing along the path. Follow it round to the right. This will take you back to the steps and down to the café.

Make the Most of Your Day

Brean is now linked to Weston-super-Mare by a cycle route that starts by the beach in Uphill, continues along the seafront in Weston and takes you to the café in Brean Down. This journey takes about an hour. Brean Down is rich in history so allow plenty of time on your walk to notice the ancient field systems and archaeological remains as well as the Iron Age hill fort. You can explore the ruined buildings of the fort and imagine what life must have been like living and working there. The fort also hosts art exhibitions. There are later examples of Britain's military defences on the Down, including gun platforms and emplacements and an arrow that directed pilots on practice flights to their ranges.

Food and Facilities

Refreshments and toilets are available at the café.

7. Leigh Woods Woodland Wander

This walk runs through beautiful woodland with rare and veteran trees as well as grassland. Stokeleigh Camp hill fort is perched on the edge of the Avon Gorge and there are dramatic views along the river. In spring the bluebell displays are not to be missed, but the woods are full of interest throughout the year.

Leigh Woods National
Nature Reserve
Bristol
BS8 3PL
0117 973 1645
leighwoods@nationaltrust.
org.uk

About this walk

Dramatic views

Wildflower displays and
rare woodland

Archaeological interest

There may be a few muddy
sections in wet weather.
A couple of uneven rocky
sections can be slippery
when wet. Look out for signs
that will let you know if
cows are on site

Dogs welcome under
close control

Distance 1 mile (1.6km)

Time 30–45 mins

Things to see

Rare Trees

Leigh Woods has long been recognised for its rich natural environment, including an abundance of rare whitebeam trees. James White described the woods in his book of 1912, *Flora of Bristol*: 'Famed Leigh Woods, a fine forest-like tract that crowns the cliffs and descends to the tideway – home to a plant community of uncommon interest.' They contain nearly every indigenous tree in the country, and offer a foliage of singular varied tint, from the darkest yew to the pale light green of lime and oak, and the silver of the whitebeam.

Flora and Fauna

At Leigh Woods National Nature Reserve, designated pathways lead you through oak, small leaf lime and ash forest, which is dotted with bluebells and wood anemones in spring and an interesting array of fungi in autumn. Former woodland pasture offers a mixture of open grassy glades surrounded by broadleaf woodland, and there are also areas of flower-rich limestone grassland around old stone quarries. Rockrose, Bristol rock-cress and black knapweed are all native to this area.

Above: Bluebells in flower in Leigh Woods.

Below: Leigh Woods, Bristol.

How to Get There

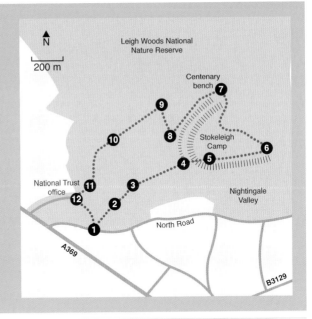

By Train Clifton Down 1⅔ miles (2.6km); Bristol Temple Meads 2¾ miles (4.5km)

By Car 2 miles (3.2km) south-west of Bristol. North Road runs from A369, Bristol to Portishead road, to Bridge Road near Clifton Suspension Bridge. Roadside parking on North Road near entrance to wood

OS Map Landranger 154

Start / End North Road entrance, **OS grid ref: ST 555730**

1. Go through the kissing gate and up the sunken track straight ahead.

2. This brings you out onto an open grassy area. Cross this, sticking to the right-hand side. You'll walk past a line of rare whitebeam trees.

3. Just past these trees, take the small path that runs along the top of the valley and straight onto another grassy area.

4. Ahead of you are the ramparts of Stokeleigh Camp, an Iron Age hill fort. Follow the narrow rocky path through these; can be slippery when wet.

5. Once through the rampart, follow the grassy path straight ahead for 220 yards (200m) to the viewpoint.

6. Turn left and follow the path along the gorge side for 330 yards (300m), back through the ramparts and past a fenced pond.

7. Turn left onto the Purple Trail, where you can see the dramatic sweep of the ramparts and Centenary bench on your left.

8. Turn right and follow the Purple Trail to the stone wall.

9. When you reach the parish wall leave the Purple Trail and turn left following the stone wall. Go straight through the gate after 220 yards (200m) and join the Blue Trail.

10. Follow the Blue Trail straight ahead. Once you reach the ancient yew that grows in the line of the wall, the path should curve away from the wall.

11. Carry on past the low wooden building, the National Trust office, where you can pick up a site leaflet. Follow the gravel road and look out for the blue-topped waymarker on the left.

12. Follow the Blue Trail back downhill to the start.

Make the Most of Your Day
Family activities are available during the year, including survival days and wildlife walks.

Food and Facilities
Leigh Woods is a great place for a picnic. Compost toilets are available next to the National Trust office on Valley Road during office hours.

8. May Hill Countryside Walk

May Hill
Gloucestershire/
Herefordshire border
GL18 1JS
01452 814213
mayhill@nationaltrust.
org.uk

About this walk
Wildflowers
Pondlife
Superb views
One steep climb; the
woodland can be muddy in
wet weather
Dogs welcome; keep under
close control near livestock

Distance 3 miles (4.8km)

Time 1 hour

Enjoy an exhilarating walk over this prominent landmark. Starting on May Hill Common, the walk climbs to the clump of trees on the summit, before crossing an open expanse of grassland. Enjoy the stunning views and the wide variety of wildflowers that thrive in this habitat. You'll then return via the woodlands of the Huntley Estate.

Things to see

May Hill
With its conspicuous clump of pine trees, May Hill rises to a height of 1,000ft (305m). The Corsican pines at its summit were planted to commemorate Queen Victoria's Golden Jubilee in 1887, with more recent planting marking Queen Elizabeth's Silver Jubilee. There was an even earlier clump of Scots pine trees in the eighteenth century, several of which still survive. Morris dancers celebrate May Day each year on top of the hill.

Grasslands
The area of acidic grassland on the summit of May Hill is the largest and finest in Gloucestershire. In spring it is covered in bluebells. Bracken grows in abundance so it is cut back every July, and plants such as heath bedstraw, heath speedwell, bilberry and heather also thrive. Listen out for breeding birds like tree and meadow pipits.

Pondlife
Along the route, and especially at point 3, there are scattered ponds and flushes where you can find uncommon plants, including lesser skullcap, bog pimpernel and bog mosses. Palmate newts and rare water beetles can also be found in this habitat.

Above: Beautiful views from May Hill.

Above left: A copse of trees at the top of May Hill.

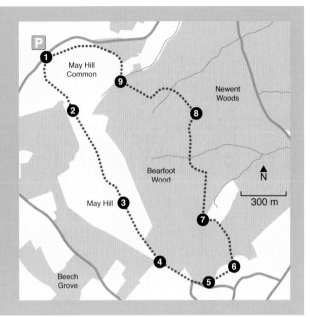

How to Get There

By Train Gloucester 10 miles (16km)

By Car May Hill is signposted off A40 Gloucester to Ross-on-Wye road, 1 mile (1.6km) west of Huntley, 3 miles (4.8km) from junction 3 of M50. Follow road up hill past Yew Tree Inn, Clifford's Mesne. Roadside parking ½ mile (800m) past cattle grid

OS Map Landranger 162, Explorer OL14

Start / End May Hill Common, **OS grid ref: SO 690221**

1. From the parking area, go past the metal gate and head straight up the fairly steep middle path to the top of May Hill Common.

2. At the top, go through the kissing gate at the end of the wall (which marks the county boundary) and head across the grassland in the direction of the clump of pine trees.

3. From the pine trees follow the main track to the southern end of the hill.

4. Pass through the gate and continue down the track, crossing straight over the crossroads by a water tank in the field to your right.

5. After about 55 yards (50m), turn left down the track and follow the public footpath waymarkers.

6. When you reach a small road, turn left along the forestry track and over a stile next to a metal gate. Continue along the track into the woodlands of the Huntley Estate.

7. At the next bend the public footpath leaves the main track. Follow the arrows until it rejoins the

forestry track. You'll pass through an impressive plantation of coast redwood trees.

8. Just after the timber stacking area, turn sharp left, still following the public footpath. Continue along this footpath, ignoring the next two footpaths leading off to the right.

9. Go over the stile onto the common, continuing along the footpath. Head straight over the track and follow the path through the bracken. Eventually the path will join the road just below the parking area.

Make the Most of Your Day
Take the time to soak up the views of the surrounding area: from May Hill it is possible to see Wales and Ross-on-Wye and the Shropshire Hills, and in the other direction, the Malvern Hills that mark the county boundary between Herefordshire and Worcestershire.

Food and Facilities
There are pubs in the surrounding villages and public toilets in Newent, 3 miles (4.8km) from May Hill.

South West

9. Lacock Riverside Walk

Hither Way
Lacock
Chippenham
Wiltshire
SN15 2LG
01249 730459
lacockabbey@nationaltrust.org.uk

About this walk
Historical interest

Riverside views

Wildflowers

Can be muddy in sections during winter

Dogs welcome; keep on leads inside Abbey grounds

Distance 2 miles (3.2km)

Time 40 mins

This walk opens up to beautiful views of the surrounding countryside and the River Avon, as it follows the riverbank through the valley of Snaylesmeade where Lacock Abbey stands. The long grass of Snaylesmead meadow alongside the river is full of wildflowers, including poppies, knapweed and columbines.

Things to see

Lacock Abbey
Packed with history, Lacock Abbey started as an abbey and nunnery and then became a Tudor family residence. The last owners were the Talbots, a caring close-knit family who loved their home in Lacock. You might know it as the birthplace of photography, where Henry Fox Talbot took the first photographic negative.

Lacock Village
A firm favourite for film and TV producers, Lacock village is renowned for its picturesque streets and historic cottages, untouched by modern alterations. The village's most famous appearances include *Downton Abbey*, the BBC's *Pride and Prejudice* and *Cranford*, and the films *Harry Potter and the Half-blood Prince* and *Wolfman*.

Above: Houses in the village at Lacock, Wiltshire.

Right: A view of the north cloister walk at Lacock Abbey.

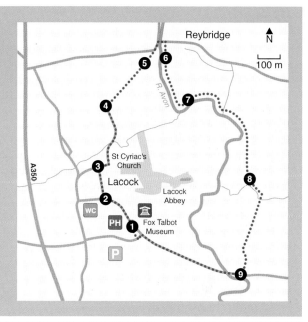

How to Get There

By Train Chippenham
3 miles (4.8km)

By Car 3 miles (4.8km)
south of Chippenham. M4,
junction 17, signposted to
Chippenham (A350). Follow
A350 (signposted Poole/
Warminster) until you reach
Lacock, then follow signs for
main car park

OS Map Landranger 173,
Explorer 156

Start / End Hither Way car
park, **OS grid ref: ST 917684**

1. From the car park, cross the road and follow the brown tourist signs into the village, where you'll emerge in front of the Fox Talbot Museum and entrance to Lacock Abbey.

2. From here, walk towards the High Street and pass the Red Lion pub on the left, where you'll see a half-timbered house on your right. Walk down East Street to your right, passing the Tithe Barn on your right-hand side and then the Village Hall.

3. At the end of East Street, with the bakery in front of you, turn right towards St Cyriac's Church. Turn left just before the church at the half-timbered house, towards the brook and the packhorse bridge. Cross the bridge, keeping the weir to your right. Walk up the hill, past allotments on your left.

4. At the top, pass through a kissing gate and onto a narrow tarmac path which leads down to the hamlet of Reybridge. As you approach another kissing gate at the end of the path, you'll see glimpses of the River Avon to your right.

5. Pass through the gate and walk down the path, past Wicket Gate Cottage. Continue along the path then turn right and then right again over the bridge. At the end of the bridge turn immediately right over the stile and into a field.

6. Keep the river on your right and walk along the riverbank. Through the clearing in the trees, look back towards the village for views of the church.

7. Exit the field through a metal kissing gate and wooden bridge. With the river still on your right, continue along its bank. After the next bend in the river, the path veers off to the left. Pass over a stile and along a waymarked path through the middle of the field. Here you can catch your first glimpse of Lacock Abbey on your right.

8. Leave the field by the metal gate and walk along the field edge to a stile and footbridge. Cross over the footbridge, where you'll see your first view of Sharington's Tower at the Abbey. With the tower on your right, cast your eye along the river, which is

South West

marked out by a line of trees in the middle distance. Scanning to the left you'll see Stone Bridge, walk towards this over the well-worn path, which goes diagonally right across a field. At this point you could take a small diversion and head straight towards the river where you'll get better views of the Abbey on the opposite side.

9. Continue on to the stone stile by the bridge, cross over it and turn right towards the village. Walk over the bridge, onto the footpath and back to the car park. Take care as this is a busy road.

Make the Most of Your Day

The woodland gardens at Lacock Abbey are at their best in spring, before the leaf canopy starts to block out the light reaching the bulbs and flowers. Under the trees you can find snowdrops, aconites, anemones, daffodils, snake's head fritillaries and one of the best displays of *Crocus vernus* in the country. Shrubs in flower during the spring and early summer include viburnums, mahonia, osmanthus, clematis, magnolia, philadelphus, forsythia, flowering crabs, cherries, hawthorn, lilac and a Judas tree on the Abbey wall. As summer arrives the garden takes on a different atmosphere, with the trees in full leaf giving essential shade to the sleeping spring bulbs. The meadow areas of the garden are left unmown until July, allowing the fritillaries and crocus to set seed. All the plants around the Abbey have been carefully chosen to blend with the stonework and the monastic atmosphere.

Food and Facilities

After your walk you can enjoy a drink and some food at the George Inn or the Red Lion – both historic pubs looked after by the National Trust. There is also a tea-room and amenities at Lacock Abbey.

Above: Sheep grazing in parkland at Lacock Abbey, Wiltshire.

10. King Alfred's Tower Walk at Stourhead

Stourhead
Stourton
Warminster
Wiltshire
BA12 6QD
01747 841152
stourhead@nationaltrust.
org.uk

About this walk
Stunning vistas

Historic interest

Steep climbs near the start
of the walk; paths can be
boggy in places

Dogs welcome under close
control

Distance 5½ miles (8.8km)

Time 2 hours

Stourhead is one of the world's finest landscape gardens. It was created in the 1740s by a team of 50 gardeners who planted and tended beech, oak, sycamore, Spanish chestnut, ash and holm oak. This walk takes you through beautiful woodlands to King Alfred's Tower, returning via Park Hill Camp Iron Age Hill Fort and Turner's Paddock.

South West

Things to see

King Alfred's Tower
The Tower is a 160ft (48.8m) high folly designed by Henry Flitcroft for Henry Hoare II in 1772, on the site where it's believed that King Alfred the Great rallied his troops. It commands spectacular views over the three counties of Wiltshire, Dorset and Somerset. It is open at weekends until the end of October.

St Peter's Church
St Peter's Church dates from 1290, is Grade I listed and also has several Grade I listed memorials, most of them from the Hoare family. The beautiful organ has been recently restored and can be heard playing during services.

Above: Visitors on the Palladian Bridge at Stourhead, enjoying the autumnal colours.

Right: King Alfred's Tower on the Stourhead Estate built to commemorate Alfred the Great's victory over the Danes in 879. It was the last work of Henry Flitcroft for Henry Hoare II.

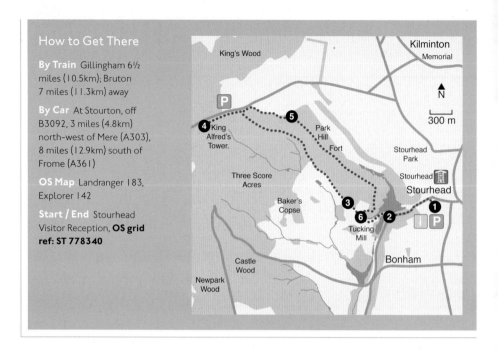

How to Get There

By Train Gillingham 6½ miles (10.5km); Bruton 7 miles (11.3km) away

By Car At Stourton, off B3092, 3 miles (4.8km) north-west of Mere (A303), 8 miles (12.9km) south of Frome (A361)

OS Map Landranger 183, Explorer 142

Start / End Stourhead Visitor Reception, **OS grid ref: ST 778340**

---

1. From the main car park, go through Visitor Reception. Take the zig-zag path down to the Spread Eagle Inn. Walk through the car park and courtyard. Watching out for traffic, turn left here and walk down the road, passing St Peter's Church on your left. Turn right just beyond the Rock Arch.

2. Continue walking with Turner's Paddock Lake and the waterwheel on your left. Keep following the track beside the cattle grid, past Beech Cottage on your right and over a stile. Where the main track forks, take the right-hand track and go through the gate. Follow the track along the top of the field. The ruins of Tucking Mill and cottages are on your left.

3. Go over the stile at the gate and through the mixed conifer woods, keeping on the main track and going straight ahead at any junctions. After a steep ascent of about 1 mile (1.6km) the track emerges on to part of Terrace Ride. Turn left and walk for approximately ½ mile (800m) until you reach King Alfred's Tower.

4. On leaving the Tower, retrace your steps along the Terrace Ride (following the blue waymarkers) to where the woodland area on your right ends. Turn right, down the forestry track on the edge of the woodland, keeping the field on your left.

5. Follow the main track as it bears 90 degrees to the right. Walk along the Broad Ride through the woodland. After approximately ½ mile (800m) you will reach Park Hill Camp Iron Age Hill Fort. Go straight through (if sheep are grazing, dog walkers will need to follow a clearly-marked small diversion). Exit the fort by the information panel, follow the main track for ½ mile (800m) and then round to the right, down the hill and through the gate into Turner's Paddock.

6. Continue along the track, bearing left where you rejoin the main track. Go through the gate beside the cattle grid, passing Turner's Paddock Lake and the waterwheel on your right. As you reach the road, turn left under the Rock Arch. Continue along the road passing St Peter's Church on your right. At the Spread Eagle Inn, turn right and go through the courtyard and car park and follow the footpath that zig-zags up the hill to visitor reception and the car park.

Make the Most of Your Day
Explore the Palladian house with its collection of treasures and a unique Regency library.

Food and Facilities
Seasonal treats can be found at the Spread Eagle Inn and Stourhead's restaurant. There are toilets at visitor reception.

11. Walk at Holt Heath

The walk explores this important lowland heath, which is one of the largest areas of its type in Dorset. Acquired in the 1630s by Sir John Bankes as part of Kingston Lacy's estate, it is now cared for by the National Trust. This important habitat is famous for its heathers and is home to all six of the UK's native reptile species.

Holt Heath
Near Wimborne
Dorset
BH21 7DB
01202 883402
kingstonlacy@nationaltrust.org.uk

About this walk

Heathland flora

Reptiles and invertebrates

Birdwatching

Boardwalks can become slippery in wet conditions

Adequate footwear recommended

Dogs welcome; keep under control near livestock

Distance 6 miles (9.7km)

Time 3 hours

South West

Things to see

Birdwatching
Some birds that can be seen on the Heath include curlews that many locals believe may nest here, along with Dartford warblers, stonechats and nightjars.

Reptiles
This site supports a rich invertebrate community and all of Britain's six reptile species can be found here: adders (also known as vipers), grass snakes, smooth snakes, sand lizards, common lizards and slow worms.

Flora on the Heath
The heathers include common (ling), bell and cross-leaved heath, with a rich lichen flora beneath. The yellow bog asphodel is prominent in the wetter areas accompanied by marsh gentian. Children really enjoy finding the sundew, a carnivorous plant that loves the wet habitats and acidic soil found at Holt Heath.

Above: Dartford Warbler on yellow gorse.

Right: Close-up view of heather.

How to Get There

By Car Travel east from the Canford Bottom roundabout on the A31 on the outskirts of Wimborne. After about ¼ mile (400m), turn left into Uddens Drive where it is signed towards Holt. Follow the windy lane for about 3 miles (4.8km) and then turn right towards Broom Hill. Follow the road for about another 3 miles (4.8km). On a sharp left-hand bend, turn right into White Sheet car park, which is free

OS Map Explorer 118 and OL22

Start / End White Sheet car park, **OS grid ref: SU 048037**

Crooked Withies
Lower Mannington
Holt Heath National Nature Reserve
Summerlug Hill
PH
Holt Heath
Higher Row
Holt Heath
Holt Heath
White Sheet Plantation

1. Leave the car park and enter the fenced area to the north through a gate and past the notice-board. Go straight on, ignoring a right fork. When you reach a T-junction turn right as directed by the waymark.

2. Follow the track and, ignoring the gate on the right, continue straight ahead. On reaching a crossroads of paths keep going straight.

3. When you reach a T-junction by the road, turn right as directed by the waymark. Follow the path and on reaching a fork you can carry straight on for the shorter route. To stay with the main walk, turn left and almost immediately right to follow the bridleway.

4. On exiting the bridleway, go straight across the gravel track and enter the Heath on the narrow dirt track, then left onto a wider sandy path. Ignoring the path almost immediately on your right, follow the edge of the heath to the east towards a small hill.

5. Skirt the bottom of the hill keeping the open heath on your right where you might see some interesting birdlife. Turn right at the utility posts and, following the fence line, through a wooded area, until Newman's Lane is reached on a bend. Take a sharp right, following the footpath over a boardwalk. The cross-heath path continues over boggy ground.

6. Turn right at the pond and then left at the junction, briefly rejoining the outward track before veering left. In a short while you will pass houses on the right, and through a gate onto a permissive path. The going underfoot varies.

7. Turn left to rejoin the shorter walk, carrying straight onto the south. For the longer walk continue straight on as the bridleway turns off to the right.

8. The walk meanders down to the Heath's southern edge, crossing a stream and through a gate. Turn immediately right on the track following the fence line and on meeting another track turn right.

9. At the next public access gate, go through and turn left through another gate and back to the car park.

Make the Most of Your Day

Combine your walk with a visit to Kingston Lacy, a lavish family home built to resemble an Italian *palazzo*. There is plenty to see including an art collection and ancient Egyptian artefacts. There are regular events and play areas for children.

Food and Facilities

There is a pub, The Cross Keys Inn, on the far side of the Heath on the road to Three-Legged Cross.

12. Brownsea Island Wildlife Walk

Located in Poole Harbour, Brownsea Island has spectacular views across to the Purbeck Hills. Thriving habitats including woodland, heathland and a lagoon create a unique haven for wildlife, such as the rare red squirrel and a wide variety of woodland and water birds.

Poole Harbour
Poole
Dorset
BH13 7EE
01202 707744
brownseaisland@
nationaltrust.org.uk

About this walk
Wildlife interest

Superb views

Varied habitats

Paths are uneven in some places

Dogs not permitted

Distance 1 mile (1.6km)

Time 30 mins

Things to see

Birds
Look out for goldcrests – Europe's smallest bird – amongst the many species of bird that visit or live in the woodland. They are distinguished by a bright yellow stripe on their head, although they can be hard to spot as they tend to live high up in the canopy. Birds that visit Brownsea in the winter include the avocet (with over 1,000 roosting in the lagoon, along with good numbers of the bar-tailed godwit), peregrine, little egret and kingfisher; while terns, gulls and oystercatchers can be seen in summer. Birds in the reed-beds include grebes, coots and the shy water rail, with its distinctive pig-squealing call.

Red Squirrels
Red squirrels need to put on plenty of weight in order to survive the winter. They're best seen in autumn when they spend time foraging on the ground for nuts. Pine trees are particularly important for red squirrels and you'll often see chewed pine cones on the woodland floor.

Wetland Areas
The wetlands on the island support sea lavender, common spotted orchids and marsh cinquefoil. Water voles are extremely shy (and rare) so it takes a lot of patience to spot them. Not to be confused with rats, water voles have a blunter, rounder face.

Above: Aerial view of Brownsea Island, Dorset. The wildlife sanctuary sits in the middle of Poole Harbour and was the birthplace of both the Scouts and Guides movements.

Below: Red squirrel on Brownsea Island, Poole Harbour, Dorset.

How to Get There

By Ferry Ferries to Brownsea Island leave from Sandbanks and Poole Quay; sailings run from mid-March to mid-November

By Train Trains to Poole or Bournemouth

By Car Poole Quay and Sandbanks are clearly signposted on roads approaching Poole. Shell Bay National Trust car park and non-National Trust car parks in Poole and Sandbanks

OS Map Landranger 195, Explorer OL15

Start / End Path next to church, **OS grid ref: SZ 022876**

East Lake

Rockets Corner **3**

2

4

Church **1**

Harley Wood

Church Hill

5

6

Farm buildings

N

100 m

---

1. Start the walk from the path next to the church and walk in the opposite direction from Brownsea Castle. Take the left fork in the path.

2. In autumn, this is a good place to see red squirrels as they feed on sweet chestnut and beech tree nuts. Carry straight along this path.

3. At Rockets Corner, take the second left and continue through ideal red squirrel territory, with mature Scots pine trees on your left.

4. Note that the pine woodland here is regenerating. This must be managed carefully to conserve the red squirrel population. Take the next path on your left.

5. Pass a track on your left, and then take the path that bears left. In this area, volunteers have removed rhododendron (an invasive foreign plant) to maintain the diversity of native plant and animal species. The lakes on Brownsea (which resulted from peat digging) attract many insects, including 24 species of dragonfly, such as the small red damselfly and the ruddy darter. There are also green tiger beetles and many species of butterfly, such as the green hairstreak and the small copper.

6. At the farm buildings turn left, then follow a path until you again reach the church at the start of your walk. Alternatively, take a right to see Brownsea Castle.

Make the Most of Your Day
As well as Brownsea's wealth of wildlife you can explore all around the island – it's only 1 mile (1.6km) long). Find your favourite viewpoint, enjoy some time on the beach, try the new natural play area or take part in one of the organised events at the Outdoor Centre, such as low ropes or archery activity days.

Food and Facilities
You will find a café and toilets at Brownsea Castle.

Opposite: Bluebells in woodland at Hughenden, Buckinghamshire (walk 19).

South East

13. Walk to the Huff Duff

This walk descends into a tranquil wooded valley at Dockens Water before crossing the stream to Rockford Common. Wet heath and gleaming bogs reveal carnivorous sundews and mysterious mosses. Enjoy a multitude of wildlife and the breathtaking views from Ibsley Common, an area steeped in military history, and visit the Huff Duff (an old directional station) and associated bunker.

Rockford Common National Trust car park
New Forest
Hampshire
BH24 3NA

About this walk

Heathland habitat

Wildlife interest

Military history

Dogs welcome under close control; keep on short leads during ground nesting bird season (March–July)

Distance 4$^1/_3$ miles (7km)

Time I hour 30 mins– 2 hours

Things to see

New Forest Flora and Fauna

Keep an eye out for buzzards and foxes among the trees and hedgerows. The woodland edge is great for minibeasts – take time to carefully turn over rotten logs to see what you can find. The yellow-flowering gorse provides a fantastic habitat for nesting birds, including stonechats, Dartford warblers and dunnocks, and you may see woodlarks in nearby trees.

The New Forest is also a nationally important habitat for fungi during autumn.

The Huff Duff

This was a Direction Finding Station during the Second World War used to assist in the tracking of Allied aircraft on their way to intercept enemy raids. They could also transmit homing signals to help Allied aircraft find their way back to base.

Above: Ponies in the early morning on Ibsley Common, New Forest, Hampshire.

Left: Rockford Common, New Forest, Hampshire, in October.

Right: Bracken at Rockford Common.

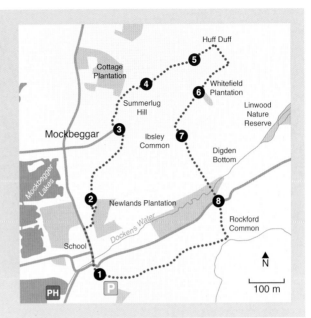

How to Get There

By Car Rockford Common National Trust car park is off Ellingham Drove/Highwood Lane, Rockford, Hampshire 10 miles (16km) west of Lyndhurst, access from A337. 3 miles (4.8km) northeast from Ringwood and 5 miles (8km) south from Fordingbridge on A338

OS Map Explorer OL22

Start / End Rockford Common National Trust car park, **OS grid ref: SU 164082**

1. Walk back towards the road, under ancient English oaks, and cross over the Dockens Water stream using the footbridge. Continue up the road ahead with Moyles Court School on your left. Before reaching the riding stables, turn right onto the Avon Valley Path (AVP) leading you uphill through horse paddocks towards the tree line of Newlands Plantation.

2. Turn left as you reach the tree line to continue following the AVP, with the tree line on your right. Go through the gate ahead and enter Ibsley Common. Follow the path that skirts along the edge of the common, keeping the fence line on your left. Look through the many ancient oak trees marking the boundary, across the plateau, to see Blashford Lakes Nature Reserve. Follow this path for about ⅓ mile (500m), cross the ditch via the boardwalk and footbridge, go straight across Mockbeggar Lane and up the other side of the bank, following the AVP.

3. Follow the contour of the land, keeping the houses on your left, and continue straight on as you reach a track ending in a large junction. Turn right through a wooden barrier gate back onto Ibsley Common. Walk onto Summerlug Hill, keeping the banks of the old gravel works on your right.

4. Bear left on a well-trodden grassy path, heading in a north-easterly direction. The path will take you slightly uphill, past a wooden bench and across the tops of two valleys to your left, known as Little Chibden Bottom and Chibden Bottom (if you find yourself heading towards a clump of pine trees on the horizon, called Whitefield Plantation, you are heading in the wrong direction – you want this on your right). The path becomes gravelly after a while and passes between birch trees. Continue onwards.

5. After about ½ mile (800m), you'll be able to see a cluster of pine trees in the distance to your left, known as Robin Hood's Clump. Ahead, you will see the Huff Duff, an octagonal brick building. Head east, to the right of the Huff Duff, towards a scrub-covered mound to find the nearby air raid bunker.

6. Continue on and turn right, heading south on a gravel path, keeping right of the Whitefield Plantation. Passing the plantation, you reach a white-stone trig point. Stop here to take in the view.

7. Continue heading south on the path bearing left, and turn left at the track crossroads, heading east towards a horizon of trees.

8. This track will take you slowly downhill through open heathland. Go straight on at the crossroads, down towards the Dockens Water stream. Pass the National Trust sign on your left and cross over the footbridge into the cover of pine trees, known as Newlands Plantation. Cross the road ahead onto Rockford Common and ascend the gravel path. When the path levels out, you will reach a crossroads; turn right and follow the gravel path south for ⅔ mile (just over 1km). Finally, go down through the sunken lane downhill, around the barrier, and back into the car park.

Make the Most of Your Day
During this walk make time to play Pooh sticks at the footbridge! The New Forest is all about nature, so make time to enjoy as much of it as possible.

Food and Facilities
Benches for picnics are available; the nearest amenities are in Lyndhurst.

14. Discover Dunsbury on the Isle of Wight

Take a breezy and invigorating farmland and downs walk over the Dunsbury Estate on the Isle of Wight, purchased through the National Trust's Neptune Coastline Campaign. Admire the magnificent views and spot butterflies along the way.

Compton Bay
Brook Chine
Military Road
Isle of Wight
Nearest postcode PO30 4EX
01983 741020
isleofwight@nationaltrust.
org.uk

About this walk
Stunning views

Beautiful beaches

Some steep slopes and muddy, slippery paths

Dogs welcome on leads

Distance 3½ miles (5.6km)

Time 1 hour 30 mins–2 hours

Things to see

The Downs
This is a coastline which is constantly changing as the sea erodes the soft cliffs. Our purchase of Dunsbury will enable us to look after more of the beautiful landscape, provide coastal access and preserve wildlife. The pond between points 2 and 3 marks the course of a stream valley that was a tributary to the Yar, but it has been cut off by coastal retreat. It would have originally formed a chine as the water poured over the cliff.

Butterfly Conservation Galore
The chalk downland coast in this part of the island is home to an amazing 33 species of butterfly. These include the rare Glanville fritillary, first discovered in England in the seventeenth century by Lady Eleanor Glanville.

This striking orange chequered butterfly specialises in breeding on the crumbling clay cliffs where its caterpillars feed on ribwort plantain and then retreat into their protective webs. In good years these butterflies are also seen on the downs.

Fundraising for Future Countryside
At Dunsbury we are planning to create the right farmland habitat for wildlife to flourish. The acquisition of Dunsbury links the land the National Trust already owns at Compton and Mottistone, providing us with a large swathe of mixed farmland, woodland and downs. The Neptune Coastal Campaign, which has been running for 50 years, has helped us make this significant purchase.

Above: Dunsbury Farm, Isle of Wight.

Below: A female Glanville fritillary in June at Compton Bay.

How to Get There

By Car Brook Chine car park is a National Trust pay and display car park (free to members) on the A3055 military road at Brookgreen. Nearest post code is PO30 4EX

OS Map Landranger 196, Explorer OL29

Start / End Brook Chine car park, **OS grid ref: SZ 385836**

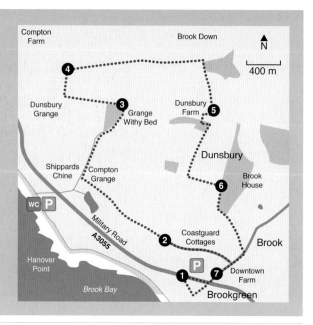

1. From the car park, take the path into the field just to the left of the track which leads down to the beach. Take the left-hand fork, following the line of the hedge and the road. Leave the field by the cattle grid and carefully cross the busy Military Road. Go along Brook Village Road and after 220 yards (200m) turn left into Coastguard Lane. Follow the track past some houses then the terrace of coastguard cottages.

2. When the tarmac ends, continue straight ahead. Go through a field gate and past a pond on your left, then through another field gate. Turn right opposite the entrance to Compton Grange and head up the field to a crossing track about 110 yards (100m) before the fence line.

3. Turn left along the track. When you reach Dunsbury Grange on your left, turn right through a gate and head steeply up a field keeping the fence close to your right.

4. Cross a stile on the ridge and turn right. Go onwards through a field gate and keep just to the left of the ridge top. Pass through another field gate and follow the grassy path through the next gate. Turn right immediately after the gate on 'BS86 Dunsbury'. Keep to the right of the track and take the higher level grassy path when the main track bears left and descends. Head downhill to Dunsbury Farm, with hedges on both sides.

5. Go through two field gates and turn right onto the tarmac farm track, then quickly left after just 40 yards (37m) – between the buildings – signposted 'BS102 Hamstead Trail'. The tarmac track bends left then right, heading downhill with buildings on both sides. Take the next left and go between hedges to a T-junction with a seat.

6. Turn right here to follow the bridleway down a sunken lane, eventually reaching Badger Lane. Bear right and follow the lane into Brook village. Turn right along the road and go past Coastguard Lane back to the Military Road.

7. Take care crossing the road to the track opposite, and head straight ahead along the track which services the houses on Brookgreen. Just before a little bridge, follow a coast path marker post on the right through a field and head back to the car park.

Make the Most of Your Day
At Compton Beach you can swim, surf, build sand castles, go rock pooling and even hunt for fossils.

Food and Facilities
The nearest toilets and refreshments can be found in Freshwater Bay, to the west of Dunsbury.

15. Mottisfont Estate Walk

Discover this beautiful and diverse estate on a varied walk through ancient woodlands, historic farmland and along the crystal-clear River Test. A great deal of work is taking place to restore and improve natural habitats for wildlife – see how many species you can spot

Mottisfont
Hampshire
SO51 0LS
01794 344757
mottisfont@nationaltrust.org.uk

About this walk

Varied walk

Historic interest

Ancient woodland

Dogs welcome on short leads, excluding rose gardens, formal lawns and play areas

Distance 6 miles (9.7km)

Time 3 hours

South East

Things to see

Mottisfont Estate

The National Trust acquired Mottisfont estate in 1957 from Mrs Maud Russell, which includes the Abbey (house), gardens, woodlands, rivers and farmlands over 1,600 acres (648ha). The Trust owns 64 houses within the estate, mostly in the village of Mottisfont. One of the oldest properties is the Fox, which you will pass once you cross Hat Lane. This was one of many pubs in the village until they were closed down around 1920. The church dates from 1150 and it is said that a tunnel connected the church with the main abbey. The oldest houses in the village date from the 1500s.

Dunbridge Springs

The three freshwater springs here feed into the surrounding ditch systems and the River Dun. The adjacent fields are managed as traditional hay and grazing meadows without intensive fertilisers, herbicides or pesticides. Such management will protect local habitats, and many wetland species can be found here.

Historic Farmland

Much of the land is farmed, either growing arable crops such as barley and wheat or for grazing cattle. The National Trust works closely with our farmers to improve the wildlife habitat and although there is much to do, many hedges have been replanted where they

once existed, and buffer strips of natural vegetation have been left uncultivated to protect rivers and woods and provide habitats for plants, insects and small mammals. These areas also offer fine opportunities to kestrels and barn owls for hunting.

Above: The house at Mottisfont, Hampshire.

Overleaf: Wintertime in the gardens at Mottisfont.

How to Get There

By Train Dunbridge station is 1½ miles (2.4km) away along the B0384. Walk up hill away from the station and Mill Arms pub

By Car Park at Spearywell car park SO51 0LS, which is not far from Mottisfont

OS Map Landranger 185

Start / End Spearywell car park, **OS grid ref: SU 316275**

1. Set off from Spearywell car park taking the left-hand path. This walk takes in much of the woodland. Follow the bear stone and post markers through the woodland until you exit the woods and come out by farmland.

2. Turn left out of the woods and onto a long path beside the fields. If you go under a railway bridge then you are on the right path.

3. Walk across the fields and under the railway tunnel turning right at the kissing gate.

4. Follow the River Dun towards the railway station.

5. Go over the level crossing and across the fields via a kissing gate a few yards from the station.

6. Walk along Oakley Road along the west perimeter of the Abbey. Turn right off the road by the marker.

7. Continue through Queenmeadow Copse and along the perimeter of Clapgate Copse, across fields to Great Copse.

8. Walk through Great Copse and into the top of Spearywell Wood. Follow the pathway back to the start point.

Make the Most of Your Day

Originally founded in the 1200s and with a great artistic tradition, Mottisfont has an extraordinary drawing room painted by Rex Whistler. It houses a permanent twentieth-century art collection and holds important exhibitions. Outside you can enjoy the gardens, as well as regular family events and activities.

Food and Facilities

A restaurant, café and toilets can be found within the grounds at Mottisfont.

16. Dutton Estate Walk at Hinton Ampner

Hinton Ampner
Bramdean
Hampshire
SO24 0LA
01962 771305
hintonampner@
nationaltrust.org.uk

About this walk
Wildflowers

Wildlife interest

Ancient woodland

Breathtaking views

Trail can be muddy in places
after heavy rainfall

Dogs welcome; keep under
under close control at all
times

Distance 4 miles (6.4km)

Time 2 hours

South East

This route takes in the historic estate at Hinton Ampner, the final part
of Ralph Dutton's vision for an estate, garden and house that would
blend harmoniously into the surrounding countryside. It starts on open
downland with endless views over the South Downs, and then weaves
through ancient woodland, along avenues lined with beech trees. In
spring, the woodland is turned into a sea of blue as native bluebells
carpet the woodland floor.

Things to see

A View from the Ridge
Take the time to stop and enjoy
the view over the stunning South
Downs. You will often see roe deer
and hares from this vantage point.

Woodland at Hinton Ampner
As part of the development of the
woodland by Ralph Dutton, Hinton
Ampner had its own saw mill and
much of the wood was grown
so that the estate could be self
sufficient. Hazel was also coppiced

and used for many things, such
as fencing; you will notice many
sections of hazel, and we hope to
use this recourse again in the future.
The woodland is a habitat for many
native species of flora and fauna;
in spring there is a dazzling display
of bluebells and wood anemones.
There are many native creatures
that inhabit the woods including
badger, roe deer, fox and the rare
barbastelle bat. Follow the path as
it meanders through the woods.

Beech Avenues
Towering beech trees line
the avenues in this section of
woodland. The leaves form an
ever-changing canopy of colour
throughout the seasons.

Above: Bluebells in the long grass,
with the house in the distance, at
Hinton Ampner, Hampshire.

How to Get There

By Train Winchester 9 miles (14.5km); Petersfield 10 miles (16km); Alresford (Mid-Hants Railway steam railway, linked via mainline services at Alton) 4 miles (6.4km). See bus details for transfers to Hinton Ampner

By Car On A272, 1 mile (1.6km) west of Bramdean village, 8 miles east of Winchester. Leave M3 at junction 9 and follow signs to Petersfield

OS Map Explorer 132

Start / End Gated entrance just off the main drive, behind the Church, **OS grid ref: SU 597275**

---

1. As you leave Visitor Reception (please note normal admission price applies to access walks from here), head straight along the main drive with the House on your right and the Church to your left. The drive begins to sweep to the left behind the church. You will notice a gate just off to the right-hand side; this is the start of the estate walk. Head through the two gates and across the field in the direction of the waymarker. There are often sheep grazing in this field, so dogs need to be kept on leads. At the end of the field turn left on to the road. Make sure you keep to the right-hand side of the road, facing the oncoming traffic, then a few yards along the road, turn right on the track denoted by the waymarker.

2. In front of you is a path leading up and along the ridge. About ½ mile (800m) down is a bench; take time to stop here and enjoy the view over the Hampshire countryside.

3. At the end of this section of path, turn right and head down the ridge. You will often see hares in the fields in the spring so keep a close eye out for them. If your dog is not used to wildlife we advise keeping it on a lead. Follow the path down till you reach the road.

4. To the left of the path you will notice a large house. This was the home of the last of the Dutton line, Joane Dutton, who was the youngest sister of Ralph Dutton, the last owner of Hinton Ampner. Cross the road at this point, again listening out for any passing traffic. Once over the road, follow the path towards the woods.

5. The woodland at Hinton Ampner is mixed and has both conifer and native broad-leaf trees. Although this is ancient woodland, Ralph Dutton did much to improve the woodland and make it a vital part of the working estate.

6. Turn right onto the last section of woodland; grand avenues lined by towering beech trees stretch as far as the eye can see. Pheasant pens used to line the trail here but they have been removed recently so walkers can enjoy this area. You will also notice woodland dens dotted through the trees – why not build your own den while you are here?

7. At the end of the avenue, exit the woodlands using the kissing gate to the right of the main gate and follow the bridleway to the left. This area can be muddy after prolonged periods of rainfall so be careful on muddy sections. Keep a watchful eye in

the field on the left as this is another excellent area for spotting hares. At the end of the path take care in crossing the road and follow the path on the opposite side.

8. Turn right onto the Wayfarers' Walk, a pathway created in memory of the first flight of Geoffrey de Havilland, an aviation pioneer, which runs from Berkshire through to Emsworth in Hampshire. It takes in many sites along its route including Watership Down; the route was in use since ancient times and would have been used by drovers to move livestock. Follow the track back up the slope towards the finishing point at Hinton Ampner.

9. Exit the path through the gate by which you entered and back onto the main driveway.

Make the Most of Your Day

The house at Hinton Ampner was lovingly rebuilt by its last owner, Ralph Dutton, after a catastrophic fire in 1960. Inside you can enjoy the beautifully proportioned rooms, which house his exquisite collection of ceramics and art, each window offering undisturbed views to the tranquil countryside beyond. Beautifully manicured lawns lead the eye down avenues of sculptured topiary, past borders full of the heady scent of roses, to breathtaking views across the South Downs. Family events, music, theatre and guided walks are held throughout the year.

Food and Facilities

Refreshments are available in the café near visitor reception. Toilet facilities are also located here.

Above: Trees in blossom at Hinton Ampner, Hampshire.

17. Hat Hill to Levin Down

Drovers Estate draws all the landscapes of the Downs together in one magical place. Among sweeps of flowers, ancient woods, rolling hills, farmland and hedgerows, Drovers is a fine retreat from everyday hustle and bustle. This all adds up to a fantastic habitat for the many species of flora and fauna that you can enjoy during this walk.

Drovers Estate
Singleton
West Sussex
01730 816638
PO18 0HA
woolbedingenquiries@
nationaltrust.org.uk

About this walk
Unspoiled chalk grassland

Birdwatching

Dogs welcome; keep under close control near livestock

Distance 4¾ miles (7.6km)

Time 2 hours 30 mins

Things to see

Ancient Woodland
The ancient woodland along this walk supports some rare and unusual species: look out for early purple orchids in spring, and butcher's broom, an evergreen prickly plant that is typical of ancient woodland. As its name implies, this plant was used to scrub clean butchers' tables after cutting meat. These woods are also fine habitat for speckled wood and ringlet butterflies.

Levin Down
A Sussex Wildlife Trust (SWT) site, Levin Down is a hill covered in natural scrubby grassland that provides superb habitat for summer birds, and is a botanical utopia for chalk grassland wildflowers, including wild thyme, marjoram, lady's bedstraw, pyramidal orchid, clustered bellflower, round-headed rampion and harebell. Here you can also see scattered juniper trees, descendants of some of the earliest species to colonise the area after the last Ice Age.

Above: A chalk grassland meadow on Hat Hill.

Right: Juniper berries. Juniper trees are a feature of Levin Down.

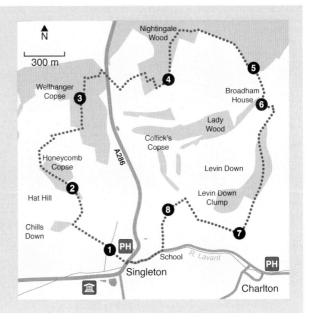

How to Get There

By Train Chichester 7 miles
(11.3km)

By Car A286 Chichester
to Midhurst road, park in
Singleton village

OS Map Explorer 120, OL8

Start Park near The Partridge
Inn. Walk up to the main
road, turn left and continue
along to the cricket pavilion,
OS grid ref: SU 874131

End Beside Singleton village
school. Turn right onto road,
bear left at the next junction,
this will take you back to the
start, **OS grid ref: SU 879132**

1. From behind the cricket pavilion go over a stile, along the edge of a field, turn right over a second stile, and cross a stream bed using the plank bridge. Enter Drovers Estate over the stile beside the National Trust omega sign and follow the way up. Turn right at the top, after passing between the red brick walls of an old railway bridge. The disused railway tunnels are now legally protected roost sites for bats.

2. With the cutting to your right, go over the stile. Above to your left is Hat Hill, an area of unspoiled flower-rich chalk grassland. Keeping the railway-cutting trees to your right, follow the path to a waymarker post. Here, take the middle path along the track opposite (don't go up or down hill), which leads slightly left and uphill to the woods. The track winds gently up beneath two ancient beech trees on a mossy, root-bound bank to your left, then past another great beech further along to your right. Keeping the woodland to your right as the path opens out into a meadow at the top of Honeycomb Copse, continue along the path and then pass through a field gate and stile into pasture. Follow the path round towards the gate and stile near the barn. Once past the barn, go left at a T-junction, then over the stile on

the right where a white marker post points across a field. Keep heading straight across towards the stile to Wellhanger Copse.

3. Go over the stile into the shady woods. After 11 yards (10m) or so bear left along a moss-edged track through open beech woodland and enjoy its stillness and leaf-green light. Under sweeping boughs at the wood's edge dogleg to your right, then left across an open ride into a path opposite by a marker post. Follow this path to a T-junction, turn right and go downhill out of the woods, crossing another track. Follow the green footpath sign down and then cross the busy A286.

4. Once safely across by the bus-stop, follow the surfaced lane, then at the marker post turn left, keeping the hedge to your left. Follow the track into Nightingale Wood; look to your right and take an uphill track by the marker post, then turn left by another marker post up a narrow path. Turn right at the T-junction and go up to the edge of the wood, looking out into an open field. Go left and follow the wood edge as it curves round at your left hand.

5. The path now bears left and downhill between tall beech trees to a T-junction. Go right here, then follow the path to another T-junction. Follow the bridleway right and up a steady incline as it comes out to the wood edge, rising up to some magnificent old pollarded beech trees.

6. Turn left out from the woods following the blue bridleway signs to the Broadham House farm and up the grey flinty farm track which winds round the hill. Turn right through the metal field gate indicated by the 'Charlton' finger of the tall waymarker post. Embrace the wind on this sweeping hillside, then follow the path to your left along the field edge to a little gateway on your left which takes you into a twisting tunnel of trees and dense scrub. The pathway is narrow and on a steep hillside, so take care.

7. From here you are in Levin Down. Step over a stile with the SWT sign and carry on walking as the path opens up into glorious steep-sided downland with views towards Singleton. Walk on and pass through

another gate. When you reach the signboard, go right and up the slope to enjoy the views once more. Turn right through a single gate into a juniper grotto, and enjoy walking through this secluded spot.

8. Continue along the path to a set of double gates, pass through and head towards the copse of trees. Bear left across the hillside towards the kissing gate in the corner. If you look west over the hillside you can see Hat Hill where you started the walk (the hill with the tallest pylon on top). Pass through the gates and follow the path down into Singleton village where you pop out at the primary school. If you turn right you will find the Partridge Inn.

Make the Most of Your Day
There are events held throughout the year in the Woolbeding countryside.

Food and Facilities
There is a pub, The Partridge Inn, in Singleton village.

Below: Speckled wood butterfly (male).

18. Hidden Hindhead Walk

Above: A Highland cow at the Devil's Punch Bowl, Hindhead, Surrey.

London Road
Hindhead
Surrey
GU26 6AB
01428 681050
hindhead@nationaltrust.
org.uk

About this walk
Stunning views
Historical interest
Rare wildlife
Some steep slopes and
uneven surfaces
Dogs welcome; keep on
leads near livestock

Distance 3 miles (4.8km)
Time 1–2 hours

South East

Hindhead Commons and the Devil's Punch Bowl offers you the chance to explore a majestic landscape and pine-clad hilltops. The important habitats here support an abundance of wildlife, including endangered bird species, such as Dartford warbler, woodlark and nightjar.

Things to see

Highland Cattle

On this walk make sure you keep an eye out for our residents, the 40 orange Highland cattle we have grazing the scrub. They help us keep it under control together with a group of Exmoor ponies.

Sailor's Stone

In 1786 a sailor was brutally murdered by three men while walking from London to the docks in Portsmouth. A stone was erected to mark the spot where the poor sailor met his death, and the three villains were tried and then hung on Gibbet Hill.

Wildife Haven

The Devil's Punch Bowl, once separated from Hindhead Commons by the A3, has become one of the top wildlife sites in south-east England. The creation of the Hindhead Tunnel by Highways England, completed in 2011, has enabled the site to regenerate. The last decade has seen the restoration of fragile and endangered historic heathland habitat, and the return of rare and diverse breeding birds such as woodlark and nightjar.

Right: The Celtic Cross at dawn on Gibbet Hill, Hindhead Common.

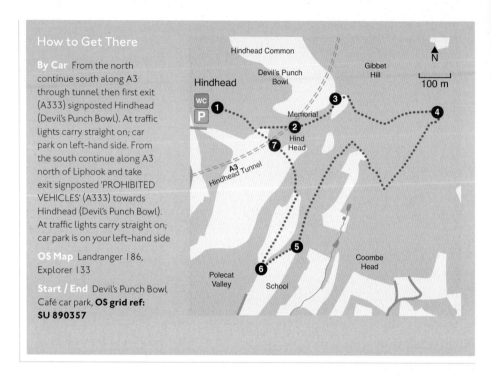

How to Get There

By Car From the north continue south along A3 through tunnel then first exit (A333) signposted Hindhead (Devil's Punch Bowl). At traffic lights carry straight on; car park on left-hand side. From the south continue along A3 north of Liphook and take exit signposted 'PROHIBITED VEHICLES' (A333) towards Hindhead (Devil's Punch Bowl). At traffic lights carry straight on; car park is on your left-hand side

OS Map Landranger 186, Explorer 133

Start / End Devil's Punch Bowl Café car park, **OS grid ref: SU 890357**

---

1. Follow the signs along the new path towards the old A3 road. It's hard to imagine that a busy road really used to be here.

2. Follow the route and head north down the Byway Open to all Traffic (surfaced road). Discover the Sailor's Stone and admire the views across the Punch Bowl. Don't miss the recently recovered old milestone just after the Sailor's Stone.

3. Continue down the old London Road until you reach some steps on your right. These lead to Gibbet Hill and far-reaching views across the Weald. Rest on the bench and admire the scenery.

4. Head down the marked path on your right – this is a fairly steep descent – and wander down through the shady trees that lead you to the plinth of the Temple of the Four Winds. Demolished in the 1970s, this lodge was where Viscount Pirrie, who owned Witley Park estate, would hold elaborate picnic lunches for his hunting friends.

5. Continue along the path around the chestnut coppice wood and past the pond on your right. Head through the gate and then on up the hill. At the unpaved road, continue up until you reach a large red brick house on your left. Turn right through the gate and follow the signs.

6. Head up over the heathland. There are several benches nearby to rest if you need to – look out for the ponies and cattle grazing on the heath.

7. Go through the gate and across the old London Road and follow the route back to the start.

Make the Most of Your Day
The shop at Hindhead Commons is a great place to find gifts and beautiful things for your home and garden.

Food and Facilities
There is a café at the Devil's Punch Bowl and toilets are available during opening times.

19. Hughenden Boundary Walk

Hughenden Manor
High Wycombe
Buckinghamshire
HP14 4LA
01494 755573
hughenden@nationaltrust.
org.uk

About this walk
Wildflower displays

Beautiful woodland

Chalk stream

Some of the route can be
muddy and slippery in or
after wet weather, and there
are some quite steep slopes
to walk up and down

Dogs welcome under close
control

Distance 4 miles (6.4km)

Time 1 hour 30 mins–
2 hours

South East

This energetic walk broadly follows the outer boundary of the Hughenden Estate. It allows you to explore beautiful woodland, open parkland, farmland and a rare chalk stream. There is plenty of nature to enjoy throughout the year, from wildflower displays and important grassland habitats, to nesting birds and soaring kites, as well as rare butterflies, such as the marbled white.

Things to see

Conservation in Action

The countryside around Hughenden features chalk grassland, managed farmland and beech woodlands. It is an area rich in wildlife, from red kites to rare butterflies. Since the Second World War, the UK has lost around 80 per cent of its rare grassland habitats. Monitoring the flowers, butterflies, moths and insects that make their homes here is an important part of our work and it means we can help to protect them and provide habitats and landscapes that let them thrive, reversing this decline.

Hughenden Parkland

The Park was first laid out in the 1820s with limes, horse chestnuts, walnuts and sycamores. Some of the trees planted then survive now, as do some field maples that pre-dated them. After Disraeli bought Hughenden in 1848 he extended the parkland southwards. He enjoyed walking here with his wife, Mary Anne, and planted many trees to commemorate visitors.

Chalk Stream

The stream along the route is rare because the chalk rock it flows over is permeable and water normally sinks down into it. The stream rises in the Hughenden Valley and flows into the River Wye in High Wycombe. Its flow is intermittent and dependent on groundwater levels that vary according to rainfall and season.

Above: The view from the Pleasure Grounds towards the parkland in May at Hughenden Manor, Buckinghamshire.

1. From the Visitor Welcome Kiosk retrace your steps towards the main car park. The Boundary Walk is marked with red waymarkers. At the T-junction of paths by the Dew Pond turn right and cross the road, heading left for 22 yards (20m) before turning right onto a path. Shortly after entering Woodcock Wood turn left at a crossing. Soon you pass a sawpit on your right. Continue through to the end of the wood ignoring any crossing paths.

2 Go through a gate then continue in a leftward direction across the field towards a gate in the field boundary, with views of Hughenden Valley to the right. Go left through the gate and walk up the right edge of a field. Cross a path and through another field, with a hedge now on your left. At the end of the field, turn right along the woodland boundary until you see a metal gate on your left.

3. Turn left through the gate to enter Flagmore Wood. You soon pass chalk pits on either side of the path. Bear right at a junction where the path bends to the right to go downhill. When you come to another junction follow the path downhill in the same direction. At the bottom of the hill, turn left on the bridleway until you reach a gate leading into a field.

4. Don't go through the gate but turn right uphill into Common Wood. When you reach the crossing boundary ditch, turn left keeping the ditch on your right. Go downhill to a crossing track. Cross the track and continue steeply uphill until you leave the wood between two fences. Take care here as the route meets a busy public road.

5. Cross the road (Coates Lane) into Littleworth Road and walk along the pavement on the left. Just after house number 78 (and opposite a brick and flint cottage) join a public footpath on the left. Cross a drive then continue along a path towards Little Tinker's Wood. Enter the woods then immediately bear left at the fork. Follow the path down then gently uphill until you reach a metal gate into a field containing the D'Israeli Monument. Here there are fine views over the estate and the Manor House.

6. Leave the Monument field through the same gate you entered then turn right to go down to the bottom of the woods. Turn right through a gate into a field then continue with a fence on your right until you reach a road, Coates Lane. Cross the road and turn left for 33 yards (30m).

7. Turn sharp right onto a track and go through a metal gate. Follow the track uphill until you reach a gate with Middle Lodge on it. Turn left here and go through a set of metal gates into Hughenden Park. Turn sharp right then follow the path downhill with a metal fence on your right and parkland on your left. Continue beneath some large field maples until you reach a stream, with an ornamental lake created by a concrete weir.

8. Turn left to walk along the left bank of the stream until you reach the main drive that you drove up.

9. Turn left to walk uphill, keeping to the left of the drive. Pass through the car park of St Michael and All Angels Church then go into the churchyard.

10. Follow the tarmac path up to the left of the church. Leave the churchyard through a small gate and continue uphill. At the top of the park go through the metal gate next to a cattle grid, join the main drive and walk straight along it until you reach the Stableyard and Walled Garden entrances on your right.

Make the Most of Your Day
Hughenden Manor was the country home of Victorian statesman Benjamin Disraeli. The house contains an extraordinary collection of personal memorabilia, and there's even a Victorian playroom for younger visitors. Historical, literary and other events take place throughout the year.

Food and Facilities
Restaurant/tea-room and toilets at the Stableyard. Dizzy's Tea-room at Hughenden Manor.

Left: Bluebells in woodland at Hughenden.

20. The Best of Coombe Hill Walk

This circular walk takes in the best Coombe Hill has to offer with incredible views across the Aylesbury Vale. Coombe Hill is the highest viewpoint in the Chilterns, while its chalk grassland and acid heathland are two of the UK's most important habitats.

Coombe Hill
Near Butlers Cross
Aylesbury
Buckinghamshire
HP17 0UR
01494 755573
chilternscountryside@
nationaltrust.org.uk

About this walk

Superb views

Military history

Chalk grassland

Some sections can be slippery

Dogs welcome under close control

Distance 1 mile (1.6km)

Time 40 mins

Things to see

The Monument

The monument was built in 1904 in memory of the 148 men of Buckinghamshire who gave their lives in the Second Boer War of 1899–1902. It was almost completely destroyed in 1938 by a lightning strike but was rebuilt later that year. A full restoration took place in 2010 when the bronze tablet was replaced and all the stone work was cleaned up and repointed. It was unveiled at a dedicated ceremony held on 20 October the same year.

Chequers

Chequers is a sixteenth-century mansion, although there has been a house on the site since the twelfth century. The house was given to the nation as a country retreat for the serving Prime Minister in 1917 and it has been used for that purpose since 1921. In that time, the mansion has been visited by numerous presidents, prime ministers, leaders and monarchs, from all corners of the world.

Chalk Grassland

Chalk grassland is one of our rarest habitats and a reason why Coombe Hill is designated as a Site of Special Scientific Interest. The large bumps you can see are home to the yellow meadow ant and the anthills themselves provide a fantastic home to many of the wildflower species. During winter months the ant hills really stand out after the summer grazing. In summer you can expect to see over 30 different species of wildflowers and up to 28 different species of butterfly on these slopes.

Above: Coombe Hill in January, Chilterns Countryside, Buckinghamshire.

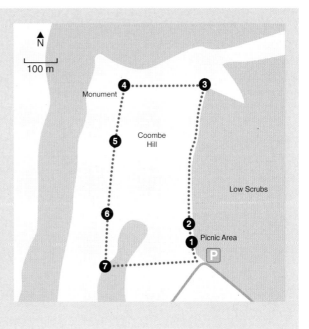

By Train Wendover 1 mile
(1.6km). Follow signs for the
Ridgeway and you will come
out at the Monument, halfway
round the trail

By Car 3 miles (4.8km) west
of Wendover and 5 miles (8km)
drive east of Princes Risborough.
Turn onto the Missenden Road.
Drive for 2 miles (3.2km) up the
hill until you reach the peak
where you need to turn left
up Lodge Hill. Drive for 1 mile
(1.6km) up Lodge Hill until you
reach the car park in front of you
on a tight right-hand bend

OS Map Explorer 181

Start / End Near car park,
OS grid ref: SP 851062

1. Go to the stone track just the other side of the picnic area next to the car park and start walking along the track with the picnic area fence on your right. Look out for the orange waymarkers along the route and follow these.

2. 65 yards (60m) after the picnic area you will see an entrance to the Natural Play Trail on your right-hand side. You can either have a go now or come back at the end of the walk. Continue along the stone track with the fence on your right.

3. Follow the stone track around to the left in the direction of the finger post. Magnificent views over the Aylesbury Vale open up on your right. Continue along the track until you reach the Monument.

4. You have now reached the highest viewpoint in the Chilterns, 853ft (260m) above sea level. Take a moment to look at the toposcope, which will explain what you can see in the landscape. When you are ready to move on, turn your back to the view and look for an orange waymarking disc on your right, just in front of some bushes. You are now on the Ridgeway National Trail and the path turns from stone into a well-worn grassy/flinty track.

5. You will reach a slight rise in the path that gives you a fantastic moment to stop and admire Chequers, the Prime Minister's country retreat. It is the large house hidden in the trees at a 1 o'clock direction to your path ahead. In the distance, just above Chequers, you can see Pulpit Hill, another National Trust property. Carry on along the path following the orange arrows.

6. You will see along your right-hand side a fantastic example of chalk grassland. Continue along the path until you meet a fence at the end.

7. Once you reach the fence line at the end of the path, turn left up a slight incline. Ignore the kissing gate on your right – this is where you leave the Ridgeway path behind. Keep going straight on weaving through trees and bushes roughly parallel to the fence on your right. The orange waymarking disc on your right-hand side will keep you on track. You have reached the end of the trail and are back at the start.

Make the Most of Your Day

Situated in the picturesque Chiltern Hills, Coombe Hill is one of a group of popular beauty spots that offer fabulous walking opportunities with lots of pubs where you can stop to have lunch. Don't forget to enjoy the Natural Play Trail at Coombe Hill on your visit. The other sites include Aston Wood and Juniper Bank, Bradenham Estate, Hogback Wood, Pulpit Wood and Watlington Hill and Woods.

Food and Facilities

There is a picnic area at Coombe Hill and there are pubs and cafés in Wendover. The nearest public toilets for Coombe Hill are also in Wendover.

Above: Second Boer War memorial at Coombe Hill.

21. Morden Hall Park Walk

The historic parkland at Morden Hall was created by the Hatfeild family in the nineteenth century. Field boundaries were removed and were planted up with narrow fringes of trees. This walk takes you along avenues lined with lime trees, as well as following a section of the River Wandle and its wetlands that are rich with wildlife.

Morden Hall Park
Morden
Surrey
SM4 5JD
020 8545 6850
mordenhallpark@
nationaltrust.org.uk

About this walk
Riverside views
Historic parkland
Wildlife interest
The ground can be muddy and slippery in wet weather
Dogs are welcome under close control

Distance Almost 2 miles (3km)

Time 1 hour

Things to see

The Stableyard

This building was constructed in about 1879 to house carriage and riding horses, and is a real demonstration of the Hatfeilds' wealth. Note the trout on the weather vane, reflecting the links with the River Wandle and fishing. Step inside to discover the gallery, café and bookshop.

The Snuff Mill

The Hatfeild fortune came from drying and grinding tobacco (using the water mills) into a fine powder known as snuff, with this particular mill remaining in use until 1922. You can see the original waterwheel that once powered the huge millstones to crush the tobacco.

Wildlife

Water lies at the heart of Morden Hall Park. During your walk you will cross over the River Wandle several times and visit the lush wetlands, vibrant riverbanks and islands, which provide homes to a variety of plants, animals, insects and birdlife. The park is one of the closest heronries to central London.

Above: Morden Hall Park, London. Morden Hall Park is an Arcadian country estate hidden behind Grade II-listed walls.

How to Get There

By Train Morden South approximately ½ mile (800m)

By Car Off the A24 and A297 south of Wimbledon and north of Sutton. From the M25, exit at junction 10 and take the A3 towards London. Join the A289 (Bushey Road) at the Merton junction. Follow the brown signs to Morden Hall Park

OS Map Landranger 176, Explorer 161

Start / End The Potting Shed Café, next to Garden Centre car park, **OS grid ref: TQ 262686**

---

1. To enter Morden Hall Park, pass through the gate between the Potting Shed Café and the Garden Centre, under an archway. Turn right. On your right you will see workshops associated with the Hatfeild family's estate.

2. Follow the sign to the Snuff Mill, which is now a Learning Centre providing activities for groups from the local area. The millstones on display outside are originally from a spice mill, but show the edge-turning arrangement of the stones used.

3. At the Snuff Mill proceed across a modern bridge over the main tributary of the River Wandle. You will pass a little building on the left where G.E. Hatfeild bred trout, then Morden Cottage on your right. The building is thought to have originally been a hunting lodge before becoming a permanent residence. Look out for the rose garden beyond the cottage.

4. Walk along the path with the rose garden on your right and go through a gate, turn right, crossing over the tarmac bridge across a stream of the Wandle and take the first path to your right. Pass through a smaller gate and back into the rose garden, on the far side of the stream that divides it in two. Continue on this path out of the garden and into the arboretum.

The eighteenth-century statues of Neptune and Venus can also be seen on an island in the river.

5. Follow the path along the course of the river, with the water on your right. When the path forks at a pond, stay left, on the hard standing. When you come up to the avenue of lime and horse chestnut trees near the gate by the Surrey Arms pub, turn left and walk along the avenue. Avenues of lime trees were a status symbol, and horse chestnuts were very fashionable trees.

6. Carry on walking down the avenue past the path coming up from Phipps Bridge tram stop. Re-cross the tarmac bridge and continue straight on. To your right, in the trees, there is a natural play area for children.

7. Cross over the ornate white Victorian bridge, and ahead you will see a second white bridge with Morden Hall beyond, surrounded by a moat. Approach Morden Hall. Cross back over the bridge into the park, turn left following the path crossing over two large wooden bridges. Once over the second bridge, turn right, following the dragonfly signpost to the wetlands, which is flooded and is home to a rich variety of wildlife. (Please note, the boardwalk through the wetlands can be wet after rain and in winter. If you would prefer not to take this route, continue straight ahead and make a circuit of North Park before continuing from this point at point 9.)

8. When you leave the wetlands you will reach a T-junction with a tram crossing to your right. Instead, turn left and follow the path with the wetlands on your left; North Park is to your right. Turn left at the end of the wetland boardwalk, cross over a wooden bridge, with glimpses of Morden Hall through the trees to your right.

9. Retrace your steps back over the two large wooden bridges to the white bridge over the Wandle. Do not cross it, instead pass straight ahead towards the Snuff Mill

10. At the Snuff Mill turn right and retrace your steps back to the Potting Shed Café and our Garden Centre, where you started.

Make the Most of Your Day

As well as enjoying the tranquillity of the deer park and exploring the River Wandle and its wildlife, you can find out more about Morden Hall by joining one of the guided history tours that take place every Sunday between April and November. There is a new boardwalk through the wetlands that allows you to get up close and personal with the flora and fauna. You can also visit the garden centre where you can find everything you need to keep your garden looking its best.

Food and Facilities

Refreshments are available at the Potting Shed Café, the Stableyard Café and the kiosk in the rose garden at the weekend. Toilets at the Stableyard, Potting Shed Café, Garden Centre and the Snuff Mill (when open).

Below: Snuff Mill and the River Wandle in Morden Hall Park, London. The Snuff Mill is an eighteenth-century water mill and is now a Learning Centre.

22. Nymans Woodland Trail

Nymans is a romantic garden with a wooded valley full of exotic trees and shrubs. Planted in the 1890s by German émigré, Ludwig Messel, it combines the formality of topiary and a rock garden with the informality of naturalistic planting and drifts of colourful plants. Messel was a keen collector who cultivated a significant number of rare plants. The work he began at Nymans continues to this day.

Handcross
Near Haywards Heath
West Sussex
RH17 6EB
01444 405250
nymans@nationaltrust.org.uk

About this walk
Spectacular woodland views

Arboretum

Wildlife interest

Areas of the route can be slippery and muddy, especially in wetter months and on the final ascent

Dogs welcome in the woods, but not in the garden; please keep on leads during nesting season (March–August)

Distance 2½ miles (4km)

Time 1 hour 30 mins

Things to see

Woodland Views
Great views can be seen across the Weald towards the South Downs. The woodland stretches before you, showing a wide variety of tree species which give a spectacular patchwork of colour in the autumn.

Above: The Lime Avenue (pictured) overlooks the woodland, which contains trees of mainly oak, sweet chestnut and beech. The woodland forms the eastern boundary of the garden overlooking the park.

The Lake
The lake was originally created as a 'hammer pond' to drive the iron furnace downstream. The power of the water behind the dam drove hammers to break locally quarried ironstone. It was widened in the 1800s to create a pond with a boathouse and bathing hut. The lake is a haven for wildlife, including dragonflies, rare beetles, fish and eels. An array of birds can be spotted and, if you are very lucky, you may see the blue flash of a kingfisher.

Cascades
The cascades are often full and fast flowing, adding movement and sound in the hush of the woods. The cascades were created for the Messel family by soldiers returning from the First World War.

Giant Redwood
As you pass the cottage look left over the field and you can see the top of the Giant Redwood standing proud, head and shoulders above the rest.

How to Get There

By Train Balcombe 5 miles (8km) (no public transport to Nymans available); Crawley 5 miles (8km); Haywards Heath 9 miles (14.5km)

By Car Signposted off London–Brighton M23/A23 at Handcross, south of Crawley

OS Map Explorer 134

Start / End Nymans car park, **OS grid ref: TQ 263296**

1. To take advantage of stunning views over the Weald towards the South Downs, enter Nymans Gardens via Visitor Reception (admission charges apply, free for members, no dogs admitted via this entrance). At Visitor Reception you can get the combination code for the gate you'll use at point 3 of the walk. Head towards the Temple in the Pinetum. Alternative access for those with dogs is via the public footpath (from the rear of car park) following Sussex Ouse Valley Way, and excludes the Arboretum loop of the walk. For this route start the walk from point 3.

2. After taking a moment to enjoy the view across from the Temple, head down the path through the Pinetum. When you reach the bottom of the slope turn to your left, leave the main path and head towards the woodland gate.

3. Exit the formal gardens at the pedestrian gate using the code obtained from the Visitor Reception. Continue ahead where you will see a waymark post 1. (Those who began this walk on the public footpath from the car park can join the trail here.)

4. Take the path to the right downhill following the Ouse Valley Way public footpath. You will eventually come to a staggered crossroads; turn right and almost immediately turn left at waymark post 24, following the blue arrows.

5. Continue down the narrow path with a stream at the bottom of the slope to your left. The path will then widen and you will find yourself on the Conifer Avenue.

6. Partway down, look to your right and you will see a magnificent Giant Redwood by a short section of boardwalk. Don't turn up this path but continue along the footpath.

7. Stay on the public footpath until you come to the lake, take the right-hand fork down the slope and at waymark post 17 turn right along the edge of the lake.

8. When you see waymark post 16 turn to your left and cross a small footbridge. Continue on until you come to a larger bridge, cross this and then head up the steps and follow the path across the meadow.

9. Head across the meadow and up the steps; at the top of the steps turn sharply left, then continue to follow the path ahead. As you follow the track,

Above: The ruins of the house can be seen across the main lawn at Nymans, West Sussex.

remember to look to your left to enjoy views across the woods. At waymark post 12, follow the orange arrow straight ahead.

10. You will eventually come to a sign that says 'Jack Reeding's Woods'; continue ahead and follow the orange arrows. After a while the path begins to head back downhill; there are some twists and turns with steps and railings to guide you and you will pass more rocks to your left.

11. Keep following the orange arrows – after a while the path turns to the left and you will see a stream far below you to your right. Eventually you will come to another flight of steps on the right at waymark post 9; this route is currently closed as it can get very boggy here. Continue straight ahead until you come to a grassy glade and join the track taking you up a slope until you come to a T-junction, where you turn right at waymark post 7 and head uphill.

12. Following the track up the hill, you will come to a clearing with a cottage and barn on the left and old dog kennels on the right. Past here the path bends to the left; keep to the main track and continue to follow the orange arrows. This will eventually almost bring you full circle as you will now be able to see the garden gate at the bottom of the Pinetum ahead of you.

13. Before you reach the garden gate ahead, there is a track sharp right; take this turn, joining the public footpath. There is a steep incline that then brings you back to the main Nymans car park.

Make the Most of Your Day
There is much to see at Nymans, including the dramatic house – part Regency, part pseudo-medieval and part ruin following a fire in 1947 – and the stunning garden. Events include painting workshops, guided walks and family trails.

Food and Facilities
There is a café at Nymans garden. Toilets in car park and café.

23. Bounding up to Belle Tout

Birling Gap
East Dean
West Sussex
BN20 0AB
01323 423197
birlinggap@nationaltrust.org.uk

About this walk
Wildflowers and wildlife
Coastal history
Breathtaking views
Some slopes, steps and uneven terrain
Dogs welcome on leads

At Birling Gap the wild forces of the sea have created unusual platforms and huge heaps of gleaming white chalk. With over 500 acres (over 200ha) of open chalk grassland, the area is rich with butterflies and downland flowers.

Distance 2 miles (3.2km)
Time 1 hour

South East

Things to see

On the Lookout
For centuries, customs officers have kept a vigil along these cliffs, whilst smugglers lurked on the beaches below. There have been cottages here since the 1820s to house the families of the coastguards who worked from Birling Gap. Notice the mossy patch and bricks on the cliff-top, the site of a lookout tower which was demolished in 1991.

Lighthouse on the Move
The lighthouse, Belle Tout, was moved inland in March 1999 to escape the receding coastline. It was originally built in the 1820s by a local character known as 'Mad' Jack Fuller, but became a private home after being superseded by the Beachy Head Lighthouse.

Wonderful Wildlife
The grassland to the sides of the grassy track leading to the

Horseshoe Plantation is a carpet of wildflowers in the spring and summer. Look out for the spotted leaves of early purple orchids in the spring, and if you're very lucky you might see the delicate green flowers of an early spider orchid. Dropwort bursts into puffs of white in the summer, and the black and white chequerboard wings of marbled white butterflies can be seen as they feed on the nectar of wild honeysuckle.

How to Get There

By Train Eastbourne 5½ miles (8.8km); Seaford 6½ miles (10.5km)

By Car 5 miles (8km) west of Eastbourne and 6 miles east of Seaford. Birling Gap car park is signposted from A259 at East Dean, between Seaford and Eastbourne

OS Map Explorer OL25

Start / End Birling Gap car park by the Coastguard Station, **OS grid ref: TV 554960**

1. From the bus-stop follow the finger post with a yellow arrow 'South Downs Way'. Walk up the path and through the gate with the National Trust sign 'The Lookout' and follow this path up the hill to another finger post. Follow this finger post and take the path bearing left along the cliff-top or through the scrub.

2. At the top, head towards the lighthouse either along the cliff-top path or through the scrub.

3. Follow the path to the left of the lighthouse. Continue to follow the new access track down the hill. Pause to enjoy wonderful views towards Beachy Head and the candy-striped lighthouse. At the bottom of the path turn left to head back towards Birling Gap.

4. Continue walking along the track around the base of the hill. This will take you through a small, delicate dappled woodland known as the Horseshoe Plantation, much loved by dragonflies and migrating birds.

5. Continue along the track and this will take you back to the car park from where you started.

Make the Most of Your Day
As well as the many different walks you can try along the Seven Sisters cliffs, you can also search the strand line, go rock pooling, hunt for fossils and spot insects in the grassland.

Food and Facilities
Birling Gap café is located beside the car park; all food is locally sourced. There are toilets in the main car park at Birling Gap.

Previous page above: View of the beach and white cliffs from the cliff-top at Birling Gap and the Seven Sisters.

Previous page below: Belle Tout Lighthouse at Birling Gap.

24. Scotney Parkland Trail

The Scotney Castle estate has a long and varied history. The Grade I-listed parkland is full of magnificent veteran trees. Sussex cattle have been a feature of the landscape since Victorian times, but sheep have been grazed for even longer. The woodlands have been home to traditional Wealden industries such as charcoal and hop production.

Scotney Castle
Lamberhurst
Kent
TN3 8JN
01892 893820
scotneycastle@
nationaltrust.org.uk

About this walk
Superb views
Historical interest
Ancient trees
Some moderate hills and a bridge with steps and stiles
Dogs welcome on leads due to livestock in the fields

Distance 2 miles (3.2km)
Time 1 hour

South East

Things to see

Salvin Gate and Carriageway

The large white gate at the top of the carriageway was designed by Anthony Salvin, the man who designed the New House at Scotney. The gate was designed to be self-closing from either direction ensuring that the footman could leave the gate to close itself. The old carriageway was eventually abandoned, as the horses would look tired after pulling the carriage up the hill to the New House. This was undesirable, so a new carriageway was built that took the carriages downhill and the horses could arrive in a more presentable manner.

Old Hornbeam Pollard

The hornbeam pollard is one of the oldest trees on the estate and is estimated to be around 600 years old. Pollards are trees that are cut at around 6ft (1.8m) high. This would have been done on a rotation and used as a crop for timber, fuel and fodder. Pollards would have been created in areas with grazing animals. By cutting them at 6ft (1.8m) the livestock would not have been able to eat the new growth. Pollarding, if done correctly, can significantly increase the lifespan of the tree.

Iconic View

Before construction of the New House began in 1837, Edward Hussey spent many months looking at suitable locations to ensure that what he created would fit into the beautiful picturesque landscape that you can see before you today. Edward Hussey sited the new house 27 yards (25m) above the fourteenth-century castle for the spectacular views over the garden, towards the woodland that is behind you, forming an Arcadian backdrop to this carefully composed picture.

Above: A robin in the garden at Scotney Castle, Kent.

How to Get There

By Train Wadhurst 5½ miles (8.8km)

By Car Signposted from A21. Main car park (limited spaces) overflow car park ¼ mile (400m) from start point

OS Map Landranger 188

Start / End Scotney Castle car park, **OS grid ref: TQ 6883539**

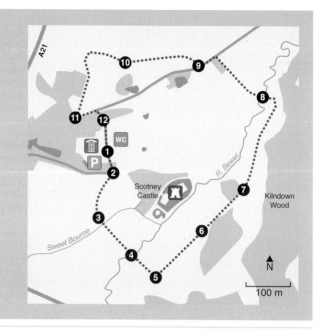

1. At the bottom of the car park follow the road to the right, passing the view of the New House on your left. At the corner head towards the large white Salvin Gate. Please be careful as there may be traffic on this section.

2. Go through the gate and onto the old carriageway. Follow the old carriageway to the bridge at the bottom of the field.

3. The stream which runs under this bridge is called the Sweet Bourne. This small stream feeds the moat which surrounds the Castle. From the bridge, continue on the old carriageway, go through the gate and head towards the next bridge. Look to the left before the next bridge for a glimpse of the old castle.

4. The river which flows under this bridge is the River Bewl. The Bewl Water reservoir is a short distance from Scotney. This bridge is interesting as when seen from a carriage you would imagine that the entire structure is built of expensive sandstone, an apparent indication of the owners' wealth; however, look over the bridge, and you will see the lower is half built of cheaper bricks. From the bridge go through the gate and walk up the hill until you reach the finger post.

5. From the finger post turn left and follow the blue-topped posts across the field. On reaching the blue post marked 8, look to the right to see the gnarly old hornbeam pollard. Continue over the crest of the field towards a gate in the fence line.

6. Go through the gap and continue straight on along the edge of the woodland pasture. Stop halfway along this field and take in the iconic view of the new house and old castle, there is a well-positioned log here for you to rest for a while. Carry on until you come to the gateway.

7. From the gateway continue to the next blue post. As you near the post, the tops of the Oast House of Little Scotney Farm should come into view. Built in 1871, the oasts are Grade II-listed, and are still used to dry the hops that are grown and picked at the farm. Continue across the field until you reach the bridge.

8. After crossing the bridge go through the field to the next gate. Go through the gate and follow the hedge line up the field towards the gate on the road. Before going through the gate, sit on the bench and admire the view of the historic parkland. At the road, turn left through the gate and continue for approximately 110 yards (100m), then turn right into the field.

9. Follow the hedge line around the field, continuing to the gate at the top of the field.

10. Walk along the top of the field following the blue posts; at post 24, stop and look at the bomb craters from the Second World War to your right. Carry on walking past these and turn left at the finger post. Walk down the hill towards the gate at the right-hand corner of the field.

11. Once over the gate, turn left and follow the old servant's entrance. Turn right onto the road, after about 55 yards (50m) turn right through the old barn.

12. After going through the old barn you have arrived back at the car park.

Make the Most of Your Day
Scotney was built by Edward Hussey III from the sandstone quarried from the grounds of the old castle. It is positioned to overlook the castle and estate and the garden was also designed and created at the same time. This meant that all the three elements – house, garden and estate – would work as one in creating a perfect picturesque country home. Events are held throughout the year.

Food and Facilities
There is a tea-room and toilets at Scotney Castle.

Opposite: Scotney Castle in winter. The estate at Scotney features a fourteenth-century moated castle, a Victorian mansion and a romantic garden.

25. Sissinghurst Castle Estate Walk

The Sissinghurst Estate is set in 460 acres (186ha) of tranquil Wealden countryside. Over recent years, great efforts have been made to transform large areas of grasslands into floral carpets and improve many established meadows in a bid to increase bio-diversity, and boost populations of butterflies, bees and moths.

Sissinghurst Castle
Biddenden Road
Near Cranbrook
Kent
TN17 2AB
01580 710700
sissinghurst@nationaltrust.org.uk

About this walk
Wildflower displays

Wildlife interest

The terrain is fairly flat but can be muddy during the wetter months. It is advisable to wear stout boots

Dogs are welcome but must be kept on a lead

Distance 3 miles (4.8km)

Time 1 hour 30 mins

Things to see

The Gazebo
Step inside the Gazebo in the corner of the garden by the Moat. It has views over the estate and wider Wealden countryside. It was built as a memorial to Harold Nicolson (diplomat, author and politician, and husband of writer Vita Sackville-West) and was used by Harold's son, Nigel Nicolson, as a writing room.

The Tower
Built in the sixteenth century, the Tower was used as a viewing platform for deer hunts on the 700 acre (283ha) deer park surrounding the Elizabethan house. Later, in the 1850s, the woodland was cleared to create the parkland that can be seen today.

Sissinghurst Castle Farm
The Vegetable Plot, visible from parts of the walk, is a new feature for the estate and supplies the restaurant with seasonal produce. Over the next few years, the farm will evolve into an organic mixed farm supplying meat, eggs, fruit and vegetables, and is managed to benefit wildlife and the environment. The arable crops are grown in rotation with grass for grazing, winter fodder and livestock bedding.

Above: The Orchard in April at Sissinghurst Castle Garden, Kent.

Above: Springtime bluebells and stitchwort in woodland.

How to Get There

By Train Regular service to Staplehurst from London Charing Cross, then take bus service 5

By Car 2 miles (3.2km) north-east of Cranbrook, 1 mile (1.6km) east of Sissinghurst village on A262

OS Map Landranger 188; Explorer 136

Start / End National Trust car park, **OS grid ref: TQ 807384**

1. From the car park follow the path towards the Castle. Walk to left of the castle and continue along the Moat, following it round to the right at the Gazebo. Continue along this path, through a gate and down the hill towards the Lake. At the bottom of the field, go through the gate and turn left around the Lower Lake.

2. After crossing the second bridge, turn right and continue along the Ride through the traditional coppice woodland.

3. After 380 yards (350m) you have two options: for the shorter route (marked on map), turn right and continue up the hill across Park Field towards the car park. To continue on the longer route (marked on map) bear left then right and continue 460 yards (420m) along the Ride until you reach the edge of the woodland. Turn right down a narrow path and continue over the stile into Park Field.

4. Bear slightly to the left across the parkland, taking in the views of the castle and estate. At the next stile cross the drive and enter Bull and Birches Woods. Follow the path for 66 yards (60m) then turn right along the public footpath up the field. At the top turn right, pass through the second double gate then bear diagonally left across the Orchard.

5. Cross the track and join the bridleway, passing the Vegetable Plots on your right and continue along this track. Turn right into the field and follow the margin until you come to a metal gate.

6. At the gate bear right onto the lane and follow this to the next gate on your right.

7. Go through this gate onto the path, taking in the views before continuing over the stream back to the castle.

Make the Most of Your Day

Sissinghurst Castle was bought by poet and writer Vita Sackville-West and her husband Harold Nicolson in the 1930s. They went on to create a world-renowned garden, and you can buy plants propagated in the garden from the plant shop. Events, exhibitions and guided walks are held throughout the year.

Food and Facilities

Hot food is available in the restaurant between 12 and 3pm as well as coffee, tea and cake all day. Toilets can be found at Visitor Reception and in the restaurant.

26. Bateman's Kipling Countryside Walk

Bateman's was the home of author and poet Rudyard Kipling. The 300 acres (121ha) of countryside around the house influenced works such as *Puck of Pook's Hill, Rewards and Fairies* and many of his poems. The ancient woodland is a haven for wildflowers, including wood anemones, early purple orchids, dog's mercury, wild garlic and celandines, and the Millpond supports many species of insect.

Bateman's Lane
Burwash
East Sussex
TN19 7DS
01435 882302
batemans@nationaltrust.org.uk

About this walk
Wildflower displays
Ancient woodland
One steady, moderate climb
Dogs welcome on a lead on the walk and in the garden at Bateman's

Distance 2½ miles (4km)
Time 1 hour

Things to see

Pook's Hill
Pook's Hill (point 1 and 2) is situated behind the Jacobean house. In Kipling's *Puck of Pook's Hill*, this hill is clearly identified as Puck's home. Kipling wrote of Bateman's in 1902, 'It is a good and peaceable place.'

Millpond
The earliest recorded mention of the Mill (point 3) at Bateman's is from the eighteenth century, but Kipling believed that the mill dated from 1196. The current Millpond is a haven for wildlife including many species of dragonfly and damselfly.

Above: Snowdrops and daffodils in the garden at Bateman's, East Sussex.

Below: A view of the estate to the west of the house at Bateman's.

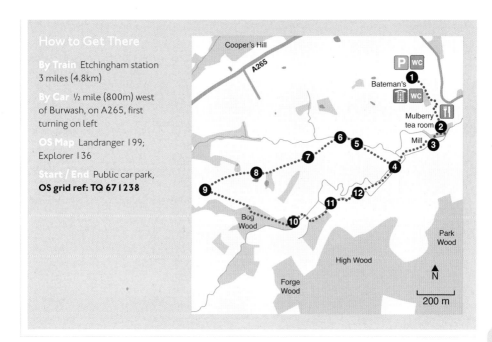

How to Get There

By Train Etchingham station
3 miles (4.8km)

By Car ½ mile (800m) west
of Burwash, on A265, first
turning on left

OS Map Landranger 199;
Explorer 136

Start / End Public car park,
OS grid ref: TQ 671238

Cooper's Hill

A265

Bateman's

Mulberry
tea room

Mill

Bog
Wood

Park
Wood

High Wood

Forge
Wood

N

200 m

1. Walk back down the drive out of the car park and turn right when you reach the road.

2. Walk across the front of the house and follow the road round to the right, crossing the bridge over the river.

3. Turn right at Corner Cottage and keep the Millpond on your left. Follow the path along the edge of the mill-stream.

4. Go over the bridge and after 55 yards (50m) turn right over the footbridge.

5. Follow the path through the field, passing the old oak and ditch. The ditch marks the manorial boundary between the customary lands of Brightling Prebend and the manor of Burwash. In the corner of the field go through the gate on your right and turn immediately left.

6. Go through another gate and follow the path.

7. You will arrive at a tarmac road with a house on your left. Cross the road and go over the stile into the field immediately in front of you. Follow the path across the field and into the woods opposite. Go through a gate and you are now outside the Bateman's estate.

8. Cross the field and go through the gate.

9. Follow the path along the top of the field; go over the stile and turn immediately left down the hill with the hedge on your left. Go through the kissing gate and follow the path to the left through the woods.

10. Go through the kissing gate and carry on straight ahead. The River Dudwell is to your right. After around 110 yards (100m), cross the river and turn left.

11. Pass through the gate and go straight ahead. After around 164 yards (150m) turn left across a bridge, go through the gate and turn immediately right.

12. Go through a kissing gate. After approximately 110 yards (100m) you will find yourself at the footbridge you crossed at point 4. From here, retrace your steps to the car park.

Make the Most of Your Day
Make time to visit the house and garden. Built in the seventeenth century, with mullioned windows and oak beams, Bateman's provided Kipling with a much-needed sanctuary.

Food and Facilities
There are tea-rooms and toilets at Bateman's.

South East

27. Woodland Trail at Ashridge

Every corner you turn, or hill you climb, will give you a view of Ashridge more breathtaking than the last. With its rich wildlife, diverse habitats and varied history there is plenty to uncover, from glorious birdsong to elusive deer.

Ashridge Estate
Ringshall
Berkhamsted
Hertfordshire
HP4 1LT
01442 851227
ashridge@nationaltrust.
org.uk

About this walk
Stunning views
Ancient woodland
Deer
Dogs welcome under close control

Distance Nearly 6 miles (9.5km)

Time 3 hours

Things to see

Beautiful Woodland
Lady's Walk is one of the most spectacular areas of the Estate, especially during the autumn. There are beech, oak and lime along the final stretch of the trail from Ashridge House to the Visitor Centre, each adding their unique shades to the overall colour palette.

Deer at Ashridge
If you are lucky you may catch glimpses of muntjac or fallow deer through the trees. In autumn the fallow deer are particularly active as the bucks are busy trying to attract females during the rut.

Above: Woodland in autumn on the Ashridge Estate, Hertfordshire.

Golden Valley
The Golden Valley was constructed by 'Capability' Brown in the eighteenth century, during the fashion for naturalistic landscape design which favoured vistas

and open parkland. The valley was reshaped by removing trees from the bottom and the sides, and thinning sections higher up the slopes to allow glimpses of Ashridge House through the trees.

Above: Looking south-east from the Golden Valley, Ashridge Estate.

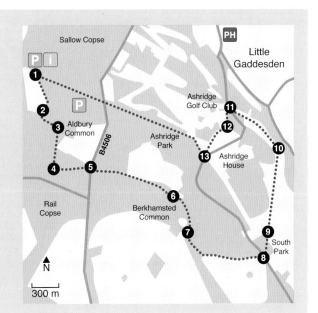

How to Get There

By Train Tring 1¾ miles (2.8km); from the station you can take a taxi or walk to the estate

By Car The Ashridge Estate Visitor Centre is between Tring and Berkhamsted, 3 miles (4.8km) north of the A41, along the B4506 from Northchurch (to Ringshall and Dagnall). It can also be reached from the B489 from Dunstable

OS Map Explorer 181

Start / End Ashridge Estate Visitor Centre, **OS grid ref: SP 970130**

---

1. Facing the Visitor Centre, turn left and walk round the back of the car park towards the gate. Beyond the gate, follow the path alongside the meadow.

2. When you reach the bottom of the meadow, take the path slightly to your left into the woods. The path continues to bear left eventually passing the edge of an area of recent coppicing on the right. You should pass a waymarker for Forester's Walk on the way.

3. At the end of this path you will arrive at Five-ways – so called because five paths meet here. You should see a roundel in front of you with a waymarker for Forester's Walk. Take the path that bears slightly right (this would be the third exit if it were a roundabout), signposted Forester's Walk. You will soon see open fields, which frequently contain livestock as well as fallow deer, so please keep dogs on leads.

4. Continue on this path until you reach a crossroad where you will see a number of waymarkers. Take the track to your left following the footpath signs into mixed woodland. Soon you will see traffic on the B4506 through the trees and a waymarker for Forester's Walk on your right. Before reaching the road you will pass a large pit and an enormous ancient beech tree at the edge of the field to your left.

5. Take care as you cross the B4506. On the other side you will find yourself in a small National Trust car park. Take the well-trodden path, called Lady's Walk, at the back of the car park close to the National Trust sign. There is a small waymarker with a white arrow highlighting this path. The left-hand side of the path is flanked by a large boundary embankment, on top of which are a number of ancient beech trees. To your right you will see a group of veteran sweet chestnuts and several pits. Please stay on the footpath and do not climb the bank as it is a delicate archaeological feature that is being worn away by footfall. Approximately 330 yards (300m) further on you will see a field ahead and to the left – keep this field on your left.

6. As you reach the corner of the field you will see a post with a blue arrow. This points to a path which veers to the right and slightly uphill, flanked by an avenue of silver birch – take this path. As this path begins to rise, it bends to the left and in a few yards you will see the outline of Woodyard Cottage through the trees. Continue forward as the path skirts to the right of the cottage. Continue until you reach a well-surfaced track. Follow this track to Great Coldharbour Farm.

7. In front of the farm is a crossroads with waymarkers. Turn left onto a well-trodden path and take the left-hand option when you reach a fork in the path. Follow this path until you see an open field ahead – this is part of Berkhamsted Common. On entering the field, turn left and keep to the field margin along this edge.

8. Continue along the field edge, ignoring several paths to the left, until you reach the corner of the field where you should see a path in front of you leading straight into woodland. This path emerges quickly onto College Road and passes in front of Ashridge House. Cross the road and continue straight ahead onto Frithsden Rise. Follow this road uphill until you reach a house on your left called Roddinghead House. Keep left alongside the house – the path soon blends into a narrow bridleway with a large field visible over the hedge to the right – this is the South Park.

9. Continue on this narrow bridleway until it reaches a kissing gate, where it ends. Please remember to keep your dog on a lead in this area as it is often grazed by cattle and other livestock. Follow the path across the field and down the hill. There are a number of beech trees here, so take the opportunity to enjoy the view down the valley towards Nettleden. At the far side of the field, pass through a gate into another open field and continue forwards following a bridleway sign around the contour of the land into Golden Valley.

10. Cross the track that dissects the valley from left to right, following the line of the valley itself. Continue to follow the valley as it winds upwards until you reach a tarmac road.

11. Cross the road and follow the worn track ahead which goes slightly uphill. You now have an open field in front of you with a golf green below and to the right. Turn left and skirt the edge of the field.

12. When you reach the top corner of the field you will find yourself at the edge of the great lawn. You will notice a track coming from the left and crossing in front of you like a T-junction. Turn right onto this track, skirting the edge of the great lawn and heading for a small stand of trees. Keeping these trees to your right and moving away from the house, continue to follow the path through an open area, then bear left into a group of impressive ancient sweet chestnuts. Pass through the trees to the iron railings round the golf course. Keeping this railing to your right, follow

Above: The Monument, erected in 1832, to the Duke of Bridgewater in the Ashridge Estate.

the path until you reach a sign directing you towards the National Trust Visitor Centre and Bridgewater Monument. Follow this path as directed.

13. Turn left onto Prince's Riding and walk towards the monument that you can see in the distance. Don't forget to look behind you to see Ashridge House framed by the trees. You will need to cross two roads, taking great care, before reaching the Visitor Centre where the trail ends.

Make the Most of Your Day

If you have time then make the most of the opportunity to climb Bridgewater Monument, where you can really appreciate the stunning views and take in the splendour of Ashridge. You can also go cycling or riding, or join an organised event, such as overnight camping or an evening wildlife hunt.

Food and Facilities

A café and toilets can be found at the Ashridge Estate Visitor Centre.

28. Hatfield Forest Golden Boots Walk

Hatfield Forest is a delicate landscape that gets busy in the winter, so this route is best enjoyed in the summer. In May and June the plains are carpeted with over 300 million buttercups. This walk takes you through the best places to see them.

Hatfield Forest
Near Bishop's Stortford
Essex
CM22 6NG
01279 870678
hatfieldforest@
nationaltrust.org.uk

About this walk
Stunning displays of buttercups

Ancient woodland

Can be muddy in wet weather

Dogs welcome, but keep on leads near livestock, around the lake and where signed

Distance 3 1/2 miles (5.4km)

Time 1 hour 30 mins

South East

Things to see

Main Plain

This stretches almost the entire length of Hatfield Forest. Warren Cottage (a private residence) was built in the nineteenth century from handmade red bricks, on the site of an earlier cottage erected in the late seventeenth century. The horse chestnuts which were planted in the 1700s have succumbed to *Phytophthora* and bleeding canker diseases. The affected trees have been monolithed (reduced to a trunk without branches) by forest staff to preserve the dead wood habitat. Hiding under the trees, obscured by scrub, are the remains of a medieval rabbit warren – a collection of linear pillow mounds.

Above: The Shell House near the Lake at Hatfield Forest, Essex.

Takeley Hill

This is actually an area of wood pasture, with a slight slope. Here you will see an abundance of

buttercups, along with Red Poll cattle. The cows do not eat the buttercups, so they flourish and re-seed each year.

Above: Buttercups in a meadow at Takeley Hill at Hatfield Forest.

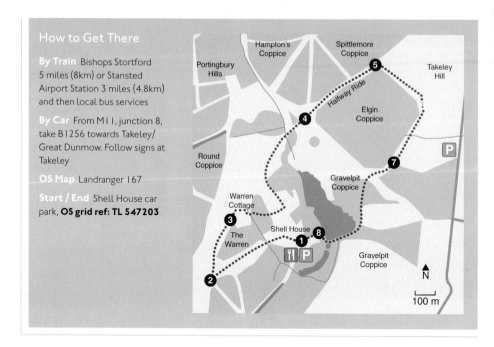

How to Get There

By Train Bishops Stortford 5 miles (8km) or Stansted Airport Station 3 miles (4.8km) and then local bus services

By Car From M11, junction 8, take B1256 towards Takeley/ Great Dunmow. Follow signs at Takeley

OS Map Landranger 167

Start / End Shell House car park, **OS grid ref: TL 547203**

1. Starting at the gate to the lakeside area car park, walk to the far left-hand corner and take the path just past a wooden bench. This path can be very muddy at most times of the year. Follow this path until reaching a more open ride, with coppice on either side. There is a metal fence on your left. Keep walking uphill until you reach the end of the ride and you see a sheep grazing sign, then turn right and walk straight in a northerly direction.

2. Continue heading north along the main plain, passing a chestnut paling fence on your left. Cross over the gravel track (which leads to Forest Lodge, a private residence).

3. Walk past a group of horse chestnut stumps to your right. From here you can see Warren Cottage. Follow the gravel track from the cottage until you reach an estate road. Turn left downhill until reaching the stream with culvert (under the road).

4. Walk uphill on the grass beside the road, until the road bears to the right. Do not follow the road, but keeping to the grass, walk straight ahead to a wide ride in front of you. This is known as 'Halfway Ride'.

5. Continue along Halfway Ride for about ½ mile

(800m) to the end (this may be muddy), and turn immediately right through the gate onto Takeley Hill.

6. Keeping to the tree line to your right, and looking out for grazing animals, walk straight ahead (south) following the distinct marked path in the grass until reaching the estate exit road. Cross over the road and continue in the same direction until reaching the estate entrance road.

7. Cross the road, and, in front of you, you should now see a boardwalk. Follow the boardwalk, go through the gate and enter the woodland.

8. Follow the boardwalk to the end, continue along the dam, keeping the lake on your right until you reach the Shell House and the car park.

Make the Most of Your Day
Bring your family to the forest and enjoy a range of outdoor activities, whether simply running around, climbing trees, building a den or exploring.

Food and Facilities
The Forest Café is next to the Shell House; there is no indoor seating but you can sit in the Fisherman's Shelter. There are toilets near Shell House car park.

29. A Walk Around Blakes Wood

Danbury and Lingwood Commons comprise 214 acres (87ha) of heath, gorse and coppice, encompassing a Site of Special Scientific Interest (SSSI), ancient woodland and military defences. Blakes Wood sits on a sloping site that includes clear streams, valleys, mighty oaks, chestnuts and coppiced hornbeam. In spring the woodland floor is a riot of colourful wildflowers, including one of the best bluebell displays in the area, primroses and yellow archangel.

Danbury Common
Danbury
Essex
CM3 4ED
01245 222669
danbury@nationaltrust.
org.uk

About this walk

Wildflower displays

Wildlife interest

Hilly in places; wear suitable footwear

Dogs welcome under close control

Distance 2½ miles (4km)

Time 1 hour 30 mins

South East

Things to see

Wildlife and Waymarking
Breeding birds here include warblers, nightingale, all three species of woodpecker, and tree-creeper. Butterflies include the purple hairstreak. The trail has recently been improved and is now marked with round National Trust footpath discs attached to wooden posts sited at various points along the route.

Coppicing
The practice of cutting trees to a cycle is known as coppicing. The 'thin-poled' coppice is often used for firewood and the thicker so-called 'standard' is used in the construction industry. For hundreds of years coppicing went on in the same way, producing a woodland habitat that alternated between light and shade, and open and densely bushy vegetation. By continuing to coppice, the National Trust is ensuring the survival of this habitat, and the wildlife that makes its home here.

Above: Great spotted woodpecker.

Above: Bluebells at Blakes Wood, Essex, in spring.

How to Get There

By Train Chelmsford 6 miles (9.7km)

By Car From Danbury Main Road (A414) via Riffham's Lane to Riffham's Chase

OS Map Landranger 168, Explorer 183

Start / End Blakes Wood car park or from Lingwood Common, **OS grid ref: TL 775064**

1. Starting from the Blakes Wood car park, go through the kissing gate Marker Post 1 and turn left. Taking the path immediately to the left (FP43) head downhill until reaching a bench and Marker Post 2.

2. Ignoring the path to your right, keep to the left-hand path until reaching another marker post, at which point (ignoring the path to your left) bear right. Continue on until reaching Marker Post 3.

3. Ignoring the path to your left, bear right until reaching Marker Post 4. Now turn to the left until you cross a culvert. The path then bears to the left and then to the right.

4. Continue on until reaching a marker post, where you will turn left. You will pass two old pond beds to the left, the path then bears right around Blakes Wood. Follow this path until reaching Marker Post 5.

5. Turn left, then right, and proceed to Marker Post 6 where the path turns to the left.

6. Carry on until reaching another culvert. Ignoring the path directly to your left, continue on until reaching Marker Post 7.

7. You now have two options. Either take the path directly to your left (over culvert) and continue to Parsonage Lane and Danbury Ridge where you will find the Generals Arms pub, or if continuing with the Blakes Wood trail, continue straight on until reaching a bench at Marker Post 8. Turn right and shortly afterwards there is a fork in the path. Take the right-hand branch and continue to Marker Post 9.

8. Make a left turn followed by a right over a footbridge and continue uphill until reaching a bench on your left – take a welcome break.

9. Continue uphill until you reach the kissing gate entrance to the car park – Marker Post 1.

Make the Most of Your Day

This is one of three walks linking Blakes Wood with Danbury and Lingwood Commons. Each walk can be undertaken separately or co-joined with this one.

Food and Facilities

Food and drink is available at the Generals Arms. There are no toilets on site, but there are toilets at the Generals Arms during opening hours.

Opposite: View along the beach at Sheringham Park, Norfolk (walk 37).

East Anglia

30. Wimpole Folly and Woodland Belt Walk

Wimpole Estate
Cambridgeshire
SG8 0BW
01223 206000
wimpolehall@nationaltrust.
org.uk

About this walk
A working estate
Historic architecture
Wildlife interest
Dogs welcome under close
control

Distance 3 miles (4.8km)

Time 1 hour 30 mins

This is a historic wildlife walk beginning at Wimpole's grand stable block. You will discover the rich history of the land, from the remains of medieval farming to lavish Georgian landscapes. You can also explore the unique contrasts between a historical and modern working estate.

Things to see

The Stable Block
This grand stable block is where you'll find most of the facilities and is the starting and finishing point to this walk. It was designed by H.E. Kendall (1776–1875) and built in 1852.

Wimpole Lakes
Home to carp, rudd, pike, tench, stickleback and the occasional eel, these lakes at the foot of Johnson's Hill have been used and loved by generations. They're also suitably placed for cattle and sheep to use them as their watering hole.

The Folly
These Gothic ruins, also known as sham ruins, were made purposefully to create a spectacular view from the Hall in 1768. They are just as stunning close up and stand as a unique portrayal of eighteenth-century style and fashion.

Above: Hebridean sheep in front of the mansion at Wimpole Estate, Cambridgeshire, in winter.

Below: Chinese Bridge in the snow at the Wimpole Estate.

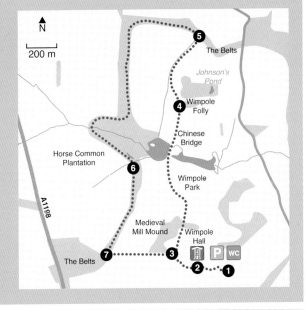

How to Get There

By Train Shepreth 5 miles (8km); Royston, with taxi service, 8 miles (12.9km)

By Car 8 miles (12.9km) south-west of Cambridge (A603); 6 miles (9.7km) north of Royston (A1198)

OS Map Landranger 154

Stand/End Kendall Stable Block, **OS grid ref: TL 336509**

1. Go through the black gate opposite the Kendall Stable Block and follow the path until you're in front of Wimpole Hall. Remember to look at the view down the stunning South Avenue.

2. Follow the path around the house until you reach a gate. Once through the gate, the ridges and furrows in the parkland are evidence of the plough pulled by oxen on Wimpole's medieval farmland.

3. Turn right and pass the ha-ha on your right, then meander to the right, following the footpath away from the hall across the field. Keep walking until you reach another ha-ha and iron bridge. Bear left ahead towards the lakes until you reach the Chinese Bridge.

4. Cross over the bridge and keep going up the hill until you reach the Folly. Then, with the folly in front of you, turn left and down the hill towards the gate at the far end.

5. Walk straight through the farmland on the grass path into the Woodland Belts, the sign here is filled with wildlife information – do stop to read. Follow the path into the woods and then turn left. Keep walking and after the path has eventually meandered around to the right, a fork in the footpath will appear; take the left turning. As you walk, the fields should be to your left behind the trees.

6. Once you've made it round the U-turn-like bend, follow the path behind the trees and up the hill. At the top of the hill the woodland belts come to an end. Jump over the stile and, in front of you, will be the Medieval Mill Mound. Turn right and head towards the gate.

7. After you go through the gate there are lines of lime trees to your left. Follow this pathway down the hill towards the hall. At the bottom bear right and go through the gate, back the way you came.

Make the Most of Your Day

Wimpole is a working estate with a Georgian mansion at its heart; there is plenty to see both inside the house and in its wonderful gardens. From the end of October until mid-February, Home Farm is open at weekends only.

Food and Facilities

Refreshments are available at the Old Rectory Restaurant and Farm Café. Toilets are available at various locations around Wimpole.

31. Wicken Fen Wildlife Walk

Wicken Fen is one of Europe's most important wetlands and supports an abundance of wildlife. There are more than 9,000 species, including a spectacular array of plants, birds and dragonflies. The raised boardwalk and lush grass droves allow easy access to a lost landscape of flowering meadows, sedge and reedbeds, where you can encounter rarities such as hen harriers, water voles and bitterns.

Wicken Fen National Nature Reserve
Wicken
Cambridgeshire
CB7 5XP
01353 720274
wickenfen@nationaltrust.org.uk

About this walk
Wildlife interest
Birdwatching
Take care near waterways and ponds
A section of this walk (between points 5 and 6) can be very muddy and will require suitable footwear
Dogs welcome on leads

Distance 2¾ miles (4.4km)

Time 1 hour 30 mins

Things to see

Fen Wildlife

Wicken Fen supports a rich array of insect life, including dragonflies such as brown hawker, common darter and banded demoiselle. Roe and muntjac deer, hares, grass snakes and water voles can also all be spotted. Look out for the herds of grazing konik ponies and Highland cattle, used to create a mosaic of different habitats.

Birdlife

There is year-round birdwatching here. Summer migrant birds include sand martins, swallows, swifts, warblers and cuckoos. Wicken Fen is also known for its feathery winter visitors, when you can spot hen harriers, starling flocks, wildfowl, particularly wigeon, and wading birds in the marshy areas, plus winter thrushes – fieldfare and redwing. Lapwing, redshank, bearded tit, heron and marsh harrier live here throughout the year. Woodpeckers nest in suitable trees, and barn, short-eared, little and tawny owls hunt over the fen and the grasslands.

Above: The sun rises behind the wind pump at Wicken Fen National Nature Reserve, Cambridgeshire.

Right: Lapwings are resident at Wicken Fen.

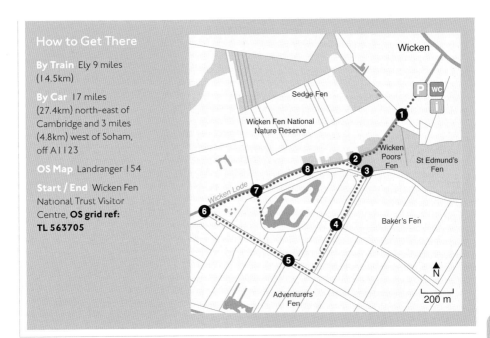

Wicken

Sedge Fen

Wicken Fen National Nature Reserve

Wicken Poors' Fen

St Edmund's Fen

Baker's Fen

Wicken Lode

Adventurers' Fen

200 m

N

East Anglia

1. As you leave the Visitor Centre, Wicken Lode is on your right. Follow the path, keeping the water to your right. Lodes are man-made fenland waterways, many medieval in origin. You will pass Wicken Poors' Fen on your left. This is common land, and traditionally the villagers had the right to collect sedge and peat from here.

2. Cross Monk's Lode at Norman's Bridge. Look out for plants like arrowhead and waterlilies in the water. The clean water of Monk's Lode comes from the chalk hills by Newmarket and supplements the water table on Sedge Fen, keeping it wet enough for the fenland plants to thrive.

3. Turn right through the double set of gates onto the grassy bank overlooking Baker's Fen. Please make sure all gates are closed due to grazing animals.

4. As the Baker's Fen fields become wetter in the autumn and winter, look out for waterfowl and waders.

5. When you get to the end of the bank, turn right onto the next path. You will go past the original site of our wind-pump, or Norman's Mill, where it was used to drain early twentieth-century turf (peat)

diggings. On your return to the Visitor Centre, spot it in its new position on Sedge Fen.

6. There are extensive reed-beds to your left. They are home to birds, including bittern, and insects such as reed leopard moth. Climb the bank and turn right to walk alongside Wicken Lode. The level of the land on Adventurers' Fen is lower than the water, a result of drainage and peat shrinkage.

7. You can take the path to West Mere Hide if you go back down the bank and through the gate on the right.

8. Cross back over Norman's Bridge and return towards the Visitor Centre.

Make the Most of Your Day
Hire a bike, or plan a longer walk to Baker's Fen Hide and Burwell Fen, to see how newer areas of restored fen are attracting wildlife. Or take a gentle boat trip (March–October) on the *Mayfly*.

Food and Facilities
There is a café and picnics are welcome. Toilets can be found in the Learning Centre behind the café and at the main car park.

32. Ickworth Off-the-beaten-track Walk

Ickworth
Horringer
Bury St Edmunds
Suffolk
IP29 5QE
01284 735270
ickworth@nationaltrust.
org.uk

About this walk
Tranquil parkland
Wildflower displays
Wildlife interest
Adequate footwear should
be worn during wet weather
Dogs welcome on leads

Distance 5 miles (8km)
Time 2 hours

This route takes you through diverse habitats and scenery, including open parkland, with some glorious views. The remote areas and ancient woodland provide likely spots for deer sightings, while closer to the house, you pass the Walled Garden; with its wonderful wildflower meadow, it is a riot of colour in summer.

Things to see

Wildlife
With the relative peace and quiet of this area of the park, it's a great location to observe wildlife. Birds, lizards, toads, small mammals and herds of deer can often be seen here. Barn owls have been spotted nesting on the estate for the first time in over 20 years. At Ickworth, the National Trust is working hard to improve natural habitats and encourage as much wildlife as possible to call this place their home.

Walled Garden
The Walled Garden contains the Earl's Summer-house, built in the early 1800s, as well as a wildflower meadow, vegetable beds and school allotments. Table grapes were grown here in Victorian times and were stored over winter in the summer-house. It's well worth a visit anytime, but the wildflower meadow is particularly stunning in July and August.

Above: Flowers in the Walled Garden at Ickworth, Suffolk.

Right: View from beyond the Canal showing the Lake, Walled Garden, Summer-house, St Mary's Church and Rotunda.

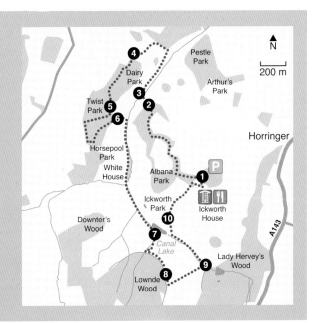

1. From the Porter's Lodge visitor reception, take the path opposite towards the Albana Wood, and follow the path going through two five-bar gates. Just after going through the second gate, take the path to the right at the small 'Albana Wood' stone. Stay on this path until you reach the large green 'Trim Trail' sign, and then turn right following the trail.

2. As the trail goes down a left-hand slope and you reach a junction, turn right off the Trim Trail, leaving the woods, and go into an open field. Follow the path down the side of the field with the trees on your right and cross the brook on the wooden bridge.

3. Once across the brook, turn right onto the wide track, and then shortly through a five-bar gate. Follow this track until you reach the next five-bar gate, where you will see a cottage beyond the gate and a bridge to your right. Do not go through the gate but turn left and walk up the hill until you intersect the main track. Turn left towards a cottage known as Dairy Wood Cottage, one of 19 on the estate.

4. As you approach the cottage, turn left across the grass and go through the gate in the corner of the field into Dairy Wood. Stay on this track and don't take any turns or junctions. You will exit the wood

briefly and keep on the track as it re-enters near the edge of the wood. Point 5 covers the loop into Twist and Horsepool Wood, so if you wish you could carry straight on, missing out point 5 and rejoining the walk just a short distance further on at the start of point 6.

5. Very soon after you have re-entered the wood look for a barely discernible track/fork to your right. Follow this track (which has a ditch on your left), as you go gently up hill. Just before you exit the wood, cross the ditch to your left and follow the track through the woods. Take the right fork when you intercept another path. Keep going until you reach the main path crossroads; turn left for a short distance and left again on a main path effectively doubling back into the same woods. Keep on this path until you exit the woods.

6. As the path leaves the wood, you will see a clear path between the cropped fields going downhill. Follow the path between the fields to the wide track at the bottom and then turn right. Stay on the wide track for a while. Shortly after passing the White House on your right you come to a crossroads. Go straight across the crossroads (stone bridge to your left/cattle grid to your right) and follow the grass track.

Above: The Rotunda at Ickworth House glimpsed through trees in the parkland.

7. With the Walled Garden and Canal Lake on your left, turn right through the gate approximately at the centre line of the gardens (opposite the Summer-house), and head up the hill towards the tree line of Lownde Wood. On reaching the wood, turn left and walk along the front of the wood with the canal and gardens at the bottom of the slope and to your left.

8. After approximately ⅓ mile (500m), you will reach the meeting of a number of fences and gates; go through the gate into the field beyond and then immediately left into the adjacent field. Go diagonally across this field to the opposite corner and cross over the stile onto the path. Turn left back towards the walled garden.

9. Follow this track until you reach the walled garden and turn right keeping the wall of the garden to your left.

10. At the end of the walled garden take the main road past the church and back up towards the Rotunda and gardens. Go through the five-bar gate turning immediately right, and enter the Italianate gardens. Continue on until you reach the West Wing where you can stop for a snack if you wish.

Make the Most of Your Day

Ickworth provides the perfect setting for a range of outdoor activities, including picnics, den building and open-air theatre. Ickworth House itself, with its impressive Rotunda, features fascinating collections and family portraits by artists including Gainsborough, Hogarth and Reynolds.

Food and Facilities

There is an outdoor café at the Porter's Lodge; food is also available at the West Wing Café and the new Squash Court Café. There are toilets in the car park, the West Wing basement and near the Bothy outside the Walled Garden.

33. Melford Hall to Lavenham Railway Walk

Long Melford
Sudbury
Suffolk
CO10 9AA
01787 379228
melford@nationaltrust.
org.uk

About this walk
Wildflower displays
Site of Special Scientific
Interest
Wildlife interest
Can get muddy through SSSI
area; adequate footwear
recommended
Dogs welcome under close
control and on leads where
signed

Distance 4½ miles (7.2km)

Time 2 hours

This walk provides the opportunity to see a variety of wildflowers, birds and other wildlife. Starting and finishing in two well-preserved medieval 'wool' towns, you can return to Long Melford by bus, or retrace your steps if you are feeling energetic.

East Anglia

Things to see

Railway Line

The line (single track with passing places) from Melford to Bury St Edmunds, via Lavenham, opened in 1865. It was closed to passengers in 1961, although it remained open for goods traffic until 1966, and then shut down completely in 1967. Long Melford Railway station building still exists (now a private house), and is located at the southern end of the village by the Old Maltings. This walk largely follows the route of the old Great Eastern Railway.

Above: A view of Melford Hall from the north-east on a bright spring day.

Site of Special Scientific Interest

This cutting is an area of heavy undergrowth and will invariably be found to be muddy or even waterlogged. Selected areas of the banks of this cutting are being returned to grass, and others left as semi-natural woodland. The grassland provides a valuable habitat for insects and wildlife.

Wildlife

Many species have been recorded along this disused railway line, including common and lesser whitethroat, blackcap, goldcrest, treecreeper, bullfinch, garden warbler and marsh tit, along with pied flycatcher, redstart, whinchat, firecrest, red warbler, waxwing, little egret and red kite.

Above: Goldcrest on a thistle.

By Train Sudbury 4 miles (6.5km)

By Car Entrance to car park and grounds opposite village green, A1092 off the A134 – 14 miles (22.5km) from Bury St Edmunds, 4 miles (6.5km) from Sudbury

OS Map Landranger 155

Start Melford Hall car park, **OS grid ref: TL 867462**

End Lavenham Guildhall, **OS grid ref: TL 916493**

1. Starting from the Melford Hall car park, turn right out of the gate and, keeping to the same side of the road, walk 660 yards (600m) until reaching the Cherry Lane Garden Centre. Entering the garden centre, walk just past the building entrance and look for the public footpath sign in front of you. This is known as Hare Drift.

2. Hare Drift continues along a concrete path until joining the main A134 Sudbury to Bury St Edmunds road. The traffic on this road can be very fast, so cross with great care. Go through the gate on the opposite side of the road and, walking straight ahead, follow the footpath, which after 100 yards (90m) or so continues downhill.

3. At the bottom of the hill turn left and follow the tree line, ignoring a footpath sign to the left (St Edmund's Way). After about another 100–200 yards (90–180m) you will find an exit through the trees on the right-hand side.

4. Going through the trees, continue across a small bridge over Chad Brook. Head slightly uphill and exit to enter a plain, with scrub to the right. You can see signs now covered with scrub, showing where the path used to be.

5. Head up the plain for about 200 yards (180m) keeping the scrub to your right, until the path runs alongside some woodland to the left.

6. Follow the path for about 400 yards (360m) until reaching a crossroads. The section after this is a permissive footpath and dogs should be kept on leads.

7. Keep on for about another 200 yards (180m) or so until the path rises up to the old railway embankment as you enter Lineage Wood to your left and Paradise Wood to your right. This is the site of an 1891 railway derailment.

8. When exiting the woodland/embankment, the route to follow is directly opposite you, but you will need to walk along the line of trees to your left, circumnavigating the open field until you reach the narrow entrance in the wood. Follow the wooded path until you reach a section of railway cutting designated as a Site of Special Scientific Interest (SSSI).

9. You will have reached the end of the SSSI section when reaching the Bridge Street railway bridge. The next section is now known as the Lavenham Walk.

10. Continue on the 'Lavenham Walk' that is now owned and maintained by Lavenham Parish Council after divestment from Suffolk County Council in 2012, until reaching some metal gates.

11. When reaching the metal gates you have reached the Park Road crossing. Crossing the road, go through the gates, and continue on for approximately 400 yards (360m), until reaching Lavenham High Street to the right of the Bury Road railway bridge.

12. Now cross the road and continue right up High Street, for approximately 300 yards (270m). Turning left into Market Lane, walk up to the Market Square. Lavenham Guildhall is across the Market Square and you have now reached the end of your walk.

Make the Most of Your Day
You can also visit Melford Hall. Devastated by fire in 1942, it was nurtured back to life by the Hyde Parker family and it remains their much-loved family home to this day. Whether you'd like to relax on a sofa in the Great Hall and soak up the atmosphere, stretch your legs on one of the guided walks, or simply potter in the garden, Melford Hall has something for everyone.

Food and Facilities
There are tea-rooms at Melford Hall and Lavenham Guildhall. Toilets are available at Melford Hall gatehouse (during opening times) and various other outlets. Please note, dogs are not allowed at Melford Hall house or gardens.

East Anglia

Left: A visitor group following the Melford Hall to Lavenham Railway Walk, Suffolk.

34. Dunwich Heath and Beach Walk

Dunwich Heath
Suffolk
IP17 3DJ
01728 648501
dunwichheath@
nationaltrust.org.uk

About this walk
Important habitat

Coastal views

One small section of
wooden steps and some
muddy tracks during wet
weather

Dogs welcome on leads

Distance 5 miles (8km)

Time 2 hours

Tucked away on the Suffolk coast, the heathland at Dunwich changes colour all year round as well as supporting a wealth of insects and breeding birds. Keep your eyes peeled too for red deer. Along this walk with its coastal views, you'll pass Dunwich Museum, Mount Pleasant Farm and Greyfriars Monastery.

Things to see

Heathland Habitat

This significant area of coastal heathland holds the largest East Anglian population of Dartford warblers, with 40–45 pairs, as well as breeding nightjars, woodlarks and stonechats. Heather and gorse flower is in abundance from July–September. They provide an excellent habitat for a variety of birds and insects.

Greyfriars Monastery

These ruins are the remains of a Franciscan monastery, built in 1290. The original monastery, built in 1227, was nearer the coast, but like so much of Dunwich, has been lost to the sea. The remains include the precinct wall, two gatehouses and the south range of the cloister, possibly the refectory.

Mount Pleasant Farm

The fields to your right are part of Mount Pleasant Farm, a 79-acre (32ha) area bought by the National Trust in 2002. Formerly used for arable and pigs, Mount Pleasant Farm is now being restored to grass and heather. The National Trust has also created a permissive bridleway around the perimeter.

Above: Dunwich Heath and Beach, Suffolk.

Right: Dog walking at Dunwich Heath.

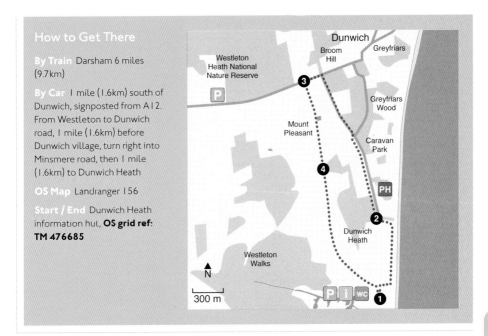

How to Get There

By Train Darsham 6 miles (9.7km)

By Car 1 mile (1.6km) south of Dunwich, signposted from A12. From Westleton to Dunwich road, 1 mile (1.6km) before Dunwich village, turn right into Minsmere road, then 1 mile (1.6km) to Dunwich Heath

OS Map Landranger 156

Start / End Dunwich Heath information hut, **OS grid ref: TM 476685**

Dunwich
Broom Hill
Greyfriars
Westleton Heath National Nature Reserve
P
❸
Greyfriars Wood
Mount Pleasant
Caravan Park
❹
PH
❷
Dunwich Heath
Westleton Walks
N
300 m
P i WC ❶

1. Head to the northern side of the Coastguard Cottages and look out for 3¼ft (1m) high oak posts with directional arrows and follow the orange route. After 165 yards (150m) you will pass by the Dell, a great place for spotting migratory birds during the autumn months. Follow the path for another 660 yards (600m) until you get to a pedestrian crossing and take care to cross the road.

2. Turn right and on your left you'll see the enclosure, which is a fine piece of open acid grassland with scattered hawthorns that is perfect for observing birds and insects. Carry along the path for 660 yards (600m) and you'll come to a bridleway crossing; head straight over and you'll start to walk past Mount Pleasant Farm where you will see fields in different stages of conversion to heathland and grassland habitat. Follow the track for another ⅔ mile (900m) and you'll arrive at Mount Pleasant Farm access track where you'll turn left.

3. Continue straight on this track for ½ mile (800m) passing residential houses and a large barn and you'll arrive at another bridleway crossing. Continue straight and you'll enter an area called Mount Pleasant Heath which the Trust bought in 2015. You may find red deer grazing in this area and there will

be many birds and insects to spot. After 330 yards (300m) you will come to a footpath crossing, where you'll need to bear left then right.

4. After ⅓ mile (500m), on your right you will pass Shooting Butts which are the remains from a training area during the First World War. After another 385 yards (350m) you will come to a small sculpture of a nightjar and will be near Heath Barn. Turn left here and you will arrive at your starting point.

Make the Most of Your Day
Explore Heath Barn and visit the lookout for its wonderful views of the sea.

Food and Facilities
Refreshments are available at the tea-room. There are toilets in the building close to the cottages. Please check for opening times.

35. Blickling Estate Walk

Blickling
Aylsham
Norfolk
NR11 6NF
01263 738030
blickling@nationaltrust.org.uk

About this walk
Wildflower displays
Ancient woodland
May be muddy in wet weather
Dogs welcome; keep on leads around livestock

Distance 4½ miles (7.2km)
Time 2 hours

Enjoy a gentle ramble around the Blickling Estate parkland. Visit points of local historical interest including the Tower, Brickyard and Mausoleum. The estate is full of wildlife, such as dragonflies, butterflies, rabbits, birds and, if you're lucky enough to spot one, red deer. There are often barn owls nesting in the woods too.

Things to see

Church of St Andrew
Although originally dating from the thirteenth to fifteenth centuries, the church was almost completely rebuilt in the nineteenth century, but has interesting brass rubbings and memorials to Blickling's former owners. The church is open daily (times may vary).

Pond Meadow and the Carr
Pond Meadow certainly matches that description. It floods to this day and in medieval times would have provided water for the moat. At this point, look to your right, and enjoy an excellent view of the Hall. The name Carr is derived from old Norse 'kjarr', which means wet (sometimes swampy) woodland.

Great Wood
Great Wood has been a feature of the park at Blickling since its earliest medieval times, and its ancient boundaries survive as low banks in the undergrowth. Great Wood has changed little since the late eighteenth century, with its mix of English oaks, groves of beech and ancient sweet chestnuts, as well as small-leaved limes on the banks on the south-west of the wood. Bluebells are a sight here from late April to early May.

Above: A sunny April day at Blickling Estate, Norfolk.

How to Get There

By Train Aylsham (Bure Valley Railway from Hoveton and Wroxham) 1¾ miles (2.8km); North Walsham 8 miles (13km)

By Car 1½ miles (2.4km) north-west of Aylsham on B1354, signposted off A140 Norwich/Cromer

OS Map Landranger 133

Start / End Blickling main car park, **OS grid ref: TG 178286**

[Map showing: Great Wood, Waterloo Wood, Hyde Park, P (9), Mausoleum (10), Beeches (11), Bunker's Hill, The Lake, The Tower, Blickling Park, (8), Long Plantation, (12) Blickling Hall (1), P (2), Blickling PH (3), (7), (6), Water Mill (5), St Andrew's (4), Hercules Wood, A1092, N, 500 m]

1. From Blickling main car park, facing the Visitor Centre, go round the left-hand side of the building and follow the path down to the lane.

2. Cross the lane and turn right past the Buckinghamshire Arms, then turn left and walk past the front of the main house driveway.

3. Now continuing on, visit the Church of St Andrew ahead.

4. Cross the road with care, and follow the minor road opposite (signposted Weaver's Way), towards Silvergate. At the end of the fence –100 yards (91m) or so – on the right-hand side, you can enter the wood and have a look at the old eighteenth-century ice house hidden in Icehouse Plantation. Used until the 1930s, this is Grade II listed. Returning to the road, turn right until reaching a waymarker with an orange arrow (with stile) on the right-hand side.

5. Cross the stile and walk through the small woodland where there is a second stile to be crossed. Continue across the meadow (Pond Meadow) where there is yet another stile to be navigated. The brick building in front of you once housed a pump, which fed water to the house during the Second World War.

Cross the Carr (just past the pump house), and turn left into the field.

6. Follow the path along the field margin until exiting onto the lane, opposite Hall Farm. Turn right along the lane for 110 yards (100m) or so and look for a waymarker on the left. Turn left up the track, go past a cottage, and just before reaching the main road, turn left and follow the path that runs alongside the road and Hercules Wood.

7. At the end of this path, turn right and, crossing the busy road with care, head towards a kissing gate ahead. Just before reaching the gate, turn left into Long Plantation and follow the path, which can be muddy.

8. After a short walk you will arrive at the Tower (on your right).

9. After leaving the Tower, continue along the waymarked path until almost reaching the road. Ignoring the path directly ahead, turn sharp right and continue along the edge of Buck's Common woodland until reaching a gate at its end. Go through the gate and continue across Hyde Park (cattle freely graze this area) until reaching another section

of woodland in the distance and another gate. Go through the gate and turn immediately right. The path now continues downhill alongside Bunker's Hill Plantation towards Great Wood.

10. When reaching the bottom of the hill, turn right and follow the edge of Great Wood uphill until reaching the second seat on the left. Now turn left and follow the path until reaching an open area with the Mausoleum to your left.

11. After visiting the mausoleum head back along the edge of the woodland and take the second path on the left. Follow the path, bearing right further on, and head towards, and then following, the edge of the arable field in front of you. Enjoy extensive views down to the River Bure and beyond, until reaching a small area of woodland known as the Beeches.

12. After entering the woodland, turn immediately right. Leaving the Beeches behind you, head downhill, watching out for grazing animals, until reaching the park gates at the bottom. Exit through the small gate and after 27 yards (25m) turn left. The entrance to the main car park will be found on your right, with the Visitor Centre, toilets and the end of your walk.

Make the Most of Your Day
At the end of your walk the café, restaurant and shops beckon, not forgetting Blickling Hall. The Buckinghamshire Arms (point 2 on the walk) dates from the 1700s and was only used occasionally 'for the horses of Gentlemen' but an ale house has stood on this site since the 1600s. Owned by the National Trust, it is a wonderful place to stay on an overnight visit to Blickling, with great food, log fires and four-poster beds.

Food and Facilities
Food is available in the restaurant and seasonal Farmyard café at Blickling and at the Buckinghamshire Arms; check for opening times. Toilets can be found in the main car park and the restaurant.

Left: The true English bluebell (*Hyacinthoides non-scripta*), rather than its Spanish relative, grows at Blickling.

36. Blakeney Freshes Coastal Wildlife Walk

Morston Quay
Quay Road
Morston
Norfolk
NR25 7BH
01263 740241
norfolkcoast@nationaltrust.org.uk

About this walk
Stunning views
Birdwatching
Dogs welcome, including on buses

Distance 3 miles (4.8km)
Time 1 hour 45 mins

This walk through Blakeney Village and around Blakeney Freshes is fantastic for spotting wildlife, especially birds, as it is an important area both for breeding birds and over-wintering wildfowl. There are also excellent views as you stroll around Blakeney and Cley harbours.

Things to see

Blakeney Quay
For several centuries, Blakeney was a busy commercial port exporting corn and wool and importing a variety of goods, including coal and timber. Today, the quay is mainly used for recreational activities, such as sailing, birdwatching and walking. Savour the stunning views across Blakeney Harbour and to the shingle spit of Blakeney Point (point 1).

Blakeney Freshes
This is a popular spot for birdwatching. In winter, large swirling flocks of golden plover move between the harbour and the marshes, while ducks, such as wigeon, black and white Brent geese, redshanks and oystercatchers graze in the fields.

St Nicholas' Church
Well worth a visit, St Nicholas' Church was built between the thirteenth and fifteenth centuries. It is large for a small village and dominates the surrounding area with its twin towers.

Left: A gull wading on the mud-flats at Morston Quay, Blakeney National Nature Reserve, Norfolk.

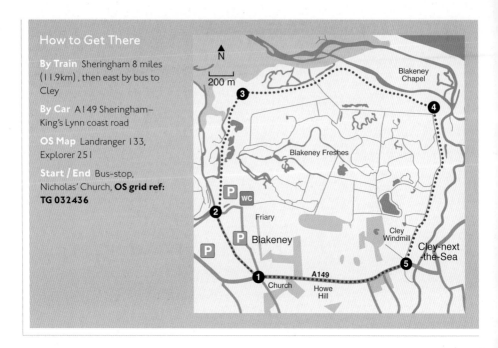

How to Get There

By Train Sheringham 8 miles
(11.9km), then east by bus to
Cley

By Car A149 Sheringham–
King's Lynn coast road

OS Map Landranger 133,
Explorer 251

Start / End Bus-stop,
Nicholas' Church, **OS grid ref:
TG 032436**

N

200 m

Blakeney
Chapel

Blakeney Freshes

Friary

Cley
Windmill

Blakeney

Cley-next
-the-Sea

A149

Church

Howe
Hill

1. From the bus-stop head away from the church
into Blakeney village and turn right down the High
Street. At the end of the High Street, you will come
out onto Blakeney Quay.

2. Cross the main car-parking area of the quay
and walk up onto the bank on the right-hand side.
From here you can see Blakeney Freshes on your
right. Take the footpath on top of the bank out
towards the harbour.

3. Follow the same footpath round to the right.

4. Stay on the coast path passing Cley Channel on
your left.

5. Keep to the footpath on the bank until you
reach the A149 between Blakeney and Cley-next-
the-sea. Cross the road and turn right, walk up
the hill and cross the road again and stay on the
pavement until you are back at the bus-stop near
St Nicholas' Church.

Make the Most of Your Day

Blakeney Point is a perfect breeding site for grey
seals, and pups are born during November, December
and early January. The best way to see the seals is to
take a ferry trip, departing from Morston Quay. Trips
continue throughout the winter, weather permitting,
but do check times and details before your visit. To
the east of the village, Friary Hills is another great
spot for birdwatching, as this part of the coast is a
convenient place for migrants flying in from or to the
Continent to stop and rest. There are also panoramic
views over Blakeney Freshes and beyond to Blakeney
Point and Harbour.

Food and Facilities

Refreshments are available in Blakeney, Morston and
Stiffkey and St Nicholas' Church, Blakeney. There are
toilets at Blakeney (not National Trust) and Morston
Quay, and St Nicholas' Church.

Previous page above: Large flocks of geese flying over
Blakeney National Nature Reserve.

Opposite: Grey seals at Blakeney National
Nature Reserve, Norfolk.

37. Sheringham Woodland and Coastal Walk

Sheringham Park
Norfolk
NR26 8TL
01263 820550
sheringhampark@
nationaltrust.org.uk

About this walk
Wildlife

Superb views

Architectural interest

Some steep slopes; can be
wet underfoot

Dogs welcome, but keep
under control

Distance 7 miles (11.2km)

Time 3 hours 30 mins

Enjoy this wonderfully varied walk through parkland, fields, woods, and along the cliff edge by the sea. Savour the views from the tree-top gazebo and absorb the history and rich variety of trees, birds and animal life.

Things to see

Wildlife

White Admiral butterflies can be spotted around the pond from late June, peaking in numbers in July. Skylarks can be seen and heard on the cliffs all year round. Mammals, such as foxes, badgers and deer, are not often visible but look out for tracks and other signs.

Below: The steam train of the North Norfolk Railway and Weybourne Windmill seen from The Gazebo.

The Gazebo

The folly or viewing tower, known as The Gazebo, is worth the climb, with views over the oak tree canopy to the sea. On a clear day the golden sands of Blakeney Point are visible, and steam trains can often be seen on the Poppy Line of the North Norfolk Railway as it runs through the northern end of Sheringham Park.

Above: View along the beach at Sheringham Park, Norfolk.

The Temple

Designed by Humphry Repton, but not built until over 160 years later. The temple was opened in 1975 to celebrate the 70th birthday of Mr Thomas Upcher, the last of his family to live in the Hall. Although built in a slightly different position than planned by Repton, the temple still provides a view as intended overlooking the parkland with the yellow gorse in flower, taking in Sheringham Hall and the coast beyond.

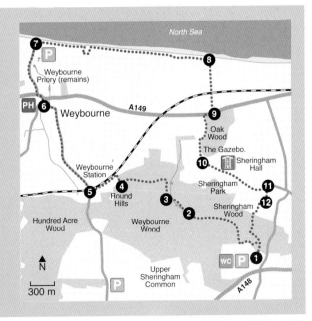

How to Get There

By Train Sheringham 2 miles (3.2km)

By Car Entrance at junction of A148/B1157 2 miles (3.2km) south-west of Sheringham, 5 miles (8km) west of Cromer and 6 miles (9.7km) east of Holt

OS Map Landranger 133, Explorer 252

Start / End Sheringham Park Visitor Centre, **OS grid ref: TG 13941**

1. From the Visitor Centre, go left past the Bower and follow the red arrows on the marker post. Go left between the rhododendrons and then bear right by the five-bar gate, going right at the bottom of the hill (in May look out for the handkerchief tree on the right - you will know it if you see it!) and on past the small shed on the right, a former saw mill. Continue to follow the red arrows to Weybourne Station.

2. Bear left at the pond and walk left of the barrier onto Weybourne Heath.

3. Go right at the National Trust sign for Weybourne Heath, pass a pond on the right, then turn left and come out of the woods with Weybourne Station on the left and a church and the sea ahead.

4. Walk on, past the shed, then leave the red marker post route and go left through the gate to the station.

5. From the station, head towards the sea. Go either over the footbridge, if the station is open, or up onto the road and over the railway bridge. Continue along the road towards the village of Weybourne and the sea; there's a good footpath all the way.

6. Follow the road into Weybourne village and go through the housing estate to the T-junction. Go right, signposted Kelling and Sheringham, then left across the A149 by the church. Go past the bus-stop and at the Ship Inn turn right, down Beach Road towards the sea. If you fancy a diversion, the site of the ruins of Weybourne Priory are on the right along Beach Road adjoining the church.

7. At the beach, turn right up the sandy path along the cliff edge and continue on. See a mill on the right, and pass a small terrace of houses on the cliff edge. Go through a kissing gate and pass a National Trust Sheringham Park sign and red marker post.

8. At the next marker post, turn right inland. Go over the railway bridge, and past the barn.

9. At the road, turn right inside the field edge (no footpath here on this busy road) then cross the road by the telegraph pole. Go through the gate on the other side of the road and carry on along this path to The Gazebo.

10. Leave the path and climb to the top of The Gazebo, then return to the path and continue left. At the gate, go through to the left and follow the path in front of Sheringham Hall. Carry straight on past the Hall (not open to the public), going through the gate with a cattle grid by a house and the Temple on the right at the top of the hill.

11. At the marker post, go right and up the hill to the temple.

12. From the Temple, follow the red, blue and orange arrows to the right, keep right across the field and go through the five-bar gate. Continue up the track (Summer-house Valley) then go left at the marker post onto the main path back to the Visitor Centre.

Make the Most of Your Day

Wander through Sheringham Park and you'll discover why it became the personal favourite of its designer, Humphry Repton. Visit the Repton exhibition to see the story of his 1812 design during a turbulent period of history. There are also events held throughout the year.

Food and Facilities

Courtyard café at Sheringham and buffet at Weybourne Station (when open). Toilets near courtyard and at Weybourne Station (when open).

Below: View from The Temple towards Sheringham Hall at Sheringham Park in Norfolk.

Opposite: A waterfall in Carding Mill Valley, Shropshire (walk 39).

The Midlands

38. Ancient Tree Walk at Croft Castle

Croft Castle and Parkland
Yarpole
Herefordshire
HR6 9PW
01568 780246
croftcastle@nationaltrust.
org.uk

About this walk
Ancient trees

Historic interest

Dogs welcome on leads in
parkland and gardens

Distance 1½ miles (2.4km)

Time 1 hour–1 hour 30
mins

This walk takes you into the heart of the parkland at Croft Castle
and passes a variety of ancient and historic trees. There's a wealth of
interesting species, including fallow deer (if you can spot them), bracket
fungi, such as birch polypore, and insects and other mini-beasts.

Things to see

Ancient Oaks
Keep an eye out in the gully just
after the lake for the Quarry Oak,
which at 1,000 years old is one of
the oldest trees at Croft. At point
7 there is a 500-year-old oak
named after Sir William Croft who
supposedly died under this tree
after being shot in the Civil War.

Chestnut Avenue
This was the original formal
approach to the Castle. It's
believed that sweet chestnuts
were taken from captured Spanish
vessels and planted at Croft
between 1580 and 1680 to
represent the formal battle plan of
the ships at the Armada.

Hawthorns
A little mystery: the old hawthorns
at point 5 are planted as if they are
within an orchard. One explanation
is they were the rootstock plants
for a medlar tree orchard and when
they died the rootstock took over.

Above: Croft Castle, Herefordshire
in autumn.

Left: Ancient trees on the walk back
towards the castle.

How to Get There

By Train Nearest station Leominster 7 miles (11.3km)

By Car Entrance off B4362, turning north at Cock Gate between Bircher and Mortimer's Cross. The property is signposted from the A49 between Ludlow and Leominster, and from A4110 at Mortimer's Cross

OS Map Landranger 149

Start / End Croft Visitor Reception, **OS grid ref: SO 451656**

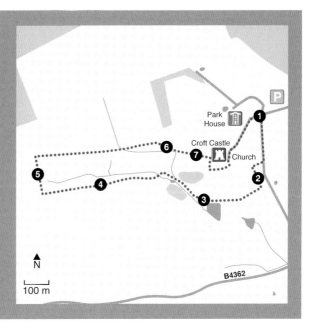

1. Start at Visitor Reception and head towards the exit drive. Walk through the gate to the left of the cattle grid and keep walking down the exit drive until you come to a waymarker on your right. Walk through the gate here and into the front meadow.

2. Follow the mown path through the meadow towards the lake, keeping the church behind you.

3. Follow the mown path alongside the lake.

4. Continue through the chestnut avenue and head across the field away from the castle. Enter the small gateway into the field in front of you.

5. Carry on towards the top of the field, keeping the fence on your right.

6. Walk through the field towards the castle. Looking to your left you can see 400 to 500-year-old chestnut trees as well as newly planted ones grown from their seeds.

7. Continue to walk towards the castle through the front meadow. Keeping the terrace wall on your left, you'll eventually come to a wrought iron gate. Walk through this and up the castle drive to the Gothic arch to finish the walk.

Make the Most of Your Day

Croft Castle had become the home of the Croft family even before the Domesday Book of 1086; guides at the house can share highlights of almost 1,000 years of family history, including the story of how the house was lost in 1746 but repurchased 177 years later. You can also enjoy the stunning gardens as well as events such as art exhibitions, theatre productions and overnight camping.

Food and Facilities

Refreshments and toilets available at the Carpenter's Tea-room.

Midlands

39. A Walk to the Waterfall at Carding Mill Valley

Carding Mill Valley
Church Stretton
Shropshire
SY6 6JG
01694 725000
cardingmill@nationaltrust.
org.uk

About this walk
Stunning views
Wildlife interest
Geological interest
Dogs welcome under close
control, especially around the
sheep that graze the common

Distance 1½ miles (2.4km)

Time 1 hour

This walk starts at Carding Mill Valley at the heart of the Long Mynd and takes you on a gentle ascent along the stream to the 13ft (4m) cascade at the picturesque Lightspout Waterfall – a sight that amazed our Victorian forebears.

Things to see

Geology of the Long Mynd
Notice the almost upright strata of hard grey rock here in the stream bed and protruding from the hillside turf. These originally horizontal, sedimentary shales and mudstones were laid down in shallow sea around 590 million years ago, when simple marine algae were the only life on Earth.

Wildlife
Long Mynd is teeming with wildlife, and depending on the time of year you can see birds such as stonechat, ring ouzel and red grouse, and a wealth of insects including emperor moths, green hairstreak, orange tip and green-veined white butterflies. Frogs, toads and newts, including the palmate newt, breed in spring.

Pole Bank
At 1,696ft (517m) above sea level, Pole Bank is the Long Mynd's highest point and a prominent feature on the walk.

Above: A waterfall in the Carding Mill Valley and the Shropshire Hills, Shropshire.

Below: The site covers 4,942 acres (2,000ha) of heather-covered hills and features iconic views of the Shropshire Hills.

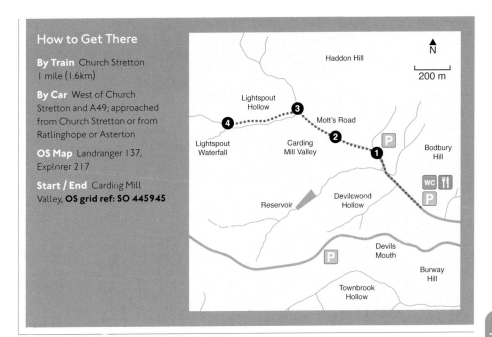

How to Get There

By Train Church Stretton
1 mile (1.6km)

By Car West of Church
Stretton and A49; approached
from Church Stretton or from
Ratlinghope or Asterton

OS Map Landranger 137,
Explorer 217

Start / End Carding Mill
Valley, **OS grid ref: SO 445945**

---

1. If you are starting from the Chalet Pavilion follow the stream uphill to the top car park. As you look up to the right you'll be looking directly at Bodbury Ring hill fort, which is more than 2,500 years old. It was in constant use throughout the Iron Age period by the Cornovii, a Celtic tribe of people found across Shropshire, Staffordshire, Cheshire and Herefordshire. They used the hill fort to guard their herds of sheep and cattle. From the top of the hill, they'd have been able to see people coming from miles away. Today sheep are used to keep the common open with their grazing, so remember to make sure dogs are kept under close control.

2. Continue up the valley (following the red trail markers) on the stony track to the left side of the stream.

3. When the valley divides ⅓ mile (500m) later, take the left-hand fork, up crude 'pitched' stone steps into the narrow Lightspout Hollow.

4. Rising above the stream, the rocky path snakes uphill around interlocking spurs before opening out, ⅓ mile (500m) on, below Lightspout Waterfall. Victorian visitors were so amazed by this cascade that it was known as 'a miniature Niagara'; after a prolonged downpour, the 13ft (4m) falls are spectacular. Return downhill by the same route.

Make the Most of Your Day
In Carding Mill Valley you can stroll along the stream, watch birds from the hide or pond dip. Up the hill there are paths for walking, cycling and horse riding. From the highest point of the Long Mynd on a clear day you can see as far as the Brecon Beacons and the Malverns. There are also four Dark Sky Discovery Sites on the Long Mynd, where it is possible to see the Milky Way with the naked eye.

Food and Facilities
There is a tea-room and toilets at Carding Mill Valley.

Midlands

113

40. River Reflections Walk at Attingham

The bridges over the River Tern at Attingham make this a perfect walk for pausing to take a photo. Attingham is host to around 5 miles (8km) of river, and the many ponds are a haven for wildlife of all sorts, from ducks, swans and otters to dragonflies.

Attingham Park
Atcham
Near Shrewsbury
Shropshire
SY4 4TP
01743 708162
attingham@nationaltrust.org.uk

About this walk
Wildlife interest

River and woodland habitat

Please be careful on the steps to the ice house

Dogs welcome

Distance 1½miles (2.4km)

Time 45 mins–1 hour

Things to see

The River Tern
Without human intervention, this river would be more of a stream – it owes its size to dams and locks that were constructed in the 1700s. These features were installed to allow access to the ironworks that were on the river near the bridges.

Attingham Deer
Attingham is home to approximately 250 semi-wild fallow deer, all direct descendants of the fallow deer here at the creation of the deer park in 1797. The last Lord Thomas was particularly fond of the deer and fed them daily in the winter months, with special favourites eating from his hand. Please note: during parts of the year sections of the deer park may be closed, please follow any signed diversions on your route.

The Ice House
This mound was an ice house probably built for Noel Hill, the first Lord Berwick in the late eighteenth century; it was converted in 1850 when a wheel pump was installed to provide the mansion with water from the River Tern. Before that, there was a corn mill on this site from the thirteenth century.

Above: Cattle in the park with the house in the background at Attingham Park, Shropshire.

Left: The River Tern divides the estate at Attingham.

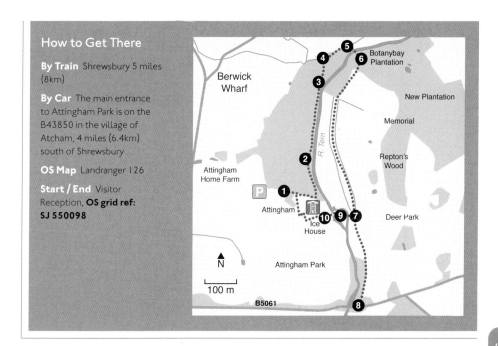

By Train Shrewsbury 5 miles (8km)

By Car The main entrance to Attingham Park is on the B43850 in the village of Atcham, 4 miles (6.4km) south of Shrewsbury

OS Map Landranger 126

Start / End Visitor Reception, **OS grid ref:** **SJ 550098**

Berwick Wharf

Botanybay Plantation

New Plantation

Memorial

Repton's Wood

Attingham Home Farm

R. Tern

Attingham

Deer Park

Ice House

N

100 m

Attingham Park

B5061

Midlands

1. From the car park make your way through the Stables Courtyard past the cottage garden and bear right. Take the cut-through on your left and bear left at the fork in the path by the cedars to join the Mile Walk along the riverside.

2. As you walk along the riverside, look out for the changing reflections of the deer park in the waters of the river. The River Tern is about 30 miles (48.3km) long, and home to wildlife of all sorts including ducks, swans, otters and dragonflies.

3. Take the path bearing right at the single cedar, following signs for the Deer Park Walk.

4. At the junction, continue to follow signs for the Deer Park Walk as you walk along the path through the trees.

5. Cross the cable stay bridge across the River Tern and enter the woodland. This bridge is a great location to stop and admire the reflections in the water – if you're lucky you may also spot an otter at this end of the river.

6. At this junction follow the signs for the short cut to leave the woodland and enter the deer park by the river. Continue along this grassy track.

7. The grass track leads you towards the large deer park gates. At this point you can extend your walk by following the instructions under point 8, or head towards the end of the route by skipping to point 9.

8. Continue past the gate and follow the grass path, which will take you under Tern Bridge, with a fantastic view of the mansion from the riverside. Re-trace your steps until you reach the deer park gates once more. This route may be closed in bad weather as floods are likely. If so, the gate will be locked.

9. Leave the deer park through the gates, and cross the two bridges over the River Tern. The Ice House is on your right.

10. Continue along the path past the front of the Regency mansion and back to the car park.

Make the Most of Your Day
Enjoy the outdoors at Attingham, with a variety of sports, trails and nature- and wildlife-themed children's activities.

Food and Facilities
The Carriage House Café and Mansion Tea-room serve a range of refreshments. Toilets can be found in the Stables Courtyard, Bothy and Brewhouse.

41. Dudmaston Hall and Dingle Walk

Surrounded by traditional woodland and a lakeside garden, Dudmaston Hall has been a family home since the seventeenth century and offers lovely walks teeming with history and wildlife. Bluebells are a favourite at Dudmaston in spring, the grounds are rich in birdlife and the estate is also home to the northernmost population of the white admiral butterfly.

Dudmaston Estate
Quatt
Near Bridgnorth
Shropshire
WV15 6QN
01746 780866
dudmaston@nationaltrust.org.uk

About this walk
Wildflower displays
Picturesque views
Wildlife interest
Please keep to footpaths
Dogs welcome on leads

Distance ⁴/₅ mile (1.3km)
Time 40 mins

Things to see

The Dingle
The wooded valley was a pet project of Frances Whitmore who, along with her husband William, resided in Dudmaston between 1775 and 1815, and she was a keen botanist. Together with their head gardener, Walter Wood, they created a picturesque route over rustic bridges and past waterfalls, urns and a hermitage.

Dudmaston's River and Pools
The river and pools at Dudmaston are home to a variety of wetland species. Dippers, grass snakes and dragonflies are regular visitors and there are signs of otters.

Above: Woodland walks around the Estate.

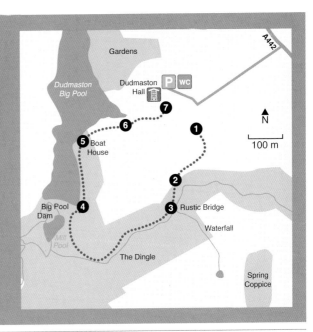

1. Leave the orchard car park via the kissing gate at the entrance. Turn right and follow the signs downhill to the Dingle.

2. Proceed through the gate (please close it behind you) and follow the trail downhill. Go through a second gate and enter the woods. Take the steps to your right before you reach the brook.

3. Continue along the path passing the Rustic Bridge on your left. Crossing the bridge takes you on one of many other walks in the grounds of Dudmaston Hall.

4. Follow the trail along the forested riverbanks of the Dingle. After passing the Mill Pool on your left you will reach the Big Pool Dam. Take the path to the right, signposted for Dudmaston.

5. Continue along the banks of the Big Pool, passing the Boat House as you go.

6. Enter the pedestrian gate and cross the meadow towards the Hall.

7. At the marked gate, you may enter the Garden and make your way to the Hall, or, alternatively, turn right and continue up the hill to your starting point at the car park.

Make the Most of Your Day

Dudmaston Hall has been a much-loved home for over 875 years; you will find the family rooms scattered with photos and perhaps an odd pair of shoes or two peeping out from under a table. The unexpected galleries create a total contrast, with their formal, crisp lines. The Gardens provide amazing vistas and tranquillity while the Orchard is the perfect place to relax and for the children to let off steam.

Food and Facilities

There is a tea-room and toilets at Dudmaston Hall.

Left: A glimpse of the house in the grounds at Dudmaston, Shropshire.

42. Rock House Trail

Rock Houses
Compton Road
Kinver
Staffordshire
DY7 6DL
01384 872553
kinveredge@nationaltrust.org.uk

About this walk

Important habitat

Spectacular views

Historical interest

Dogs welcome; keep under close control near livestock

Distance 2½ miles (4km)

Time 1 hour 30 mins– 2 hours 30 mins

This walk takes in everything this fascinating area has to offer, from the heathland buzzing with insects and the scent of gorse and heather, to leafy woodland paths with children's natural play areas. There are two different rock house complexes to explore as well as spectacular views to enjoy.

Things to see

Heathland Wildlife
This fragile heathland habitat is home to many rare species, and more familiar plants and animals can be found in the surrounding woodland. Lizards and snakes, including the adder, can be seen on the heath, and natterer's and brown long-eared bats live in the woods. Bird species include cuckoo, woodcock, willow warbler and skylark, and during the warm summer evenings you can enjoy a host of butterflies and moths and the buzz of insects, including many solitary bees and wasps.

The Rock Houses
Holy Austin Rock Houses were lived in until the 1960s, and have since been restored to feel like the cosy, simple dwellings they were. Carved straight into the rock, they were warm in winter and cool in summer. Volunteers are on hand to

tell the stories of the families who lived here, and children can have a go with traditional toys and games. Please check the opening times before you pop in.

Above: Looking across the valley from Kinver Edge and the Rock Houses, Staffordshire.

Below: The middle storey rock houses at Kinver Edge.

How to Get There

By Car From Stourbridge take the A458 towards Stourton, then the A449 to Kinver. In Kinver village follow signs to the Holy Austin Rock Houses, and park on the free lay-by parking. There is a signed overflow car park around the corner, you can also pick up the woodland walk from here by crossing the road and following the orange arrow waymarkers

OS Map Landranger 138, Explorer 218

Start / End Compton Road notice-board, **OS grid ref: SO 835836**

Kniver

Holy Austin Rock

Gorse Covert

Fort

Kinver Edge

Nanny's Rock

Kingsfield Forest Park

N

100 m

1. From the notice-board, turn right across the sandy area and take the uphill path into the woods, waymarked with a purple arrow. Keep following the purple waymarkers straight over the crossroads and past the children's natural play areas.

2. At the five-ways, follow the arrow to Nanny's Rock. There is a short, steep descent here.

3. Re-enter the National Trust boundary and walk along the top of the Edge, with spectacular views opening up to your left. Beyond the fence on your right will be an area of heathland restoration. You will then pass into the more mature heath, following a very sandy track through heather and gorse shrubs.

4. As you approach the Warden's Lodge you will cross short grassland. Head down into the woods at the war memorial. This woodland path is full of bluebells in spring.

5. Continue down the slope to approach the restored Rock Houses, and a further couple of minutes passed them you will return to the car park, which is signed from the Rock House Tea-rooms.

Make the Most of Your Day
Inside the restored Rock Houses you can absorb the atmosphere of these unusual homes with objects to play with and volunteers ready to share anecdotes of the families that lived here until as recently as the 1960s. The Iron Age Hill Fort is a scheduled ancient monument (SAM) that is kept deliberately clear of vegetation to protect its impressive ramparts. It sits on a historic county border and would have been an important trading post as well as having a defensive role.

Food and Facilities
Refreshments and toilets are available at the Rock House Tea-room.

43. Spring Walk at Croome

National Trust Croome
Visitor Centre
Near High Green
Worcester
Worcestershire
WR8 9DW
01905 371006
croome@nationaltrust.
org.uk

About this walk
Wildflower displays

Superb views

Wildlife interest

Ground will be muddy in
wet weather

Dogs welcome

Distance 4 miles (6.4km)

Time 1 hour 30 mins–
2 hours

Midlands

The estate at Croome includes over 730 acres (nearly 300ha) of parkland and a diverse habitat. A mixture of open farmed grassland, wildflower meadows, wetlands, large trees, copses and scrubland supports a huge variety of wildlife.

Things to see

The Rotunda
Built by 'Capability' Brown in the 1750s, the Rotunda is a Grade I-listed building. Once on the verge of collapse, it has undergone extensive restoration by the National Trust since 2007.

The Chinese Bridge
This is an exact replica of the original bridge, created using images from a painting by Richard Wilson in 1758 of Croome and also a book from 1749 called *Developments in Architecture and Carpentry*.

Above: The Temple Greenhouse at Croome, Worcestershire.

Opposite: Oxeye daisies surrounding Croome's Rotunda.

Below: The replica of the original Chinese Bridge at Croome.

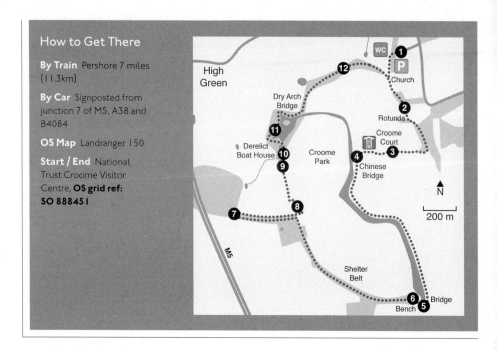

How to Get There

By Train Pershore 7 miles (11.3km)

By Car Signposted from junction 7 of M5, A38 and B4084

OS Map Landranger 150

Start / End National Trust Croome Visitor Centre, **OS grid ref: SO 888451**

1. From the Visitor Centre, follow the path through the Wilderness Walk shrubbery (look out for spring flowering bulbs) to a gate, which brings you to the top of Church Hill. Walk around the front of the church and pass through a metal gate into Church Shrubbery. Follow the path eventually passing the bird hide on your left.

2. Follow the path, crossing a tarmac road. Continue along the path until you reach the Rotunda. Keep a look out for our squirrels that frolic around in the trees. From the Rotunda follow the path to the right, down through the Home Shrubbery to the iron gate at the bottom.

3. Go through the iron gate into the park and follow the path to the right towards the Court. Continue along the path from the Court to the Chinese Bridge.

4. From the Chinese Bridge, staying on the Court side of the river, follow the mown path alongside the river for about ¾ mile (1.2km) until you reach a stile. Along the way you will see a lot of our birdlife, if you are lucky you will see a kingfisher or a heron. Cross the stile and walk clockwise around the pool.

5. Cross over a small bridge. Just before the bridge there is a bench, a great spot to sit a while and if you are lucky you will hear nightingales singing.

6. Just after the bridge turn left across a wooden platform into the shelter belt, this is a narrow wooded area , where if you are quiet you might spot muntjac deer. Follow the path for about 1 mile (1.6km) through the woods until you reach the end of the Shelter Belt.

7. At the end of the shelter belt you will see, on the left, a National Trust sign. Turn right, away from the sign, go through the gate and turn right into the field, follow the fence along the shelter belt back in the direction you have just walked.

8. Shortly you will reach three gates on the right, go through the gates until you reach the farm road.

9. Turn left and walk along this road (there may be a further closed gate across the road, go through it). Walk along the road until you see a large gate on the right back into the park. Go through the gate, turn left and in a few yards on the left you will see another gate into the lake area.

10. Enter the lake area and follow the path to the right, past the remains of the derelict Boat House. On a walk in spring look out for primroses, daffodils and, as the season progresses, bluebells.

11. Where you meet the main path round the lake, turn left and cross the two white bridges linking the island to the main path. Follow the path around the lake, past the Grotto, until you reach the Dry Arch Bridge. Turn left under the bridge and follow the path, past the Temple Greenhouse.

12. Continue through the evergreen shrubbery back to the church. From here, return to the Visitor Centre.

Make the Most of Your Day
There's more than meets the eye at Croome: a secret wartime airbase, now a Visitor Centre, was once a hub of activity for thousands of people. Outside is the grandest of English landscapes, 'Capability' Brown's masterful first commission, with commanding views over the Malverns. At the heart of the park lies Croome Court, once home to the Earls of Coventry with four floors to explore. The 6th Earl of Coventry was an eighteenth-century trendsetter and today Croome follows his lead by using artists and craftspeople in the house to tell the story of its eclectic past in inventive ways, perfect for making new discoveries.

Food and Facilities
There is a restaurant at the Visitor Centre and a tea-room at Croome Court.

Midlands

Above: View over the lake towards the house at Croome.

44. Clent Hills Nature Walk

Romsley
Worcestershire
DY9 9JR
01562 712822
clenthills@nationaltrust.
org.uk

About this walk
Ancient woodland

Wildlife interest

Some steep climbs and
uneven paths that can be
muddy

Dogs welcome; please keep
on leads in car parks and
under close control near
livestock

Distance 1 mile (1.6km)

Time 30 mins

Only 8 miles (12.8km) outside Birmingham, the Clent Hills offer a haven of peace, with beautiful woodland and plenty of wildlife. This short walk leads through woodland to the top of a hill where, on a clear day, the Welsh Black Mountains are visible on the horizon.

Things to see

Ancient Woodland
As you wander through the ancient woodlands, you will notice deadwood lying around the woodland floor; this forms an important part of the cycle of tree health by adding nutrients back into the soil and providing a habitat for many invertebrate species, which in turn attract birds and mammals.

Clent Wildlife
The open grassland and woodland provides plenty of opportunities for wildlife spotting, in particular wintering birds. Redwing, thrush and fieldfare can all be spotted from October onwards. Migrating birds, such as wheatear and ring ouzels, might also make an appearance.

Above: Visitors enjoying the views at Clent Hills, Worcester.

Below: Mature beech tree at Clent Hills.

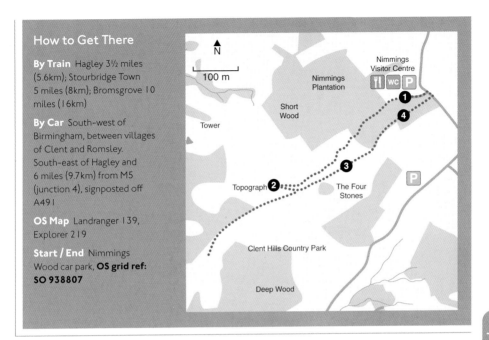

How to Get There

By Train Hagley 3½ miles (5.6km); Stourbridge Town 5 miles (8km); Bromsgrove 10 miles (16km)

By Car South-west of Birmingham, between villages of Clent and Romsley. South-east of Hagley and 6 miles (9.7km) from M5 (junction 4), signposted off A491

OS Map Landranger 139, Explorer 219

Start / End Nimmings Wood car park, **OS grid ref: SO 938807**

Map labels

N
100 m
Nimmings Visitor Centre
Nimmings Plantation
Short Wood
Tower
Topograph **2**
The Four Stones
3
1
4
Clent Hills Country Park
Deep Wood

1. Climb up a gentle zig-zag slope into the woodland from Nimmings Wood Café and information point. Turn right and follow an easy access path through the trees, with some fine views and resting points on the way. The National Trust is working hard to restore the valuable acid heathland habitat here, which is a great environment for a variety of birds and insect life.

2. Emerging from the woods you reach a sweeping panorama looking west towards Wenlock Edge and the Malvern Hills. Return to your start point via the all-ability path you came on, or turn left and walk up to what appears to be some prehistoric standing stones (these were actually created in the eighteenth century for Lord Lyttleton as a folly to be viewed from down in the valley by visitors). The views from here are some of the best in the Clent Hills. To the west is the Severn Valley and the Welsh border, while to the north is Birmingham and the Black Country.

3. Skirt to the left of the clump of trees behind the standing stones and enter through a gate into Horses Mane Woodland. Listen out for, or try to spot, birds like thrush, nuthatch, yellowhammer or perhaps even a great spotted woodpecker.

4. While taking care not to trip on exposed tree roots, look up through the woodland canopy and you may catch sight of buzzard circling above. Head left and return to the car park. Why not stop off at Nimmings Wood Café for a hot drink and delicious home-made snack to warm you up after your walk?

Make the Most of Your Day
Den building is a popular pastime here, and there is a large natural play space behind the café at Nimmings Wood. You can also walk up to the top of the hill and follow the natural play trail – when you have finished enjoying the views! You can also admire the eighteenth-century follies that form the backdrop to Hagley Hall.

Food and Facilities
Near the car park there is a café, picnic area and toilets (open Tuesday–Sunday).

Midlands

45. A Walk Through the Parkland at Charlecote

Charlecote Park
Warwickshire
CV35 9ER
01789 470277
charlecotepark@
nationaltrust.org.uk

About this walk
Wildlife interest

Walk can be lengthened at two points

Take care along the unfenced riverside and ensure children are supervised at all times

No dogs allowed

Distance ¾ mile–just over 1 mile (1.2–1.8km)

Time 40 mins–1 hour

Come for a gentle amble and allow plenty of time to see the fallow deer and Jacob sheep at Charlecote. Any time of year is perfect for spotting wildlife. The grounds provide ideal habitats and conditions for a wide variety of birds, insects and mammals.

Things to see

Royal Connection
The coat-of-arms over the front porch commemorates the visit of Elizabeth I here on her way to Kenilworth Castle in 1572.

Charlecote's Fallow Deer
On the opposite side of the river is Camp Ground where Roundhead soldiers are said to have camped before the Civil War battle of Edge Hill in 1642. There is no public access to this area as it is used as a safe haven for the deer particularly when their fawns are born. There has been a deer herd in the park since the mid-1400s. There are hares living in this part of the parkland too. Why not bring your binoculars for a closer look.

Above: The west, or entrance front, seen from the garden at Charlecote Park, Warwickshire.

Wildlife on the River
The waterfall or weir acts as a dam to maintain the water level of the lake. The river habitat is a haven for wildlife – from a heron poised motionless on the riverbank to a flash of blue kingfisher – it's always worth pausing to see what's around.

St Leonard's Church
This was rebuilt in 1862 with the help of the Lucy family. Please note the gate into the churchyard is one way. It does not allow re-entry into the park. The Jacob sheep were brought into the park from Portugal in 1756 by George Lucy – the first flock of spotted sheep to be introduced into England.

Above: Deer in the parkland at Charlecote Park.

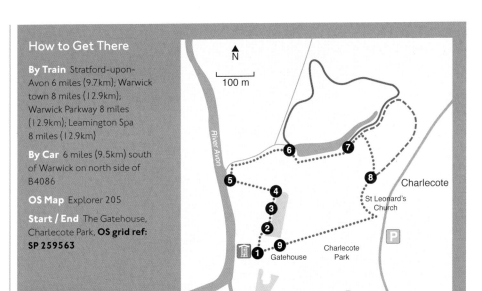

How to Get There

By Train Stratford-upon-Avon 6 miles (9.7km); Warwick town 8 miles (12.9km); Warwick Parkway 8 miles (12.9km); Leamington Spa 8 miles (12.9km)

By Car 6 miles (9.5km) south of Warwick on north side of B4086

OS Map Explorer 205

Start / End The Gatehouse, Charlecote Park, **OS grid ref: SP 259563**

Map labels: N · 100 m · River Avon · Charlecote · St Leonard's Church · Charlecote Park · Gatehouse · P

1. Start from the Gatehouse and walk towards the main house. The house was built in the 1550s for the first Sir Thomas Lucy. It was one of the first great Elizabethan houses and although it has undergone many changes, some of the original brickwork remains.

2. Turn right through the iron gates and walk between the Cedar Lawn and croquet lawn.

3. Walk along the path ahead of you to the left of the summer-house along the length of the Long Border. Go through the metal gate on your left to drop down into the parkland.

4. Walk down the gentle slope towards the River Avon. Look out for the fallen tree.

5. Turn away from the house and follow the mown path along the riverbank and round the edge of the park. Walk towards the waterfall.

6. Follow the mown path by the side of the lake for the short walk. Alternatively, bear left at the head of the lake to follow the longer (Hill Park) walk (an additional 20 minutes). The mown paths are easy to follow but there are no waymarkers, so do check your map. You'll rejoin the short walk at point 7, halfway along the lake.

7. To continue the short walk, stay on the mown path away from the lake towards St Leonard's church. To take the long walk carry on along the lakeside and bear right as you reach the boundary fence, continuing to follow the mown path towards St Leonard's church. You rejoin the short walk at the churchyard.

8. With your back to the church, follow the mown path down the avenue of trees back towards the Gatehouse (point 9 on the map).

Although no dogs are permitted on this route, there is a separate dog-friendly walk available at Charlecote.

Make the Most of Your Day
There is plenty to enjoy at Charlecote Park. During the warmer months the gardens are especially beautiful, with something new in flower every week. Bring a picnic and enjoy one of the outdoor events. The house is filled with treasures collected by the Lucy family who have owned Charlecote for 900 years.

Food and Facilities
There are toilets signposted to the left of the Gatehouse; the Orangery Tea-room can be found at Charlecote Park, to the right of the main house.

Midlands

46. Orchid Walk at Calke Abbey

Calke Abbey
Ticknall
Derby
South Derbyshire
DE73 7JF
01332 863822
calkeabbey@nationaltrust.
org.uk

About this walk
Rare flora

Ancient trees

Dogs welcome but please
keep on leads

Distance 2¾ miles (4.4km)

Time 2 hours

On the Calke Estate there are over 600 acres (243ha) of historic
parkland in which to enjoy a peaceful stroll. This walk will take you
through a varied landscape of grasslands, arable farmland and one of
Europe's rarest habitats – wood pasture. Calke is known for its varied
flora and particularly its beautiful orchids which flower during the
summer months.

Things to see

Twayblade
This plant takes its name from the
two large oval leaves that are at
the base of the flower stem. The
small yellow-green flowers look
a bit like little people. Sometimes
the stem can become damaged by
feeding froghopper nymphs found
in cuckoo spit.

Fragrant Orchid
This orchid, as the name suggests,
is heavily scented. It is most
perfumed in the early evening and
the smell is often described as
similar to mock orange blossom.
The flowers vary in colour from
pink to purple and grow in a
compact spike on a straight stem.

Common Spotted Orchid
This is the most abundant of
the British orchids. The flowers
are pink with purple markings and
the leaves are spotted – hence
the name. These flowers peak from
late June to early July at which
time we expect to see more than
5,000 common spotted orchids on
this site.

Above: Visitors in the garden
at Calke, Derbyshire.

Right: Common spotted orchid.

How to Get There

By Car 10 miles (16km) south of Derby on A514 at Ticknall. M42/A42 exit 13 and A50 Derby South

OS Map Landranger 128

Start / End Calke Abbey main car park, **OS grid ref: SK 367226**

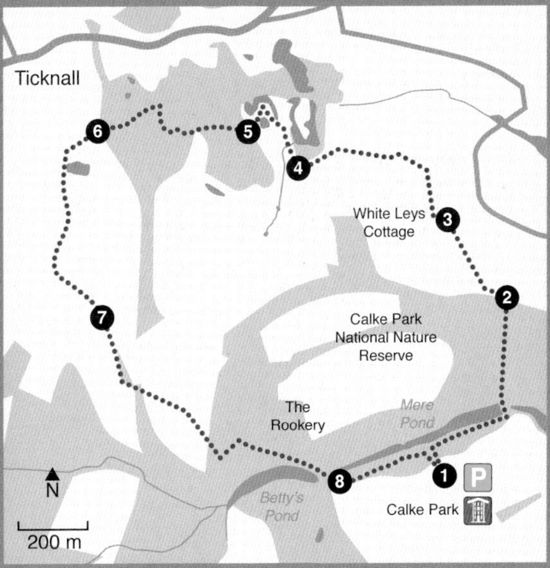

1. Begin at the northern edge of the main car park with your back to the ticket office. Follow the gravel path then down steps to the pond. Turn right and follow the deer fencing to the top of the hill, until it meets the old park boundary wall close to an interpretation board.

2. Turn left for 22 yards (20m) then go through the gate on the right. Turn left, cross the stile and walk down the field to cross the lane leading to White Leys Cottage on the left. Continue ahead.

3. At the wall turn right and follow the footpath along the wall on the left. Go over a stile and now keep the hedge on the right to meet woodland at the edge of Ticknall Limeyards.

4. Continue ahead along the wide stoned track that bears right. Look out for a path descending on the left. This leads to a stile by a gate. For a slight detour to see the orchids in summer, turn right after the stile. Return to the path and turn right.

5. Follow the path (a quarry face over on the left). Cross another stile. The path weaves its way through the woodland. Walk under a bridge then through a gate past the old limekiln. Continue on the stoned path and cross another bridge as you progress.

6. Eventually you meet a tunnel. Go through it to another stile. Cross it and after 11 yards (10m) turn left following a stoned path up to a gate. Turn right to walk along the stoned path by the hedgerow. This is the route of the National Forest Way, marked by yellow-topped posts with orange discs.

7. Follow the route through open parkland, use the narrow gate and cross the open area aiming downhill to reach the next marker post at the edge of the woodland pasture. Walk on, cross a track to eventually pass between two ponds. Next ascend steps after a gate. A number of Calke's ancient trees (some more than 800 years old) can be seen on the left.

8. Keep to the upper path to return to the car park.

Make the Most of Your Day
The faded grandeur and peeling paint inside Calke Abbey are a vivid illustration of the decline of many country house estates during the twentieth century. Around the house you can visit the beautiful walled gardens and explore the orangery, auricula theatre and the kitchen gardens.

Food and Facilities
There is a restaurant and toilets at Calke Abbey.

47. The Bluebell Woods of Clumber

Clumber Park
Hardwick Village
Worksop
Nottinghamshire
S80 3AZ
01909 544917
clumberpark@nationaltrust.
org.uk

About this walk
Wildflower displays
Wonderful views
Wildlife interest
Some uneven surfaces; take
care crossing roads
Dogs welcome

Distance 3 miles (4.8km)

Time 2 hours

A beautiful place to visit at any time of year, the appropriately named 'Bluebell Woods' at Clumber Park are transformed in the spring. The carpet of intense blue under the opening tree canopy is a spectacular sight. The traditional early flowering of bluebells makes the most of the sunlight that reaches the woodland floor before the trees cast their shade. Millions of bulbs may grow closely together in one wood, creating one of nature's most stunning displays. This walk takes in the estate village of Hardwick and the adjacent woodland.

Things to see

Semi-ancient Woodland
During spring the semi-ancient woodland along the route is a carpet of bluebells. These flowers are an indicator of woods that have remained undisturbed for centuries. These veteran trees provide home to many species of wildlife from owls and woodpeckers to butterflies. A tree next to the path at point 2 on the walk is home to more than 300 bats that roost here during the daytime. From dusk these bats feed on insects within the woods and a single bat can eat 3,000 insects in one night.

New Native Woodland
The section on the left of the track is being restored to native woodland. The woodland originally consisted of mature oak trees, but unfortunately these were felled in the early 1900s and replanted with conifer trees, such as Scots pine and larch, for commercial timber production. These reached maturity in 1990 and the trees were felled once again. The area was planted with over 1,000 young trees to return it to native woodland. As this matures, the amount of wildlife will increase.

Heathland
Another major habitat within Clumber is heathland. This fragile habitat has suffered a national decline over the last few hundred years, with areas planted with commercial woodland or ploughed to turn it into farmland. Late August sees the heather in bloom with insects collecting the nectar from the pink flowers.

Causeway
Once a mixture of trees and grassland, in the mid-1980s the area around the causeway was affected by mining subsidence, which caused a change in water levels. When the water is clear, you can see old tree stumps beneath the surface. Look closely at the fallen tree in the middle of the pond as occasionally a kingfisher sits waiting for a fish.

Above: Bluebells flowering in the parkland of Clumber Park, Nottinghamshire.

How to Get There

By Train Worksop 4½ miles (7km)

By Car 4½ miles (7.2km) south-east of Worksop, 6½ miles (10.5km) south-west of Retford, 1 mile (1.6km) from A1/A57, 11 miles (17.7km) from M1, junction 30

OS Map Landranger 120

Start /End Hardwick village car park, **OS grid ref: SK 637755**

1. Walk out of the car park with the farm on your right and up through the village of Hardwick. The village was originally for the workers on the estate during the time Clumber was owned by the Dukes of Newcastle. Walking through the village, you walk past an old red phone box and a green post box; both are still used. A short distance after the second speed ramp you can see the War Memorial on the right.

2. Shortly after the war memorial, take a right turn at a metal public footpath sign which is pointing in the direction you need to walk. Some of the oak trees in this woodland are around 500 years old and are the remains of a fragment of ancient woodland present before the park was enclosed in 1707.

3. Leaving the fragment of old oak woodland, you are now in an area of much younger native trees. Continue along this path towards the open field in the distance.

4. When you get to the boundary of the woodland the path goes across a field. If visiting in spring, take a quick glance to the left and you'll see a strip of bluebells running along the field edge. The coppiced trees almost form a tunnel over them. Head towards the School House following a yellow waymarker as the path goes round the fence line, and then across the field still following yellow markers. The path eventually meets up with a limestone farm track. Here you turn left.

5. Watch out for traffic on this section of the walk. Continue along the farm track for around ¾ mile (1.2 km) until you eventually come to a tarmac road. At this junction carefully cross the road and head downhill. After 200 yards (180m) a wooden bridleway sign on your right will point you in the right direction, through Scots pine woodland. Follow the path down the slope and at the path junction turn right.

6. Continuing along the track, you eventually get to Lime Tree Avenue, which has a double row of trees. Here you turn left to walk between the rows of trees. As you go up the hill you reach a wooden swing barrier and a path on the left. Take this path with a clump of large mature beech trees on your right and continue along this track.

7. When you reach the road, carefully cross the road and head straight into the next woodland. The section of the woodland on your left has a good show of bluebells in spring. The shade cast by the young beech trees help to restrict the growth of bracken and brambles enabling the flowers to be easily seen. Once you emerge from this woodland you're on open grassland. Head towards the road turning left along it. Again be aware of vehicles using this road.

8. Walking down the slight gradient you will see the lake in front of you and a road crossing it along a raised causeway. Continuing along the road you will reach the other side of the lake. Take the lakeside path through the car park and keep the lake on your right.

9. This is the last section of the walk, and takes you back along the lakeside. When you reach Hardwick village toilets on your left, walk along the tarmac path back to the car park. Before taking this path, a short detour takes you down to the weir and a wooden bridge, which you can see just round the corner. From here there are good views up the lake towards the chapel, or downstream towards

farmland and trees in the distance. If you have a pair of binoculars, look over the farmland for buzzards soaring above.

Make the Most of Your Day
Clumber was once the country estate of the Dukes of Newcastle. Although the house was demolished in 1938, there are many glimpses of its grand past to explore. The house, lake and gardens all wait to be discovered.

Food and Facilities
At Clumber Park there is a fully licensed café serving a range of hot and cold snacks and meals using fresh, seasonal local produce, and kiosks serving drinks, snacks, soup and ice-creams open at peak times. Picnics and barbecues are welcome in the sites provided. Toilet facilities are available near Hardwick village and at Clumber Park.

Above: Lakeside path towards Hardwick village at Clumber Park, Nottinghamshire.

48. Belton Park Walk

Belton House
Grantham
Lincolnshire
NG32 2LS
01476 566116
belton@nationaltrust.org.uk

About this walk
A quintessential country estate

Pretty views

Historical interest

Dogs welcome but must be kept on leads at all times

Distance 3 1/5 miles (5.1 km)

Time 1 hour 30 mins

Midlands

This delightful walk at Belton Park passes ancient woodland and the site of a deserted medieval village. The wetland areas are full of wildlife, including birds such as the treecreeper, insects including the speckled wood butterfly, and mammals, such as water voles.

Things to see

Belton House
Built in the 1680s, Belton House is the former home of the Brownlow family and is often cited as being the perfect example of an English country-house estate. The seventeenth-century Carolean treasure house contains fine collections of porcelain, silver, paintings and books.

Above: The south front of Belton House in the January snow prior to redecoration.

Right: Fallow deer on a misty morning.

Towthorpe Ponds
Created around 1820, Towthorpe Ponds have been a haven for white-clawed crayfish since special reefs were built in 2009.

Fallow Deer
Look out for the direct descendants of the wild deer herd enclosed here in 1690. They have large, flat antlers and can be a variety of colours. They often seek sanctuary in Old Wood so please take care not to disturb them, especially if you visit during June when they are fawning. The breeding season, known as the rut, runs from the last week in September until the middle of November. The bucks bellow and roar to attract the attention of the female does.

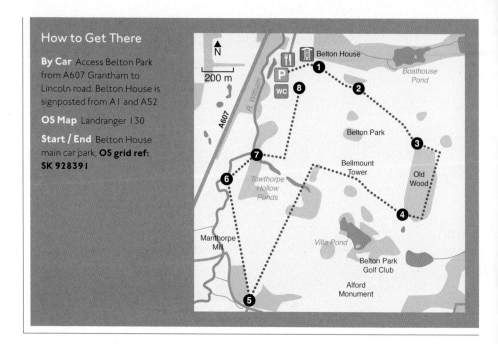

How to Get There

By Car Access Belton Park from A607 Grantham to Lincoln road. Belton House is signposted from A1 and A52

OS Map Landranger 130

Start / End Belton House main car park, **OS grid ref: SK 928391**

Belton House
Boathouse Pond
Belton Park
Bellmount Tower
Old Wood
Towthorpe Hollow Ponds
Manthorpe Mill
Villa Pond
Belton Park Golf Club
Alford Monument
R. Witham
A607

1. Make your way from Visitor Reception towards the front steps of Belton House. As you look at the mansion, follow the small gravel path on your right into the park, keeping the estate railing on your left. Follow the tree-line all the way to a gate in the wooden fence.

2. Go through the gate and on your left you'll see a ha-ha. Built in c.1800, this Grade II-listed landscape feature provides uninterrupted views from the mansion along the tree-lined avenue to Bellmount Tower in the distance. Make your way across the parkland towards the brow of the hill.

3. Pick up the woodland path and head around the back of Old Wood, identified as such on estate maps dating back to 1690. Once you reach the other side of the wood, you'll see the fence line that denotes the edge of the golf course. Head right and follow the fence line down the hill.

4. You'll see the Alford Monument within the golf course; this memorial was erected by Baron Brownlow in 1851 in memory of his son, Viscount Alford. Head left at the corner of the golf course, following the fence line and through a gate at Towthorpe Hollow Ponds, heading down towards the Lion Gates.

5. With your back to the Lion Gates, head left along the grass path towards the River Witham.

6. Here lays the site of the deserted medieval village of Towthorpe that was mentioned in the Domesday Book of 1086. Continue to walk beside the riverbank and head towards a gate in the small wood.

7. Go through the gate and head right along Towthorpe Hollow Ponds. Make your way towards the old carriageway of the south drive and head north through the gate and back towards the mansion.

8. You're now back at the top of the oval where, during the spring and summer months, you can watch Belton Park Cricket Club play their home matches.

Make the Most of Your Day
Below stairs tours at Belton take place all year round and you can see where the servants worked and lived.

Food and Facilities
Refreshments are available at the Stables Restaurant, the Ride Play Café and the Muddy Hands Outdoor Café. There are toilets at a number of locations.

Opposite: Llyn Ogwen, Snowdonia (walk 55).

Wales

49. Marloes Peninsula Coastal Walk

See the very best of the Marloes Peninsula on this circular walk. Look for seals and their pups in the secluded bays around the coastline in early autumn. This beautiful heathland peninsula has amazing views over the Pembrokeshire coast and is teeming with wildlife.

Marloes
Haverfordwest
Pembrokeshire
SA62 3BH
01437 720385
marloessands@
nationaltrust.org.uk

About this walk
Spectacular views

Geological interest

Moderate to rugged paths, some gradients and steps

Dogs welcome on leads

Distance 4 miles (6.4km)

Time 2 hours

Things to see

Seals and Jack Sound
About 50 Atlantic grey seal pups are born each year on the beaches around the peninsula, making the cliffs above the beaches on the Deer Park excellent for cliff-top seal watching. The treacherous waters of Jack Sound lie between the Deer Park and Midland Isle, and are a popular haunt for porpoises, while Wooltack Point offers spectacular views across St Bride's Bay.

Welsh Mountain Ponies
Look out for Welsh mountain ponies on the Deer Park. Their grazing is essential for keeping the coastal heathland vegetation in good order.

Geology
The geology of the peninsula presents strong contrasts: the south side is made up of sedimentary sandstones; the north side, Deer Park and Skomer are igneous rocks, which are the remains of old volcanoes.

Above: Looking towards the beach from the cliff-top at Marloes Sands and Mere, Pembrokeshire.

Right: Young swans on Marloes Mere.

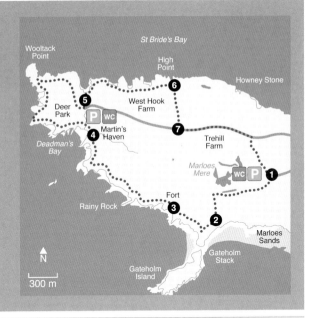

How to Get There

By Train Haverfordwest
12 miles (19.3km); Milford
Haven 9 miles (14.5km);
Pembroke Dock 13 miles
(20.9km)

By Car B4327 from
Haverfordwest, along
numerous country roads

OS Map Landranger 157,
Explorer OL36

Start / End Marloes
Sands car park, **OS grid
ref: SM 789082**

St Bride's Bay
Wooltack Point
High Point
Howney Stone
Deer Park
West Hook Farm
Deadman's Bay
Martin's Haven
Trehill Farm
Marloes Mere
Fort
Rainy Rock
Marloes Sands
Gateholm Stack
Gateholm Island

N
300 m

1. From the south end of Marloes Sands car park turn right by the emergency phone, following signs to the toilets. A short distance past the toilets, take a path to the left, through a self-closing gate signposted to the beach.

2. On reaching the coast path, you'll see Marloes Sands to your left. Turn right and continue towards Gateholm Island.

3. Continue along the coast path and through the Iron Age fort. Enjoy the dramatic sedimentary rock formations along the coast. Skomer Island and Midland Isle gradually come into view.

4. At a footbridge, shortly before a white cottage, take the left fork towards more Iron Age ramparts. Follow the path round the coastline of the Deer Park.

5. Go through the gate onto the road and turn left towards Martin's Haven and the Skomer embarkation point. Just before the beach follow the coast path right and up the steps. The path continues east, with St Bride's Bay to the left and West Hook Farm to the right. Enjoy the magnificent views across St Bride's Bay towards Newgale, the Solva Coast, St David's Peninsula and Ramsey Island.

6. After just over 1 mile (1.6km), leave the coast path. Turn right through a self-closing gate by a 'West Hook Farm' National Trust omega sign. Then cross three fields to the road.

7. Turn left and walk along the road past Trehill Farm. ¼ mile (400m) past the farm, turn right by two semi-detached cottages and down the lane leading back to the car park. (Just over 100 yards (90m) past the turning, a track to the right leads to a hide overlooking Marloes Mere.)

Make the Most of Your Day
From spring to early autumn you can enjoy boat trips from Martin's Haven to different spots around the islands. Marloes Mere is a fantastic spot for wildlife watching and you can also enjoy walking along the beach at Marloes Sands.

Food and Facilities
There is a pub and a café in Marloes village. There are toilets signposted at point 1 on the walk.

Wales

50. Bosherston Lily Ponds

Stackpole is both a listed designed landscape and an internationally important nature reserve. This relaxing stroll showcases Bosherston's beautiful lily ponds, with options to explore the dunes and pools of the Mere Pool Valley behind Broadhaven Beach.

Bosherston Car Park
Pembrokeshire
SA71 5DR
01646 623110
stackpole@nationaltrust.org.uk

About this walk
Lovely views
Beautiful waterlilies
Wildlife interest
Dogs welcome on leads

Distance 1 mile (1.6km);
2–2½ miles (3.2–4km) if you include the Mere Pool Valley

Time 30 mins (1–1 hour 30 mins for longer route)

Things to see

Waterlilies
In early summer there are hundreds of waterlilies in flower on the lake.

Warblers
In summer the reed-bed on your right at point 6 is full of chattering reed warblers and sedge warblers.

Mere Pool Valley
This is a great place to see dragon and damselflies.

Otters at Stackpole
Otters are very shy creatures. You need to be very quiet - and lucky - to see a family group.

Above: Waterlilies on Bosherston Lakes, Stackpole, Pembrokeshire.

Below: The view across Bosherston Lakes in July.

How to Get There

By Train Pembroke 6 miles (9.7km)

By Car Follow the B4319 Pembroke to Stackpole

OS Map Landranger 158

Start / End Bosherston Car Park, **OS grid ref: SR 966948**

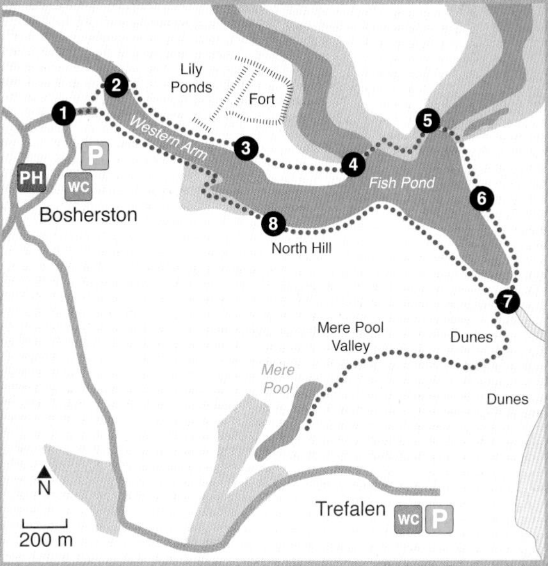

Map labels: Lily Ponds, Fort, Western Arm, Fish Pond, PH, WC, P, Bosherston, North Hill, Mere Pool Valley, Dunes, Mere Pool, Dunes, Trefalen, WC, P, N, 200 m

1. From the car park turn left and follow the path to the lake. Turn left.

2. Cross the western arm of the lake by the Bosherston causeway. The waterlilies are at their best in June and July, but the lakes and lakeside woodlands are full of wildlife all year round.

3. Follow the path up to the limestone bluff. Look down into the clear water to see the billowing green mats of rare stonewort, and if you're lucky a pike waiting in ambush. A path through the bushes to your left leads up to the Fishpond Camp, an old coastal fort built 3,000 years ago when the lakes were a tidal inlet.

4. Continue down to the central causeway and cross it. From April to September look for dragonflies and damselflies, with swallows and house martins skimming overhead.

5. Turn right at the next junction and descend to the Grassy Bridge. When the lakes were first created in the 1780s this was the barrier between lake and sea – the final dam wasn't built until 1860.

6. Continue towards the sea. In winter you may be lucky enough to see (and hear) a bittern. Listen out too for the pig-like squeals of water rails, secretive water birds that live in the reeds.

7. Cross over the lake outlet by a narrow stone bridge and continue right up the lakeside path towards Bosherston. You can also continue onto the beach, bearing right to explore the wildlife of the Mere Pool Valley.

8. Return to the car park by the western arm path, stopping often to enjoy the wildlife. You may even see an otter.

Make the Most of Your Day

Take time to discover the cliffs, coves and sand dunes along the 8 miles (12.9km) of coastline that the Stackpole Estate has to offer.

Food and Facilities

On the Stackpole Estate you will find the Stackpole Walled Garden, a café run by Mencap, and there is the Boathouse Tea-room at Stackpole Quay. There are toilets at Bosherston Lily Ponds car park.

Wales

51. Rhossili Headland Walk

Rhossili
Swansea
SA3 1PR
01792 390707
rhossili.shop@nationaltrust.org.uk

About this walk
Dramatic, coastal views

Shipwrecks

Archaeological interest

Dogs welcome under close control

Distance 3½ miles (5.6km)

Time 1 hour 30 mins

If you love the coast, you don't want to miss a stroll along one of Wales' best beaches, taking in the beautiful views as you go. Rhossili Down is lowland heath and home to a variety of birds and insects, such as the rare black bog ant. The south Gower coast hosts many rare plants and birds, including yellow whitlow grass and choughs.

Above: View towards Worms Head, Gower.

Below: The ocean-stripped oak carcass of the wreck of the *Helvetia*, Rhossili Bay.

Things to see

Rhossili Beach
One of the best beaches in Wales, Rhossili is a haven for people who want to enjoy the coast – walking, surfing or just building sand castles.

Serpents, Seascapes and Shipwrecks
The name 'Worms Head' comes from the Nordic word 'Wurm', which means serpent or dragon. The Worms Head is a tidal island with access possible for approximately two half-hour periods either side of low tide. The coastguard lookout has tide tables available and will offer advice as to the best time to cross.

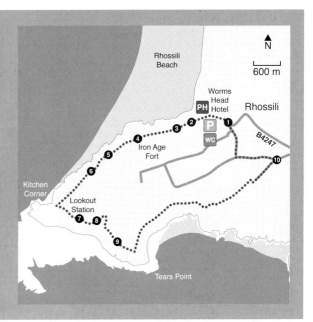

How to Get There

By Train The nearest train stations are Swansea or Gowerton 19½ miles (30.6km) away

By Car From Swansea follow A4118 and B4247. The car park is situated at the end of the village, fee payable

OS Map Landranger 159, Explorer 186

Start / End National Trust shop, Rhossili, **OS grid ref: SS 414 881**

Rhossili Beach

Worms Head Hotel

Rhossili

Iron Age Fort

Kitchen Corner

Lookout Station

Tears Point

N

600 m

B4247

1. With your back to the bus-stop, turn right and walk along the road, continuing between the car park and the Worms Head Hotel. The National Trust shop is a little further on your left.

2. Looking to your right you will see the 3 mile (4.8km) beach of Rhossili. The remains of the *Helvetia*, a Norwegian oak barque that ran aground here in 1887, can still be seen at low tide.

3. Continue to follow the path through the gateway on the surfaced path.

4. To the right of the path there are a series of mounds. These are the remains of an Iron Age fort.

5. As you continue along the surfaced track you will see fields and hedge banks that are part of a medieval open field strip system known as The Vile.

6. Where the surfaced track bears sharp left, walk straight on following a wide grass path towards the coastguard lookout with views of the Worms Head.

7. At the lookout, turn left along the cliff-top to join the path that runs alongside a stone wall. The path heads down a short slope to a kissing gate.

8. Continue to follow the path alongside the wall. After a few minutes the path descends quite steeply and then follows the wall sharply to the left. Follow the well-worn path, ascending gradually. Be careful on the stones here as they are often slippery.

9. Keep to the left and the path eventually brings you to a metal ladder and wooden steps over a wall. Cross the wall and follow the footpath as it heads back inland to Middleton.

10. Before you reach Middleton take a sharp left at the fork in the track and walk back to Rhossili village.

Make the Most of Your Day
Spend more time down on the beach or climb Rhossili Down and admire the views. There are also many archaeological features, including the fort seen along the route, together with Neolithic burial chambers and Bronze Age cairns.

Food and Facilities
There is a self-service drinks machine at the Visitor Centre and a pub opposite the car park. There are toilets between the car park and the National Trust shop.

52. 'Capability' Brown Walk at Dinefwr

Dinefwr was the first parkland National Nature Reserve in Wales and is bursting with colourful flowering plants; the show begins in spring with blossoming trees and a carpet of bluebells. Lancelot 'Capability' Brown suggested this walk, and the specimen trees to be planted along it as markers, when he visited Dinefwr in 1775.

Dinefwr Park
Llandeilo
Carmarthenshire
SA19 6RT
01558 824512
dinefwr@nationaltrust.
org.uk

About this walk
Wildflower displays
Superb views
Wildlife interest
Dogs not allowed in the deer park

Distance 1½ miles (2.4km)
Time 1 hour 30 mins

Things to see

The Deer Park
The Deer Park at Dinefwr is home to a herd of over 100 fallow deer. In spring the males shed their large, shovel-like antlers and you might find a set on your walk.

White Park Cattle
The cows winter in the agricultural sheds and return to the landscape at Newton House in April. The calves start to arrive in spring and definitely win prizes for cuteness.

Wildlife and Birds
Dinefwr has an array of habitats where you can sit and spot your favourite creatures, from otters and frogs at the millpond to badgers and butterflies in the woodland. Keep an eye on the sky, too, because you might spot red kites, woodpeckers, ravens, owls and garden birds flying above.

Above: A glimpse of Newton House through trees at Dinefwr, Carmarthenshire.

Left: The west front of Newton House, the Victorian Gothic mansion in Dinefwr Park with White Park cattle grazing in the foreground.

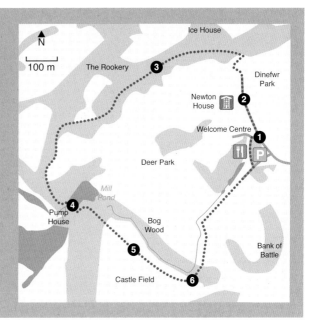

How to Get There

By Train Llandeilo (Heart of Wales line) 2 miles (3.2km)

By Car On western outskirts of Llandeilo A40(T); from Swansea take M4 to Pont Abraham, then A48(T) to Cross Hands and A476 to Llandeilo. Entrance on Carmarthen Road opposite fire and ambulance stations

OS Map Explorer 186

Start / End Welcome Centre car park at Dinefwr Park, **OS grid ref: SN 615224**

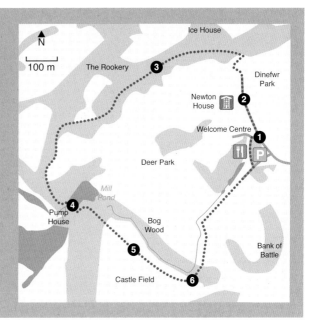

1. From the Welcome Centre, follow the driveway up past the front gates of Newton House. Go through the metal gate across the drive. To the right, back towards the town of Llandeilo, you'll see the outer park where the White Park cattle graze for much of the year. The clumps of trees and tree-lined avenues were laid out in about 1770 by George and Cecil Rice. The Deer Park is on your left.

2. Carry on up the drive and through the wooden gate, then turn left. Instead of following the sign to the ice-house, head straight on and go through the gate into the deer park. Follow the brown path through the woods, stopping at the breaks in the trees below you to admire the different views of the park.

3. Follow the path through the woods down to the Millpond. Look out for the herd of fallow deer that roam the park

4. Go out of the metal gate and turn across the bridge between the millpond and the Pump House below. The waterwheel in the pump house was used to send drinking water from a spring on the flood plain up to Newton House.

5. Follow the track around the millpond and out onto Castle Field. We're managing the field as a flower-rich hay meadow. The abundance of the flowering plant yellow-rattle in the grass from May onwards is a good indication of biodiversity.

6. Follow the track round to the left, through two gates, and back up to the car park.

Make the Most of Your Day
The walk suggested by 'Capability' Brown went along the ridge above the field at point 6, passing the Castle. You can take a detour here to go up to the castle and admire the views over the Tywi Valley. The 'hands-on' Newton House gives visitors an atmospheric, c.1912 experience and exhibitions on the first floor tell Dinefwr's story.

Food and Facilities
A café, tea-rooms and toilets can be found at Dinefwr.

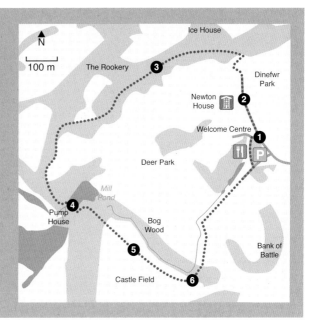

53. Cemlyn and Llanrhwydrus Circular Walk

Cemlyn
Anglesey
LL67 0DY
01248 714795
plasnewydd@nationaltrust.org.uk

About this walk
Superb costal views

Geological interest

Birdwatching

Dogs welcome
on leads

Distance 3 miles (4.8km)

Time 2 hours

Year round, waders and wildfowl can be seen around the lagoon at Cemlyn and the adjacent shorelines, while surrounding areas of gorse and grassland provide rich habitat for a range of butterflies and birds.

Things to see

Llanrhwydrus (St Rhwydrus) Church
This lovely little building is one of Anglesey's oldest spiritual sites and one of very few pre-Reformation churches on the island.

Henborth Drumlin
Drumlins are glacial deposits that expose the geological make-up of their surroundings going back hundreds of millions of years. They are rare things in Britain and this is a particularly fine example.

Birdlife
Look out across Cemlyn Lagoon: in spring more than 1,000 sandwich terns come to nest on the islands here, while in winter it provides a sheltered haven for many varieties of water fowl.

Above: Sunset at Cemlyn Bay with the lagoon to the left of the gravel bank and the sea to the right.

Below: Grey seals can often be seen in the sea around Cemlyn. They breed on rocky islands in autumn.

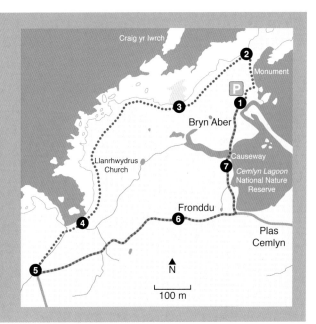

How to Get There

By Train Holyhead 12 miles (19.3km)

By Car A5025 from Valley, follow sign to Cemlyn National Nature Reserve in Tregele (opposite Douglas Inn). On approach to Cemlyn NNR, take second turning to the right then turn right again, after farm buildings, past Bryn Aber walled garden to the car park

OS Map Landranger 114

Start / End Bryn Aber car park, **OS grid ref: SH 329936**

Craig yr Iwrch · Monument · Bryn Aber · Llanrhwydrus Church · Causeway · Cemlyn Lagoon National Nature Reserve · Fronddu · Plas Cemlyn · N · 100 m

1. From the car park, walk out past the Monument towards the headland.

2. Turn left through the kissing gate and either follow the coastal path or walk along the beach. You might see grey seals hauled up on Craig yr Iwrch, the rocky island on your right.

3. Enjoy the wonderful sea views as you walk along the coast. If you have time, it's well worth making a short detour to Llanrhwydrus Church.

4. When you reach the little bay of Henborth be sure to look for the Henborth Drumlin. Turn left through the kissing gate.

5. Walk on through the kissing gate towards Hen Felin (Old Mill) and cross the bridge. Turn left onto the lane and walk back towards Cemlyn Bay and the National Nature Reserve sheltered by the shingle ridge.

6. After you pass Fronddu, turn left up the lane. This takes you past the Cemlyn Lagoon, established in the 1930s by Captain Vivian Hewitt of Bryn Aber.

7. Follow the lane over the causeway and back to the car park.

Make the Most of Your Day
Plas Newydd House is an enchanting mansion with fine gardens. The interior is famous for its association with the artist Rex Whistler. It contains his exquisite romantic mural and the largest exhibition of his works. There is also a military museum with relics from the 1st Marquess of Anglesey's tenure, who commanded the cavalry at the Battle of Waterloo. There is a whole range of events throughout the year.

Food and Facilities
A shop, tea-room and toilets are all available at Plas Newydd House.

Wales

54. Menai Strait Wildlife and Woodland Walk

Glan Faenol
Near Bangor
Gwynedd
LL57 4BP
01248 714795
plasnewydd@nationaltrust.org.uk

About this walk
Birdwatching

Superb views

Wildlife interest

Woodland paths can be muddy and are often wet

Dogs welcome but keep on leads when crossing fields

Distance 1½ miles (2.4km)

Time 1 hour–1 hour 30 mins

Wales

Explore the walled woodland that is Glan Faenol. Catch a glimpse of a seal in the Menai Strait, or see how many bird species you can identify from the hides and platforms. This short walk offers views of the house and gardens at Plas Newydd as well as the hills of Snowdonia.

Things to see

Bird Hides at Glan Faenol
The bird hides allow you to take a look over the imposing wall that surrounds the entire Faenol Estate. The wall itself is a listed monument and on its completion was the largest structure of its type in Wales. Look out for a wide variety of seabirds – oystercatchers, cormorants and curlews are just a few of the birds commonly seen in the shallows – or even a local seal swimming past.

View Across the Menai Strait
You'll be able to appreciate the splendour and grandeur of Lord Anglesey's residence Plas Newydd from Glan Faenol. And if, in turn, you visit Plas Newydd, take a walk in the manicured gardens and beautiful woodlands. From there you can look across to Glan Faenol, where you are now, and appreciate the stunning views of Snowdonia.

The Woodland of Glan Faenol
You are guaranteed a good show of colour if you walk around the Glan Faenol Estate during autumn; the rich mix of broad-leaved trees provides a spectacular display. You'll also see a wide variety of flowers beneath the woodland canopy during spring and be struck by the smell of wild garlic.

Above: Autumn at Plas Newydd, Anglesey.

Opposite: Wintery scene across the Menai Strait at Plas Newydd.

How to Get There

By Train Bangor Station 3⅓ miles (5.4km); Llanfairpwll 4⅔ miles (7.4km)

By Car Leave the A55 at junction 9. Take the Parc Menai turning at the roundabout. Go straight over the mini-roundabout and take the first left (Ffordd y Plas) and follow Glan Faenol signs to the picnic area

OS Map Landranger 114 and 115

Start / End Picnic area at Glan Faenol, **OS grid ref: SH 532698**

1. Head to the bottom of the picnic area and through the kissing gate, continue straight down the field (with dogs on leads) towards the Menai Strait.

2. As you approach the edge of the field you'll see the Faenol Wall (a listed monument and an example of the wealth of the estate in its heyday). Climb the steps to the bird hide to peak over the wall and see what wildlife you can glimpse. After enjoying the view, leave the hide and take the gate into the woodland.

3. As you follow the path through the trees, see if you can spot an interesting traditional structure hidden in the woodland on the other side of the Strait (the raised bench is a good place to do this).

4. You can now climb the viewing platform to peek over the wall at the Marquess of Anglesey's historic home, Plas Newydd. Now turn your back on the Strait and walk up the field 50 yards (45m) or so to a bridge and kissing gate on your right. Go through the gate and enter Boathouse Wood.

5. As you follow the path through the wood eventually you'll cross another bridge and then come to a track. You can cut the walk short here by turning left and following the track up until you reach some green gates. Go through the gates (which date back to when the estate had a menagerie of exotic animals and deer for hunting). Follow the tree-lined avenue to another gate; here you can turn left to return to the car park.

6. Cross over the track and plunge into another different woodland area. After climbing some steps go through a kissing gate into a field.

7. Keeping dogs on leads, walk up the field, following the fence on your left. You're now in an area of ancient parkland surrounded on all sides by woodland. Take a moment to enjoy the beauty and seclusion as you walk up the field.

8. At the top of the field enter Cefn Gwyn Woodland through another kissing gate. Follow the path past the mature oak, ash and sycamore trees until you reach another kissing gate.

9. Through this gate follow the fence across the top of the field to another kissing gate. Through this gate turn left and walk diagonally across the field to the gate under the trees.

10. You'll see a triangular gate that is designed to allow sheep access but prevent cattle from entering the path. Go through this gate and follow the path until you reach a large kissing gate.

11. Go through this last gate and turn left to take a well-deserved rest in the picnic area.

Make the Most of Your Day

Plas Newydd is an enchanting mansion and a great place to explore after your walk. Outside there is an impressive display of plants in the walled and terrace gardens, as well as a tree house and play area. Inside you can wander through the grand rooms and see how the 7th Marquess of Anglesey and his family would have lived.

Food and Facilities

A tea-room and toilets can be found at Plas Newydd House.

Above: The battlements at Plas Newydd Country House and Gardens, Anglesey, with the trees of Glan Faenol in the background.

55. Llyn Ogwen Circular Walk

Enjoy superb views of Tryfan and the Glyderau mountains with no hills to climb. Botanists have long been fascinated with this area. The cliffs and rocks support Arctic-alpine species, such as nationally rare saxifrages (tufted, purple and alpine) and the Snowdon lily. Also look out for birds such as merlins, buzzards and peregrine falcons, and mammals including brown hares, polecats and feral goats.

Ogwen Cottage
Nant Ffrancon
Bethesda
Gwynedd
LL57 3LZ
01248 600954
eryri@nationaltrust.org.uk

About this walk
Superb views

Historical interest

There are boulders to clamber over in the first section of the walk

Dogs welcome on leads

Distance 2⅞ mile (4.6km)

Time 1–2 hours

Things to see

Ogwen Cottage
Purchased by the National Trust in 2014, this is now an Outdoor Pursuits Centre that offers mountain experiences to young people.

Pont Pen y Benglog
Under the modern road bridge is the drovers bridge that was used to move livestock, known as Hen Pont Pen y Benglog.

Pill Box
This was built during the Second World War to defend the important A5 road in case of an invasion.

Above: View of Llyn Ogwen looking towards Tryfan, Carneddau and Glyderau, Gwynedd.

Right: Y Garn, the tenth highest peak in Wales seen from the edge of Llyn Ogwen.

By Car From Bangor: Travel on the A55 then turn towards Bethesda along the A5 trunk road. Continue on A5 into the Nant Ffrancon Valley. From Betws-y-Coed: Travel along the A5 to Capel Curig. Continue on A5 to Ogwen Lake

OS Map Landranger 115, Explorer OL17

Start / End Ogwen Cottage and Ranger Base, **OS grid ref: SH 650603**

1. From Ogwen Cottage, cross the main road and turn left, cross the bridge then turn right over the stile (gap in the wall).

2. Follow the river upstream to the lake by clambering over the large boulders, which can be quite challenging. It can be easy to lose the path here but keep heading for the lake and the path will become clearer with occasional waymarkers.

3. Follow the lake-shore and the waymarkers for ½ mile (800m) before climbing a slight hill away from the lake, cross the stile and continue.

4. As you approach the farmhouse at the end of the lake, cross another stile then bear left towards the footbridge and follow the upper path, which avoids the farmyard then crosses a stile before dropping down to join the farm track.

5. Follow this track away from the farmhouse until you reach the main road. Turn right and follow the pavement along the lake shore back to Ogwen Cottage.

Make the Most of Your Day

The National Trust maintains over 62 miles (100km) of footpaths in the Carneddau and Glyderau, so there are endless opportunities for hikers in north Snowdonia. The old store room at Ogwen Cottage has been converted into a ranger base and information point. Call in for the latest weather updates and wildlife sightings before setting off on your walk. From here there is also a footpath up to Cwm Idwal, a glaciated lake with a mountainous backdrop. The iconic Tryfan is where Edmund Hillary and his team trained for their ascent of Everest in 1953. Often voted the UK's favourite mountain, its rocky terrain makes for a challenging walk and various levels of scrambling. Increasingly popular among the very brave and hardy, the lakes and rivers in the area, set in magnificent surroundings, can't be rivalled by indoor heated pools. Like other mountainous activities, be prepared and don't swim alone.

Food and Facilities

There is a café at Ogwen Cottage that is open every weekend and school holiday between April and September. There are toilets in the car park.

Wales

56. Rhaeadr Ddu and Coed Ganllwyd Walk

Ganllwyd
Gwynedd
LL40 2HE
eryri@nationaltrust.org.uk
tymawrwybrnant@
nationaltrust.org.uk

About this walk
Spectacular falls

Woodland views

Grassy paths may be muddy;
some rocky slopes

Dogs welcome under close
control in woodland and on
short leads on farmland

Distance 2 miles (3.2km)

Time 1 hour 30 mins

This is a great waterside walk, taking you alongside the turbulent River Gamlan, past the magnificent Rhaeadr Ddu waterfalls and through glorious oak woodland. After rain the falls cascade powerfully into a dark pool – Rhaeadr Ddu means 'black falls' in English.

Things to see

River Gamlan
The rocky outcrops along the course of the River Gamlan make it very turbulent; it is particularly spectacular during rough weather.

Rhaeadr Ddu
These cascading falls on the River Gamlan are impressive in all weathers. There are two waterfalls which cascade over 60ft (18m). Take care on this section as the rocks can be slippery.

Above: Highland longhorn cow, Ganllwyd, Gwynedd.

Right: Rhaeadr Ddu waterfalls on the Gamlan River, Dolmelynllyn, Gwynedd.

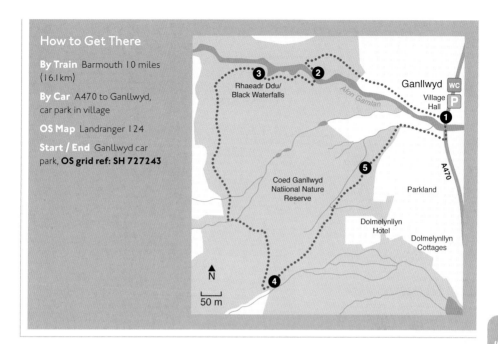

Wales

1. Cross the road from the car park towards the recently restored, corrugated iron village hall.

2. Follow the tarmac road alongside the river then follow the waymarks over the stone bridge, heading for a wooden bridge. Look out for a lichen–covered rock which has a Latin inscription carved on it.

3. Cross the wooden bridge and veer right towards the waterfalls. Rhaeadr Ddu, Black Falls in English, are two waterfalls which cascade over 60ft (18.3m). Take care on this section as the rocks can be slippery.

4. Continue along the path following the waymarkers. Go through the kissing gate and shortly afterwards take the path to the left, following the waymarkers down through the open oak woodland.

5. At the crossroads, go straight ahead through the wooden gate. Follow the path, through two more gates, to the main road. Turn left here to go back to the car park.

Make the Most of Your Day

South Snowdonia has a wealth of wild places to explore. The Dolmelynllyn Estate and Dinas Oleu are excellent places for birdwatching, and for the artistically inclined there are awe-inspiring views of the Mawddach estuary, Barmouth Bay and Dinas Oleu from the Cregennan lakes.

Food and Facilities

There are food outlets along the road to and from Ganllwyd, and in Dolgellau. There are toilets in the car park.

57. The Begwns Walk

The Begwns
Painscastle
Powys
LD2 3JN
01874 625515
brecon@nationaltrust.
org.uk

About this walk

Wildflower displays

Superb views

Wildlife interest

Dogs welcome but keep
under control around
livestock

Distance 2 miles (3.2km)

Time 1 hour

It is possible to see almost the entire Brecon Beacons National Park from the Roundabout at the start of this walk – giving you all of the views with none of the climb. The Begwyn ponds are a special site for freshwater wildlife and are home to some rare plants including pillwort, tubular water-dropwort, mudwort, floating club-rush, unbranched burreed, and the stonewort *Nitella opaca*.

Things to see

The Common
The Begwns is a 1,433 acre (580ha) common that was given to the National Trust in 1992 by the De Winton family. The common has five scheduled ancient monuments (SAMs) including a deserted medieval village on the western side.

The Roundabout
This was built by volunteers and staff to celebrate the millennium. A stone circular seat designed by a local architect was also built in 2000. The views are spectacular and you can see from Hay Bluff all the way to the Black Mountains in Carmarthenshire with the Brecon Beacons in the centre.

Monks Pond
Referred to locally as the Monks Pond, this pond is man-made and supports a variety of wildlife. Curlew have been seen here and during very cold spells the footprints of an otter have also been sighted.

Above: The highest point on the Begwns – the Roundabout.

Below: Otter emerging from the water.

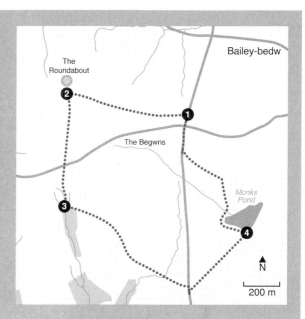

How to Get There

By Train Hereford
21 miles (34km)

By Car Take minor road
from Clyro to Painscastle
¾ mile (1.2km). Before
entering Painscastle take
left turn and a left turn
again up hill to the car park,
on the grass verge on the
right, at the top of the hill

OS Map Landranger 148,
Explorer OL13

Start / End Car park, **OS
grid ref: SO 162443**

The Roundabout

Bailey-bedw

The Begwns

Monks Pond

N

200 m

1. Starting from the grass verge car park, the Roundabout surrounded by a drystone wall with trees inside will be your first goal at the top of the hill. (This the highest point on the Begwns.)

2. Once you have reached the Roundabout, take time to rest and absorb the views if the weather permits. When you have done this, from the Roundabout retrace your steps for about 100 yards (90m) downhill until you see a track heading right towards the woodland on the far side of the common.

3. When you reach the wall by the woodland, follow the fence line downhill and left, until you meet the tarmac road. Cross the road and follow the grass track uphill until Monks Pond comes into view; walk down to the pond and turn left.

4. Follow the edge of the pond until you reach a bank at the top of the pond, turn right and follow this track across the wet ground onto a grass track. Turn left and follow the grass track that heads back to the tarmac road and turn right back towards the car park.

Make the Most of Your Day

When you have finished your walk, take some time to unwind in the pretty town of Hay-on-Wye (renowned for its annual literary festival). There is a regular street market on Thursdays where you can buy some excellent local produce. To the south is the Brecon Beacons National Park and all that it has to offer, including walking, outdoor activities, historic houses and a rich cultural and industrial history.

Food and Facilities

There is a good variety of shops, pubs and cafés in nearby Hay-on-Wye.

58. Cwm Llwch Horseshoe Walk

Pen y Fan is the highest mountain in southern Britain. With careful planning, clothing and equipment – particularly during the colder months – you can put yourself through your paces and enjoy this wonderful experience while looking out for local wildlife.

Cwm Gwdi
Brecon Beacons
Powys
LD3 8LE
01874 625515
brecon@nationaltrust.org.uk

About this walk
Highest peak in southern Britain

Archaeological interest

Paths are well made but come prepared by wearing sturdy walking boots and bringing warm clothing, waterproofs and supplies

Dogs welcome under close control

Distance 8 miles (12.9km)

Time 5 hours

Things to see

Corn Du
The second highest peak in the Brecon Beacons, Corn Du (2,864ft/873m) is often overshadowed by its more famous neighbour, Pen y Fan, nevertheless it has a special beauty of its own.

Pen y Fan
At 2,907ft (886m), Pen y Fan is deservedly popular with walkers. The views from the summit are truly spectacular. The old red sandstone cliffs of Pen y Fan and the surrounding mountains are reported to support the most southerly representation of calcareous rocky slopes with Arctic-alpine flora and fauna in the UK, including some nationally rare species.

Above: Walkers exploring the challenging route from Cwm Gwdi to Pen y Fan.

Below: Sunrise over Pen y Fan and Corn Du.

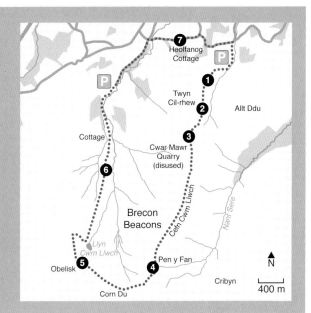

How to Get There

By Train Merthyr Tydfil 20 miles (32.2km), then bus to Brecon. Abergavenny 22 miles (35.4km), then bus to Brecon. From Brecon bus station approximately 4 miles (6.4km) to Cwm Gwdi car park

By Car 3 miles (4.8km) from Brecon via the Ffrwdgrech Road

OS Map Landranger 160, Explorer OL12

Start / End Cwm Gwdi car park, **OS grid ref: SO 025248**

1. From the pay and display car park, take the tarmac road up to the gate and stile, then along the side of a field. In this area, among the gorse you will find rifle and artillery abutments. Up to the late 1980s these were used for military firing practice.

2. Step over the stile and slightly to your right there is a grass track crossing several shallow grassed gullies, amongst the bracken heading up to a platform that once housed the quarry ponies. Keep right, close to the edge and follow the old pony and sledge track up past several small quarry sites. Take care, as there is loose stone underfoot.

3. Keep rising up and pass through a large quarry. Once you reach the top, turn right and follow the obvious path along the ridge known as Cefn Cwm Llwch, all the way up to the summit of Pen y Fan. As you tackle the last very steep section on your left you can look down on the river of Nant Sere and across to the peak of Cribyn.

4. Once you have taken a rest on the summit of Pen y Fan, with your back to the National Trust sign, take the path straight ahead, descending slightly before rising up to the summit of Corn Du, which stands at 2,864ft (873m). Keep walking straight ahead (with the steep edge on your right) past the burial chamber.

Follow the stone path down and keeping right where it divides, close to the edge of Craig Cwm Llwch. Follow this path downhill to the obelisk of Tommy Jones.

5. From the obelisk, follow the path down and to the right, to the lake known as Llyn Cwm Llwch. Turn left and continue to follow the path down, crossing the stile and leaving National Trust land. Keep heading downhill, past Cwm Llwch Cottage and then a car park until you reach the tarmac road.

6. Continue along the tarmac road until you reach a crossroads. Turn right and follow the road for ½ mile (800m) until you reach a right turn opposite Heolfanog Cottage. Take the right turn and continue on the tarmac road for another ½ mile (800m) until you reach a sharp left. The entrance to Cwm Gwdi car park is on your right

Make the Most of Your Day
Explore the lake of Cwm Llwch or wander through the beautiful Upper Tarell Valley which lies to the west of Cwm Gwdi. Discover Henrhyd Falls near Coelbren that plunges 90ft (27.4m) into the heavily wooded gorge of the Nant Llech.

Food and Facilities
There are pubs, cafés and restaurants in Brecon.

Wales

59. Sugar Loaf Circuit

Llanwenarth car park
Abergavenny
Monmouthshire
NP7 7LA
01874 625515
brecon@nationaltrust.
org.uk

About this walk
Ancient woodland

Superb views

Historic interest

Some steep climbs and
rocky sections and a small
stream to cross

Dogs welcome on leads

Distance 4 miles (6.4km)

Time 3–4 hours

The woodlands of St Mary's Vale provide a canopy from the rest of the world. This circular walk takes you out onto open moorland and up the iconic Sugar Loaf Mountain with its wonderful views. The mountain is a haven for upland birdlife. Singing skylarks soar in the sky, housemartins and swallows flit to and fro and red grouse skulk in the heather, while buzzards and the occasional red kite fly overhead.

Above: Grazing sheep near the Sugar Loaf in the Brecon Beacons.

Things to see

Ancient Oaks
As well as beech, St Mary's Vale is dominated by oak. Smaller trees can be between 80 and 100 years old, but you'll also see these wonderful large, older trees scattered throughout the woodland. In the past, these woods were a hive of activity with charcoal making. Keep your eye out for the charcoal platforms cut into the hillside as you walk through the vale.

Heather Moorland
From the Sugar Loaf summit you'll be able to look down across the mountain and at certain times of the year you can see a large expanse of purple heather. Circular patches and rough strips are regularly cut to break up the uniformity of the heather, slow wildfires and create a wider range of habitats for wildlife.

Medieval Boundaries
As you descend the Sugar Loaf, the path crosses an ancient ditch and bank structure. It might not look like much, but it stretches

for 2 miles (3.2km) right from the mountain's summit down to the common boundary and is thought to be early medieval or older.

Above: The woodland at St Mary's Vale in the Brecon Beacons.

How to Get There

By Train Abergavenny is approximately 2 miles (3.2km)

By Car Take the narrow turning for the Sugar Loaf Vineyards off the A40, turn left in front of the house then turn left again at the T-junction and go past the vineyard and up the steep hill. Around a sharp bend keep to the right and follow the road until you reach the top car park

OS Map Explorer OL13

Start / End Llanwenarth car park, **OS grid ref: SO 269167**

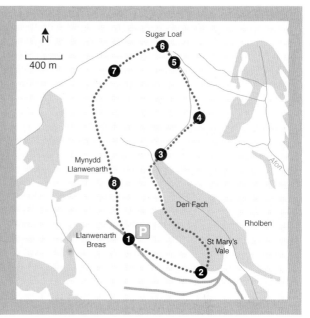

1. From the car park walk a short distance down the road you arrived on and head up onto the grass on the left-hand side. Continue along this straight and wide grass path as it gently climbs above the road. Follow the path as it descends and curves to the right, passing some old quarries, until you reach another large track. Turn left onto this track and walk along the woodland edge before turning left into the woodland.

2. Follow the footpath through the oak woodland, staying on the main path and avoiding the network of other tracks that run downhill. When you reach the woodland edge, turn right and continue down the path towards the stream.

3. Follow the path straight up the stream valley heading north-east. It's a steep climb up onto the ridge, but once you're onto the ridge, the summit of the Sugar Loaf will come into view. Look behind you for views of Abergavenny and the Usk Valley.

4. Continue up the final steep and occasionally rocky, ascent to the summit of the Sugar Loaf.

5. Once you reach the summit, head for the trig point and take in the fantastic views all around you.

6. Standing at the trig point looking at the National Trust sign, take the path to the left which descends with the summit on your right. The path then joins a wide grassy track running alongside a clearly visible ditch and bank – an ancient boundary stretching for nearly 2 miles (3.2km).

7. Follow the path that runs alongside the bank and continues along the top of the ridge. Eventually you'll see a fence running to the right of you. Walk along the track roughly parallel to this fence, until the fence turns a corner down the hill.

8. At this point, follow the direction of the path before dropping down into the car park where you started this walk.

Make the Most of Your Day
There are many places to visit nearby: Skirrid, a peak on the edge of the Black Mountains, a site steeped in myth and legend; the Clytha Estate, an eighteenth-century, landscaped park with a beautiful house and outstanding folly; and Parc Lodge Farm, at the head of the Cibi Valley, that was once a medieval deer park.

Food and Facilities
The nearest amenities can be found in Abergavenny.

60. Clytha and Coed-y-Bwnydd Walk

Ramble through an eighteenth-century estate, taking in the wildlife-rich River Usk and Coed-y-Bwnydd – the largest and one of the best-preserved hill forts in Monmouthshire – which is surrounded by a carpet of wildflowers in summer. There are beautiful views of Sugar Loaf, the wider Usk Valley and Clytha Castle.

Clytha riverside car park
Monmouthshire
NP7 9BW
01874 625515
brecon@nationaltrust.org.uk

About this walk
Wildflower displays

Stunning views

Wildlife interest

A few steep slopes and several stiles to cross

Some areas will be muddy in wet weather

Dogs welcome under close control

Distance 7½ miles (12km)

Time 4 hours

Things to see

The River Usk
The Usk flows past the western edge of Clytha Estate. It is incredibly important for nature conservation in the area and is a particularly tranquil place. Designated a Site of Special Scientific Interest and a Special Area of Conservation, it is also well known for its salmon and trout. Wildlife watching can be very rewarding, with otters, dippers, sand martins, kingfishers and bats all living in or near this stretch of the river.

Coed-y-Bwnydd Hill Fort
This scheduled ancient monument (SAM) has a history of human involvement stretching back more than 2,000 years. Today it is the perfect place to drink in the views.

Wildflowers
This is an area extremely rich in flora. In summer a carpet of red campion and orchids adds a dazzling array of colour. If you come earlier in the year during spring, you will see a stunning display of bluebells.

Above: Red campion.

Above: A view of the Usk valley.

How to Get There

By Train Abergavenny 5 miles (8km)

By Car From the east head west along the A40 to Raglan. At Raglan take the fourth exit off the roundabout signposted for Clytha and follow the National Trust signs. From the west, take the B4598 from Abergavenny. After approximately 5 miles (8km) turn right for Bettws Newydd and follow the National Trust signs

OS Map Explorer OL13

Start / End Clytha riverside car park, **OS grid ref: SO 361085**

1. Please note sections of this walk crosses land not owned by the National Trust. From the car park take the gate next to the interpretation panel and continue on until you reach a gate down on your left. Follow the Usk Valley Walk waymarkers, which run adjacent to the river for approximately 1¾ miles (2.8km), until you meet the road.

2. Turn left up the road and continue for about ½ mile (800m). As the road flattens out at the top of the hill, just before you start descending into Bettws Newydd, look out for a gate on your right next to a telegraph pole, partly covered by a hedge. Follow the path through the gate and across the field. Continue into the golf club car park and exit onto the minor road. Turn right and continue for 55 yards (50m), then turn left into a lane leading up to the church.

3. Enter the church gates and go over the stile at the other end of the churchyard. Turn right then immediately left and continue until you reach a stile on your left. Continue uphill, cross the stiles and head down the road on the other side of the hill. Follow the narrow lane uphill between two buildings until you reach Coed-y-Bwnydd Hill Fort on your left. Follow the circular path round the hill fort and return by the field gate close to the original fort entrance.

4. Go through the gate and follow the permissive path past the barn at the other end of the field. Go over the stile and turn left onto the lane. Continue walking and keep left where the lane forks until you reach a kissing gate on your left. Cross the stile and follow the path down the grassy hill, through the gap in the line of trees and continue over two stiles until you reach the woods behind Clytha Castle. Follow the wooden signposts to Clytha.

5. Once you've enjoyed the view, follow the path that runs behind the castle through the woods to the wooden gate, continuing along a grassy track above the trees to the driveway. Cross the drive keeping the fenced wood on your right and follow the line of trees diagonally uphill to a gate in the top corner of the grounds. Follow the waymarked route through three gates, leading to steep steps and the busy B4598.

6. Carefully cross this road to the road turning for Clytha Arms on the opposite side. Pass through the metal gate immediately in front of you and continue over the stile. Follow the waymarked route crossing a horse paddock and several fields until you reach a wood near Chapel Farm.

7. Pass through the kissing gates into the wood and follow the path through the trees running parallel with the A40. Just after the path opens out and passes close to the A40, it joins Clawdd Brook, and follows it until reaching a gate at the woodland edge.

8. Continue along the waymarked route round the back of Rose Cottage and through an old milk churn dock, to a gate leading to the edge of the main road. Cross the road and pass through the metal wicket gate. Turn right and follow the metal railings along the edge of the field. Pass through a wooden gate leading back onto the Usk Valley Walk and follow the path around the sharp left bend back to the car park.

Make the Most of Your Day

Clytha House and Clytha Castle can both be seen along this walk. The former is Grade I-listed and was rebuilt in the classic Greek style in the 1830s by Edward Haycock. The latter is considered one of the outstanding eighteenth-century follies of Wales.

Food and Facilities

Local pubs, Clytha Arms and the Black Bear at Bettws Newydd, are located along the route.

Below: A view of Sugar Loaf from the east.

Opposite: View over Derwent Water (walk 64).

North West

61. Undiscovered Formby

National Trust Formby
Victoria Road
Freshfield
Formby
Liverpool
L37 1LJ
01704 878591
formby@nationaltrust.
org.uk

About this walk
Rare plants and animals

Superb views

Geological interest

Dogs welcome but please
keep under close control

Distance 3 miles (4.8km)

Time 1 hour 45 mins

This is a varied walk through a number of different habitats. The dunes support many protected species, including the natterjack toad and the sand lizard. Along the shore there is a huge variety of birdlife to see, and the pine woodlands are home to even more birds and everyone's favourite, the red squirrel.

Things to see

Pine Woodland
The pine woodlands were planted from the late 1800s by the Weld Blundell family, whose estate covered this area. Before the trees were planted there would have been fixed sand dunes covered in grassland, and if you look closely you can still make out the shape of the dunes underneath the trees. These trees are home to the native red squirrel.

Stunning Sand Dunes
The sand dunes at Formby are recognised internationally as being an important habitat for a number of rare animal and plant species. These include the vernal mining bee, northern dune tiger beetle, dune helleborine and hound's tongue. Nature puts on her best display here in spring and summer when the dunes are awash with the colour of many wildflowers and the air is alive with the buzzing of insects. You might even be lucky enough to hear the call of the rare natterjack toad that breeds in the dune pools nearby.

Prehistoric Footprints
Whilst on the beach you may be lucky enough to see a piece of prehistoric life frozen in time. On a number of days throughout the year, silt beds are exposed beneath the sand, approximately 110-160 yards (100-145m) from the base of the dunes, which hold human and animal footprints that date from the late Mesolithic to the Neolithic, 7,500-4,500 years ago. Alongside the human trails, there are the footprints of animal and bird species, including red deer, crane and aurochs, the ancestor of the modern domestic cow.

Above: Sunset over the sand dunes at Formby, Liverpool.

Opposite: Pine woodland at Formby.

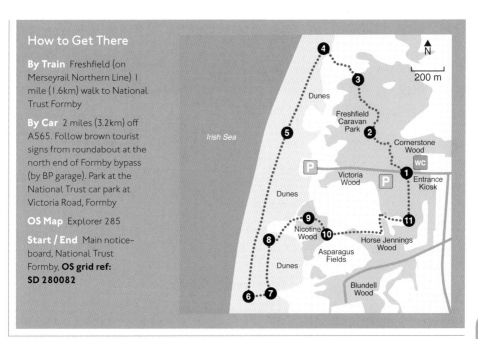

How to Get There

By Train Freshfield (on Merseyrail Northern Line) 1 mile (1.6km) walk to National Trust Formby

By Car 2 miles (3.2km) off A565. Follow brown tourist signs from roundabout at the north end of Formby bypass (by BP garage). Park at the National Trust car park at Victoria Road, Formby

OS Map Explorer 285

Start / End Main notice-board, National Trust Formby, **OS grid ref: SD 280082**

1. Cross the road and take the path (marked Cornerstone path) to the left of the toilets, heading down a ramp into the woodland. Continue to follow this clear, broad path with its white and purple marker posts through the woodland until you meet another path at a T-junction with a set of large wooden chimes on your left-hand side.

2. Turn right at this junction and follow the wide stone path. Continue along this path following waymarkers for the Sefton Coastal Path (yellow arrows on a white and grey background).

3. Following the Sefton Coastal Path you'll eventually leave the woodland and head out into the open dunes. Continue along this path as it passes through a small cut in the dunes and an old natterjack toad pool on the right. At this point the path bends to the left. When you get to a path junction by a bench, leave the Sefton Coastal Path and take the path straight ahead, over the dunes and onto the beach.

4. Turn left and, keeping the dunes on your left, continue along the beach. You will notice as you walk that there are marker posts along the beach denoting the main paths over the dunes.

5. Continue along the beach.

6. After you have walked approximately ¾ mile (1.2km) along the beach you will reach the Blundell Path marker. Turn left and leave the beach via the path over the dunes.

7. As you come over the dune you will see a clear path going off to the left through a thickly vegetated area. Take this path and follow it as it passes along the landward base of the sand dunes.

8. Continue along the path as it makes a sharp right bend before going up a slope. When the path descends take the clear path on the right heading into a woodland of gnarled black poplar trees.

9. At a path fork, take the right path that leads out onto a T-junction with a wide stone path. Turn right at this junction. After a short distance the path curves round to the right, and at this point take the sandy path to the left, which leads between two fenced fields.

10. Continue on and follow the fence on your left until the end of the field. At this point turn left along a grass/sand path until it meets a stone path at a T-junction. Turn right at the junction and pass through a small area of woodland before coming out onto a grassy field. Continue straight ahead.

11. At the end of the field take the stone path on the left that ascends a short steep slope into the pine woodland. Continue along this path until you reach a fenced path at a crossroads with a bench on your right. Go straight ahead at this junction and follow the fenced path as it makes a left-hand bend. Shortly after the bend there is a path going off to the right. Take this path to return to the walk start.

Make the Most of Your Day

As well as the many walks and the chance to seek out footprints from prehistory, you can hunt along the sands for treasure; in summer come to see the butterflies – 20 of the 66 species that occur in the UK can be found along this part of the coast.

Food and Facilities

Refreshments are available from a coffee cart in the picnic site adjacent to the woodland car park (weekends only out of high season); there are also ice-cream vans during peak periods. Toilets available during car park opening hours.

62. Wildlife Ramble at Arnside Knott

Arnside Knott
Near Arnside
Cumbria
01524 702815
arnsidesilverdale@
nationaltrust.org.uk
www.nationaltrust.org.uk/
arnside-and-silverdale

This diverse wildlife walk takes in beautiful landscapes and offers an escape from the hustle and bustle of modern life. The route takes you across Arnside Knott, a shapely 500ft (152m) limestone hill that affords stunning views of the surrounding area. The key to the Knott's diversity is its limestone landscape, which comprises a mosaic of habitats including woodland and flower-studded grassland.

About this walk
Good for spotting butterflies and birds

Breathtaking views

Steep in places, with height gain of 230ft (70m)

Dogs welcome under close control

Distance 2 miles (3.2km)

Time 1 hour

North West

Above: View from Arnside Knott over Morecambe Bay in Cumbria.

Below: A great spotted woodpecker.

Things to see

Wildflowers
Grazing livestock help keep the limestone grasslands in optimum condition for wildflowers. As such, the grassland is great for orchids such as early purple varieties, which flower from late April to May, and also bird's nest and fragrant orchids. Look out for the scarce blue moor-grass with its bright grass-heads in March and April.

Insects
Nationally important butterflies such as the Scotch argus can be seen at the beginning of August in great numbers at the top of Arnside Knott. Rare butterflies like the high brown fritillary are also to be found in the summertime. Look for the caterpillars of the painted lady on nettles and purple hairstreaks on oaks. Also keep an eye out for southern wood ants, which can be seen foraging for food and even climbing trees. The warm summer evenings are great for watching glow-worms on grass stems.

Birds
Nuthatch, bullfinch, marsh tit, great spotted woodpecker and many other woodland birds can be seen in and around Red Hill Wood; the spring birdsong is superb. Also listen out for the call of marsh tits (a loud 'pitchoo' sound), and the mewing sound of common buzzards that can be heard when the birds are displaying.

How to Get There

By Train Arnside 1 mile
(1.6km)

By Car Exit M6 at junction
36 on A65 towards Kendal;
take B6385 to Milnthorpe
then B5782 to Arnside

OS Map Landranger 97,
Explorer OL7

Start / End National Trust
car park at Arnside Knott,
OS grid ref: SD 450774

1. Turn left out of the National Trust car park and after a short walk along the entrance track, climb up the bank on your right to a mountain indicator. There are great views over the estuary towards the Lake District here.

2. Keep zig-zagging up the hillside to a stone toposcope and a breathtaking panorama. The slopes here are made of frost-shattered limestone, with areas of distinctive blue moor-grass, yew and juniper.

3. Bear left on the path and climb through woodland up to open grassland (a good spot for picnics) along the crest of the ridge.

4. When you reach the highest point on the walk, at a bench, continue a short way then head right, downhill, with a wall on your left.

5. The route angles right before reaching a gate to enter Red Hills Wood. Soon after, turn left at a crossroads and tour the woodland, always following paths round to the right. This area is home to a fantastic range of flora, such as dog's mercury, dog's violet and primrose. The trees are a mix of yew, holly, rowan, hazel and sessile oak. Dead and decaying wood makes an excellent habitat for fungi, hoverflies and beetles.

6. Silverdale Road appears down to your right as you emerge onto open hillside. Pass the Shilla Slopes. Only some plants such as marjoram and thyme can anchor in this rubble; both types attract butterflies.

7. Take the broad uphill track back towards the car park, going through several gates and avoiding the left-hand turns leading to Heathwaite and Copridding Wood.

Make the Most of Your Day
If you fancy visiting a country house estate after your walk, try Sizergh, 8 miles (12.8km) north en route to Kendal. See walk 63 for details.

Food and Facilities
There are a number of pubs and cafés in and around Arnside village. Otherwise, you'll find plenty of choice at Sizergh. Public toilets can be found in Arnside.

63. Sizergh Wildlife Walk

Sizergh Castle is a great starting point for a walk in the Lake District. The castle, still lived in by the Strickland family, is surrounded by a traditional agricultural estate with stunning views across the countryside, taking in the coast at Morecambe Bay, the Lakeland Fells and the Pennines. Discover an amazing array of natural history throughout the year in this quiet corner of the South Lakes.

Sizergh
Near Kendal
Cumbria LA8 8AE
sizergh@nationaltrust.org.uk
www.nationaltrust.org.uk/sizergh

About this walk
Amazing views

Good for bird watching all year round

A short, steepish climb near to the start of the walk

Distance 2½ miles (4km)

Time 1 hour 30 minutes

North West

Things to see

Special Visitors
Look out for a very special visitor lurking in the trees in the car park. Hawfinches are very shy birds, best seen in winter when the trees have shed their leaves; look for them on the highest branches. Sizergh is a nationally important breeding site for these birds.

Wildflowers and Ant Hills
Purple swathes of field scabious and harebell, and a yellow haze of buttercups, bedstraws and cowslips fill the characteristic ant-hill fields on Sizergh Fell in early summer.

Above: View across the lake to the south-east front of Sizergh Castle in Cumbria.

Fritillary Butterflies
Fritillary butterfly species fly effortlessly through the woodland glades in summer, basking and feeding in warm open areas. Sunlight encourages the growth of food plants such as violets and cowslip on the woodland floor – these are both valuable plants for egg laying and caterpillar feeding. The trees are cut down in lines called glades, connecting valuable open feeding areas. Sheltered areas provide a rich nectaring source for adult fritillaries as they feed on brambles.

Below: A male hawfinch.

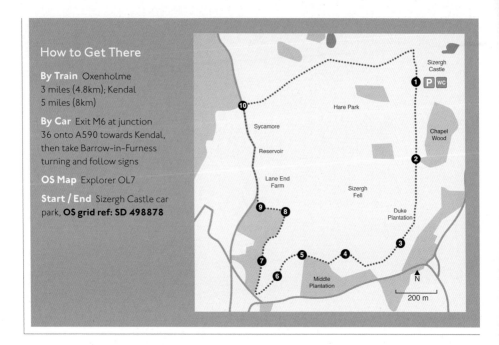

By Train Oxenholme
3 miles (4.8km); Kendal
5 miles (8km)

By Car Exit M6 at junction
36 onto A590 towards Kendal,
then take Barrow-in-Furness
turning and follow signs

OS Map Explorer OL7

Start / End Sizergh Castle car
park, **OS grid ref: SD 498878**

1. From Sizergh Castle car park, leave by the footpath gate and walk into a field at the south end, near to the coach parking bays. This field can be very wet and muddy. Walk straight on, with the wall on your left. During spring and summer, buzzards and pheasants are a common sight along this stretch of footpath, as they nest in the woodland to your left.

2. Go through the next gate into another field (which can also be very muddy) and then immediately through another gate to your left, onto Sizergh Fell. Notice the difference between the two fields either side of the fence boundary, where one has been improved.

3. Wander uphill with the fence on your right and go through a field. The many bumps to be seen in this field are actually ant hills. During the summer, the field is filled with magnificent wildflowers, bees and butterflies. You might even be able to spot a green woodpecker feeding on the ants.

4. As you continue uphill towards the clump of trees at the top, you pass some hawthorn trees. These are excellent for attracting nesting birds in spring and then fieldfare and redwings in winter, when they are plentiful with berries. Once you reach the top, stop

to admire the amazing views out to Morecambe Bay ahead of you and the Howgills and Pennines behind.

5. From the top, walk past the clump of trees on the right-hand side. Follow the footpath with the telephone lines on your left and the stunning Lake District Fells ahead of you. Continue across the top and then downhill until you reach a gate in the wall.

6. Go through the gate and head diagonally on the path towards the left, through the field of ant hills towards the woodland in the distance. Go through the gate into the woodland glade and turn immediately right. This takes you through an area that has recently been cleared to diversify the woodland edge and enhance the butterfly populations. Look out for fritillary species here in the summer.

7. Continue with the wall on your right-hand side. Many woodland bird species can be spotted here including great spotted woodpecker, nuthatch and treecreeper.

8. Once you get to the end of the wall, turn left and walk downhill, following the wall on your right towards the road, until you reach the gate on the right-hand side. Go through the gate into the field and then continue walking downhill to the next gate, which takes you onto the tarmacked road.

9. Turn right here, and walk along the road on the right-hand side, facing the oncoming traffic, for about a third of a mile (0.5km). Pass Lane End Farm on your left – a National Trust tenanted farm. Continue along the road until you reach the big wooden gate on the right and go through onto Ashbank Lane.

10. Walk along the lane with the hedgerow full of life on your left. Walk through three more gates along the track, with the old deer park wall on your right, heading all the way back to Sizergh Castle and well-earned refreshments at the café.

Make the Most of Your Day

Make time to visit Sizergh, a beautiful medieval house owned by the Strickland family. It has many tales to tell and certainly feels lived in, with centuries-old portraits and fine furniture sitting alongside modern family photographs. Its rich and beautiful garden includes a pond, lake, a national collection of hardy ferns and a superb limestone rock garden.

Food and Facilities

The recently refurbished café has been designed to give a taste of Sizergh's history and treasures. There is also a pub and farm tea-room. Toilets are available for visitors.

Above: The rock garden at Sizergh Castle in June.

64. Stargazing Walk at Friar's Crag

Near Keswick
Cumbria
CA12 5DL
01768774649
borrowdale@nationaltrust.org.uk

About this walk
Low levels of light pollution make this a perfect place for star-gazing

Choose a clear night and remember to bring binoculars and a torch

Take care around the unprotected edge at the end of the walk

Distance ¾ mile (1.2km)

Time 15 mins

On a clear night it's possible to see some 4,000 stars sparkling in our Solar System. Perfect for families and anyone unfamiliar with astronomy, this easy walk will introduce you to stargazing at Friar's Crag, which offers one of the most scenic views in the Lake District.

Things to see

Ruskin and Rawnsley

During your evening walk use your torch to see if you can find the Canon Rawnsley or Ruskin memorials. Ruskin (1819–1900) had many associations with Keswick and his memorial was erected by Rawnsley, who was one of the founders of the National Trust. The land around here was the first area of the Lake District to be placed in the care of the National Trust.

Summer Triangle

Look up to see the Summer Triangle. It is made up of three bright stars positioned in a triangle shape, directly overhead. The stars are called Deneb, Vega and Altair, and also form part of other constellations. Listen out for the distinctive 'too-whit-twhoo' of the tawny owl, which is actually a duet between a male and female. These are the largest common owls in the UK and they feed on small mammals, frogs, insects and birds, sometimes including other owls.

Milky Way and North Star

The Milky Way is a ribbon of millions of stars, threading its way across the night sky. The North Star, also known as the Pole Star or Polaris, is a very bright star and is always fixed above the north point of the horizon. It has been used for over 2,000 years to help navigators at sea and on land find their way.

Above: Visitors enjoying the view from Friar's Crag, Cumbria.

Opposite: View over Derwent Water.

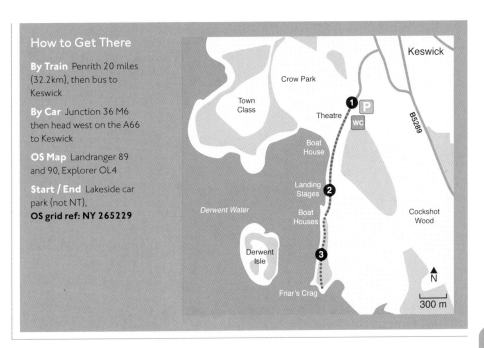

How to Get There

By Train Penrith 20 miles (32.2km), then bus to Keswick

By Car Junction 36 M6 then head west on the A66 to Keswick

OS Map Landranger 89 and 90, Explorer OL4

Start / End Lakeside car park (not NT), **OS grid ref: NY 265229**

Keswick

Crow Park

Town Class

Theatre

WC

P

B5289

Boat House

Landing Stages

Derwent Water

Boat Houses

Cockshot Wood

Derwent Isle

Friar's Crag

N

300 m

1. From Lakeside car park walk down towards the Theatre by the Lake, which will be on your left as you pass it.

2. Continue along the road with the launch jetties and lake on your right until the tarmac road runs out.

3. Then continue straight on, along an unsurfaced track to the end of Friar's Crag. This is your star-gazing spot. Lay a blanket on the ground and take in the views of the wide open sky. Return the way you came.

Make the Most of Your Day

During the day you can hire a canoe and explore the islands of Derwent Water that provided the setting for the 2016 film *Swallows and Amazons*. Bring an evening picnic and experience an atmospheric sunset before your night of star-gazing.

Food and Facilities

There is a café at Theatre by the Lake that is open until 9pm. Toilets and restaurants are also available in Keswick.

65. Ambleside to Troutbeck and Back via Wansfell

This walk from Ambleside to Troutbeck takes you along tracks and lanes through woods and fields, with panoramic views over Windermere at Jenkin Crag. A wonderful walk throughout the year, a visit to Skelghyll Woods is a real treat in spring when carpets of wildflowers, such as bluebells, wood sorrel and daffodils, come into bloom.

Ambleside
Cumbria
LA22 9BT
01539432628
townend@nationaltrust.org.uk

About this walk
Superb views
Wildflower displays
Social history
Some of the walk is on uneven ground and can be muddy
Dogs welcome; keep under close control near livestock

Distance 5¾ miles (9.3km)

Time 4–5 hours

North West

Things to see

Troutbeck Post Office
The Post Office is a Victorian building and was originally built as the Village Institute. It once was home to a Reading, Assembly and Billiards Room. The post office and village shop are still very much the centre of Troutbeck, and provide invaluable services to the local community.

Wansfell Pike
From the top of Wansfell you have great views over Windermere, Ambleside and the Kirkstone Pass.

Above left: Bluebells and wild garlic growing in Skelghyll Woods near Ambleside, Cumbria.

Above: A view of the south front of Townend, a yeoman farmer's house, built c.1626.

Opposite: The winding path from Ambleside to Troutbeck.

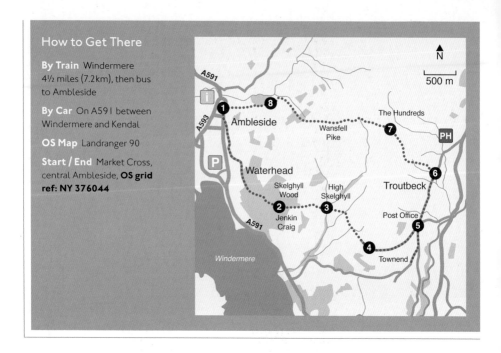

How to Get There

By Train Windermere 4½ miles (7.2km), then bus to Ambleside

By Car On A591 between Windermere and Kendal

OS Map Landranger 90

Start / End Market Cross, central Ambleside, **OS grid ref: NY 376044**

---

1. From the Market Cross in Ambleside, follow the A591 towards Windermere, out of the town along Lake Road and take the Old Lake Road on the left. After a big car park there is a small road to the left, signposted to 'Jenkin Crag, Skelghyll and Troutbeck (bridleway)'.

2. Follow the signposts on this path through Skelghyll Wood, past Jenkin Crag, where you can pause to admire the view. Follow the path through the woods to High Skelghyll Farm.

3. Go across the farmyard at High Skelghyll, following the signposted footpath. At the crossing of paths at High Skelghyll, follow the public bridleway to Troutbeck. This path turns left just across the bridge, through a gate, then goes uphill. At the end of this path, cross the kissing gate into Robin Lane.

4. Follow the gravelled track that is Robin Lane, past the pillar, to Troutbeck Post Office.

5. From the post office you can visit Townend. Turn right and follow the road. Townend is on the right, at the road junction.

6. For the return leg of the walk, return to the Post Office, and continue on the road into Troutbeck

village. Between two houses, near the Mortal Man Inn, is a footpath on the left leading up Nanny Lane to Wansfell. The names of the roads and the pubs have a story to tell in themselves.

7. The gravelled track climbs steadily. Take the footpath to the left and go uphill to reach the summit of Wansfell Pike, with superb views over Ambleside and the surrounding fells. From here take the steep path down to Ambleside until you meet the road.

8. Turn left on the road. Take the road marked 'Styrigg' on the left, and follow the footpath back to the centre of Ambleside.

Make the Most of Your Day

Just before you reach Styrigg road, there is an entrance on the right to Stock Ghyll Force. This magnificent waterfall is worth a visit. Townend in the Troutbeck Valley is a traditional Lake District stone and slate farmhouse. Here you can learn about the members of the Browne family who lived here for more than 400 years. Their house tells the stories of their social climbing, love of traditions and education.

Food and Facilities

There are shops, cafés, restaurants and toilets in Ambleside.

66. Southern Woods Walk at Quarry Bank

The Southern Woods provide a great opportunity to explore the wider estate at Quarry Bank and to watch the river twist and turn, making its way to the mill. Water birds congregate around the Millpond and the wet woodland habitat allows a host of less common species to thrive here.

Visitor Reception
Quarry Bank
Styal
Wilmslow
Cheshire
SK9 4LA
01625 527468
quarrybank@nationaltrust.org.uk

About this walk
Wildflower displays

Wildlife interest

Industrial heritage site

Dogs welcome

Distance 1 ½ miles (2.5km)

Time 50 mins

North West

Things to see

The Millpond
Moorhen, little grebe and mallard hide amongst the red-stemmed dogwood and alder at the Millpond. The pond was created in 1801 when the weir was built to raise the water level to the top of a new waterwheel.

Wet Woodland
Known as Willow Carr, the wet, decaying wood on the river flood plain at Quarry Bank provides ideal conditions for many rare plants, insects and invertebrates, including ancient species of snails. Unusual birds such as the willow tit, lesser redpoll and siskin can also be found here.

Above: View of the mill at Quarry Bank, Cheshire.

Above: Snowdrops in the garden with the mill owner's house in the background at Quarry Bank.

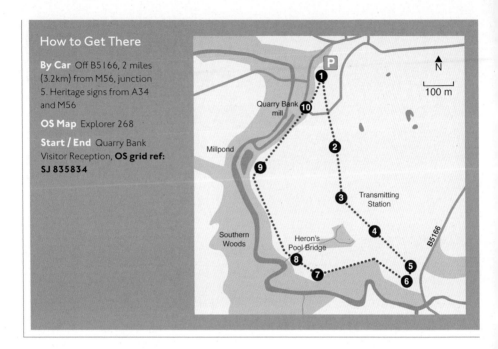

How to Get There

By Car Off B5166, 2 miles (3.2km) from M56, junction 5. Heritage signs from A34 and M56

OS Map Explorer 268

Start / End Quarry Bank Visitor Reception, **OS grid ref: SJ 835834**

1. From the Visitor Reception walk through the car park and past the small square reservoir pond on your right, towards a set of gates.

2. Pass through the gates and walk across the field where you will reach another gate, go through the gate and head along the path.

3. Across the field on your left you will see a large house. This used to be the transmitter and control station for Manchester Airport during the Second World War.

4. At this point pass through the small iron gate; drop down the hill and follow the footpath straight across the meadow. If you are walking in the evening keep an eye out for bats.

5. At the gate, turn right along the concrete cycle track. Walk for approximately 44 yards (40m) and you will see another gate on your right. If you go over the river you have gone too far.

6. Pass through the kissing gate and the River Bollin will be on your left. This area is called Willow Carr.

7. As you walk along the low-lying path you will reach a large granite boulder. This is called an erratic

stone that was deposited here during the last Ice Age from the Lake District. To your right there is a steep woodland bank; during late April and throughout May this is a carpet of bluebells. Keep following the path straight ahead.

8. As you follow the path it will rise up steeply and you will pass over Heron's Pool Bridge, where you can see herons feeding and also bats later in the evening.

9. You will reach the millpond on your left, which is a great place for pond dipping. Keep on heading straight and past the playground on your left until you reach the mill.

10. Head up the mill drive and back to the visitor reception to complete your walk.

Make the Most of Your Day

Quarry Bank overflows with the atmosphere of the Industrial Revolution. Explore the progression of the cotton industry from the pre-industrial era through to the nineteenth century; speak to the knowledgeable demonstrators to find out more.

Food and Facilities

There are toilets and a café in the mill yard.

67. The Stubbins Estate Walk

Stubbins Estate
Near Ramsbottom
Lancashire
BL0 9DS
gawthorpehall@
nationaltrust.org.uk

About this walk
Mature woodland

Superb views

Industrial history

Footpaths with climbs and descents

Dogs welcome; please keep on leads when crossing open farmland

Distance 2 miles (3.2km)

Time 1 hour

Less than 30 minutes' drive from Gawthorpe Hall in Lancashire lies the Stubbins Estate and Holcombe Moor. The wooded hillside is a spectacular sight, and on a clear day you can see as far as Wales. This walk circles part of the Estate and takes in both natural woodland and a relic of Lancashire's industrial past.

Things to see

Views of the Local Countryside
The viewpoint at point 2 on this walk provides extensive vistas of the local countryside. On a clear day the centre of Manchester is visible to the south with the Derbyshire Pennines on the distant horizon.

Buckden Wood
Mature oak, birch, alder and aspen grow in Buckden Wood and to the west there is a beech and sycamore plantation. Hawthorn, holly and willow provide good cover for wildlife, while floral ground cover includes bracken, heather, bilberry and bluebells. Wildlife includes an increasing number of roe deer, and look out for birds such as green woodpecker, jay and tawny owl.

The Tentering Tower
The Tentering Tower is an unusual building in that its purpose seems to have been two-fold. It served both as part of the textile industry and also to act as a point of focus in the landscape. Tentering involved the stretching and drying of cloth fixed to wooden frames by a series of sharply pointed hooks. The factory, of which it was part, was built in 1877 by a local textile manufacturing family, the Porritts.

Above: The grand Entrance Front at Gawthorpe Hall.

Previous page: Beside the River Bollin at Quarry Bank Mill, Cheshire.

Opposite: A group of beech trees in autumn.

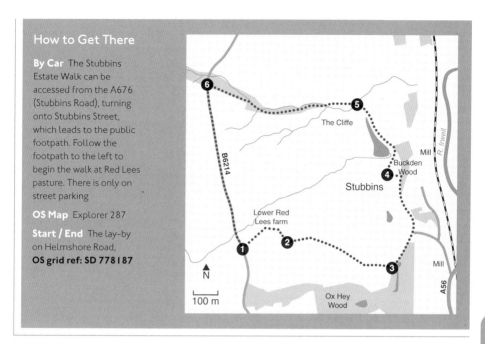

How to Get There

By Car The Stubbins Estate Walk can be accessed from the A676 (Stubbins Road), turning onto Stubbins Street, which leads to the public footpath. Follow the footpath to the left to begin the walk at Red Lees pasture. There is only on street parking

OS Map Explorer 287

Start / End The lay-by on Helmshore Road, **OS grid ref: SD 778187**

1. Start at the bottom of Red Lees pasture.

2. Proceed west for approximately ½ mile (800m), past Lower Red Lees farm, to the Helmshore Road.

3. From here the route follows Helmshore Road for almost ½ mile (800m) to the north of Buckden Wood.

4. From here there is a short descent for another ½ mile (800m) east through Buckden Wood to The Cliffe.

5. Here the route veers to the south.

6. At the end of Porritt's Lodge the route goes through a gate on the right and passes the rear of the castellated Tentering Tower back to Red Lees pasture.

Make the Most of Your Day
Gawthorpe Hall was redesigned in the 1850s by Sir Charles Barry, designer of the Houses of Parliament and Highclere Castle. The Hall houses the North West's largest collection of portraits on loan from the National Portrait Gallery as well as the Gawthorpe Textiles Collection, a wonderful collection of intricate lace, embroidery and needlework amassed by Miss Rachel Kay-Shuttleworth.

Food and Facilities
There is a tea-room and toilets at Gawthorpe Hall.

North West

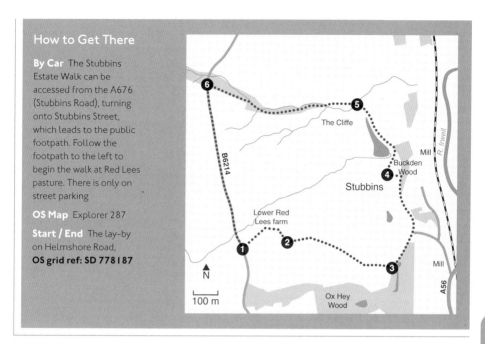

68. A Walk to the Lantern at Lyme

Lyme is home to an abundance of wildlife. From the mightiest stag to the smallest tadpole, the residents of Lyme are great in number and personality. Look out for the ancient deer herd and enjoy far-reaching views over Cheshire and Derbyshire.

Lyme
Disley
Stockport
SK12 2NX
01663 762023
lyme@nationaltrust.org.uk

About this walk
Lovely views

Georgian design

Wildlife interest

Dogs welcome under close control

Distance 1⅔ miles (2.7km)

Time 1 hour 30 mins

Above left: A view of the South Front of Lyme Park from across the lake with snow-covered ground.

Things to see

Lyme House
The house at Lyme has been altered by succeeding generations of the Legh family who owned it for 600 years before giving it to the National Trust in 1946. The statue of Minerva with her shield and spear over the central gateway was erected at the end of the eighteenth century.

The Lantern
Tradition has it that the top third of the Lantern tower used to be on the roof of the house where Minerva's statue now stands.

Birdlife at Lyme
Look for big flocks of mixed tits including great, blue, long-tailed and coal tits, as well as the odd treecreeper flitting through the woods searching for insects. In conifers you may spot the UK's smallest bird, the goldcrest. During colder months bird numbers will be swelled by migrating birds from Scandinavia, visitors who come to devour the berries here and escape the harsh winter weather back home.

Fieldfare and redwing in particular can be seen moving between feeding sites. Summer visitors include pied flycatcher, redstart, whitethroat, garden warbler, swallows and house martins.

Above: Deer in front of The Cage, an old hunting lodge at Lyme Park.

How to Get There

By Train Disley train station ½ mile (800m) from entrance to the park, main car park 1 mile (1.6km) from park entrance

By Car Entrance on A6 only, parking: 200 yards (180m) from house

OS Map Explorer OL1

Start / End Main car park, **OS grid ref: SJ 965824**

1. From the main car park, follow the sloping path at the side of the Information Centre that takes you up towards the house.

2. With the house to your right, head along the tarmac road that leads uphill to the left. You will pass The Stables before coming to a gateway on your right-hand side. Go through this gate, with The Stables on your right and the old Nursery Garden on your left.

3. Continue along the track and through the next gate into Turfhouse Meadow. Keep going along the track.

4. Continue until you reach a gate and stile. Climb over the stile onto the moor and head straight up the hill, following the wall. Keeping Lantern Wood to your left, you'll pass a deer leap in the wall, before reaching another stile. Climb this stile and continue along the path through the woodland.

5. Wander through the magnificent woodland. Eventually you will stumble across The Lantern (downhill on your left). Take some time to explore around it and take in the views down towards the house.

6. Once you've finished exploring, continue along the same path through to the other side of Lantern Wood. Climb over the stile onto Caters Slack.

7. The path through Caters Slack bears down to the left. Walk along here until you reach the final stile.

8. After climbing over the last stile, make your way to the road ahead. On the right is Lyme's Deer Sanctuary, and if you are lucky you may be able to spot some of the medieval herd of red deer. Please stay on the paths so they are not disturbed. At the road turn left. Follow it past The Stables, down the hill past the house and back to your starting point in the main car park.

Make the Most of Your Day
To visit Lyme is to step back in time to the Regency era: enjoy lavish interiors, try out the billiards table in the Long Gallery, or visit the Dressing Room. Outside there are elegant gardens as well as the beautiful parkland. There are also regular events, such as tours, walks and family activities.

Food and Facilities
Refreshments and toilets are available at the Timber Yard Café. There are also tea-rooms in the Servant's Hall and the Salting Room.

183

69. Marsden Moor Heritage Walk

This circular walk takes you across open moorland that is bursting with wildlife. Marsden Moor is the ideal habitat for plants and animals that can cope with heavy rainfall, little shelter and acidic soil. See if you can spot mountain hares, curlews, golden plovers and stoats.

Marsden Moor
West Yorkshire
HD7 6DH
01484 847016
marsdenmoor@
nationaltrust.org.uk

About this walk
Fine views

Industrial history

Birdlife

The route crosses open moorland where the weather can change very quickly; come prepared by wearing sturdy walking boots and bringing warm clothing and waterproofs

Dogs welcome on leads

Distance 10 miles (16.1 km)

Time 4–5 hours

Things to see

History of the Moors
The moorland has been used for thousands of years, from hunter-gatherers ambushing prey, to traders on the packhorse roads taking goods to market. The reservoirs and conduits supply water to the people of Yorkshire, feeding the Huddersfield Narrow Canal.

Flora and Fauna
Marsden is host to an array of moorland species such as curlew, grouse, golden plover, dunlin, merlin, short-eared owl and even the rare twite. Mammals include the stoat and mountain hare. You may find common upland plant species like heather, bilberry, crowberry and a variety of grasses and, if you are lucky, you might even come across the carnivorous sundew.

Previous page: Daffodils in bloom at Lyme Park, Cheshire.

Above: Purple heather blooming on Marsden Moor, West Yorkshire.

Right: Golden plover on moorland grass.

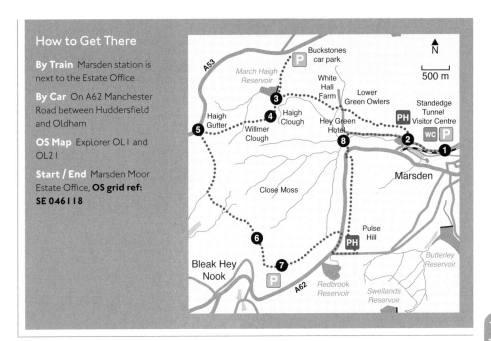

How to Get There

By Train Marsden station is next to the Estate Office

By Car On A62 Manchester Road between Huddersfield and Oldham

OS Map Explorer OL1 and OL21

Start / End Marsden Moor Estate Office, **OS grid ref: SE 046 118**

Map labels: Buckstones car park, March Haigh Reservoir, A53, White Hall Farm, Lower Green Owlers, Standedge Tunnel Visitor Centre, Haigh Gutter, Haigh Clough, Willmer Clough, Hey Green Hotel, Marsden, Close Moss, Pulse Hill, Bleak Hey Nook, Redbrook Reservoir, Swellands Reservoir, Butterley Reservoir, A62, 500 m, N

1. From the Estate Office head towards the train station and then onwards along the canal until you reach the Standedge Tunnel Visitor Centre.

2. Leave the car park and head up to Waters Road. Walk up the drive beside what was the Tunnel End pub, now a private home, and then take the path immediately behind it. Head up and across some fields to a group of houses. Go through a green metal gate and then immediately right through another gate beside the house to bring you out onto a lane. Follow the lane left past Berry Greave. When the lane starts to descend downhill, turn right and follow this lane past the first house and round to a path at the back of the next house. Climb gently across the fields and at the small footbridge keep to high ground before you drop sharply down to a stream and back up again to the right of the phone mast. Turn right down Blake Lee Lane, past Lower Green Owlers to a road junction. Turn left and climb up the track to White Hall Farm. In front of the farm, go through the gate leading onto the moor and through some rushes, following the path along the edge of Haigh Clough to the southern corner of March Haigh Reservoir.

3. Here you have the option to head up to Buckstones car park for magnificent views across the estate. Cross the dam wall and take the path heading steeply up through the rocks to the car park. Once you have caught your breath and taken in the views, retrace your steps back to the dam wall.

4. Continue to head south to meet up with the Packhorse Trail where you turn right and follow the trail across Willmer Clough and up to the top to one of the old marker stones. Continue straight ahead until you come out at Haigh Gutter.

5. Here, turn sharp left to follow the Pennine Way south, making sure that when you come to a square marker stone you follow the path to the left keeping Millstone Edge on your right. You will shortly arrive at the trig point at Dinner Stones.

6. Continue along Millstone Edge through a kissing gate into a field where mild-mannered cows normally reside. Take care around livestock especially if they have calves or you have dogs. Go through the next gate and turn left along a path, over a stile and down Thieves Clough. Follow a broken down wall until you come to the old engine house.

7. Follow the track over Redbrook Clough and onto the A62. Turn right in front of the Carriage House pub (also a hotel and campsite) and continue for a short distance before turning left down Mount Road. Continue along the road for $^1/_3$ mile (500m) where you can take a path left along the Standedge Trail. The path here is boggy to begin with but soon dries out to contour around the front of Pule Hill. Continue round, passing the incline that was used to transport materials from the quarry and walk between the air vents for the tunnel deep below. Be careful not to wander up the hill but stay level roughly under the telephone wires, going over two stiles. Walk behind two houses before taking the path left onto the A62. Take care crossing the road and walk downhill a short distance to a path called Dark Lane that leads you steeply down between two walls to Easter Gate. Cross the river at the bottom – it can be quite high after rain so you may end up with wet socks even when crossing at the shallowest point on the right.

8. Cross over the packhorse bridge, following the path to the road and then down to Hey Green Hotel. Continue along Waters Road until you pass the former coach house and turn right onto a path that runs alongside the river back to the Tunnel End. Retrace your steps along the canal to Marsden.

Make the Most of Your Day

There is so much to explore at Marsden Moor and many ways to do it. You can go cycling, try Nordic walking, discover the Stanedge Tunnel, go geocaching or follow the Stanza Stone Trail at Pule Edge Quarry.

Food and Facilities

Refreshments are available in Marsden, Tunnel End and near Redbrook Reservoir. There are toilets in the pubs and cafés in the area.

Above: Visitors walking on Pule Hill, Marsden Moor, West Yorkshire.

Opposite: Yockenthwaite in Upper Wharfedale, Yorkshire Dales (walk 76).

North East

70. Inner Farne Wildlife Walk

North Sea
Off the Northumberland
Coast between Bamburgh
and Seahouses
NE68 7SR
01665 720651
farneislands@nationaltrust.
org.uk

About this walk
Wildlife haven

Breathtaking views

Take care on cobbles and
near cliff-top viewpoints

No dogs allowed due to
the sensitive nature of the
colony

Distance ½ mile (800m)

Time I hour

The Farne Islands are one of the natural highlights of the Northumbrian coast. Famed for providing sanctuary to St Cuthbert in the seventh century, Inner Farne is now renowned as a haven for nesting seabirds along with a host of other coastal wildlife.

Things to see

Breeding Seabirds

There can be as many as 50,000 birds on Inner Farne during the breeding season, including three different types of tern, puffin, shag, guillemot, razorbill, fulmar, eider duck, and waders like oystercatcher and ringed plover. They arrive in spring, lay eggs, hatch chicks and care for them, before departing in late summer to spend the rest of the year out in the North Sea or on difficult journeys across Europe and Africa. The Arctic tern even travels down as far as the Antarctic.

Above: Inner Farne showing the Chapel of St Cuthbert, medieval Pele Tower and Victorian lighthouse from Bamburgh beach, Northumberland.

Right: Arctic terns can be spotted on the Farne Islands from May to August.

Grey Seal Colonies

The Farnes are home to one of the biggest grey seal colonies in the British Isles. They've been here for at least 800 years, but were hunted for oil and skins for most of that time. Now they're protected and you can see them peeking out of the water or huddling together lazily on rocks.

Puffins

Puffins can be seen between April and early August. They dig burrows underground in which to lay their eggs. You may spot adults, mouths filled with sand eels, ducking into holes to feed their chicks. You're unlikely to spot the young as they stay well hidden to avoid being eaten by gulls.

How to Get There

By Ferry Seahouses harbour to Inner Farne, boat trips daily (at additional cost), April to September, weather permitting

By Car Car park (non-National Trust) close to where the boats depart for Inner Farne in Seahouses harbour

OS Map Landranger 75, Explorer 340

Start Island jetty, **OS grid ref: NU 218359**

End Information Centre, **OS grid ref: NU 217358**

Farne Haven

St Cuthbert's Chapel

WC ②   ①

⑦   ⑧

⑥

Quarry Viewpoint   ③

⑤

Lighthouse

Inner Sound   ④

N

50 m

---

1. Take care stepping off the boat onto the jetties and climb up the boardwalk. The small stone building on your left is the Fishe House. It stands on the site of the medieval guesthouse where visiting monks would stay. From April to July this is the first place you meet breeding Arctic terns. They nest near the path and can be very defensive of their eggs or chicks. You may be dive-bombed, but don't panic; just slowly wave a hand above your head and move steadily away.

2. Visit St Cuthbert's Chapel, see the Pele Tower and check out the Information Centre, or go left and start your circuit of the island. Again this is an Arctic tern nesting zone, and in early summer chicks could be dotted around the cobbles, so watch where you step and never run. Don't linger for too long.

3. Look left to the one spot on Inner Farne where sandwich and common terns cluster together to breed.

4. Walk up the island to the lighthouse. Before it was built in 1825 a beacon was lit on top of the Pele Tower to warn off ships. Turn left to Lighthouse Cliff Viewpoint; you can see Dunstanburgh Castle in the distance on a clear day. These are the tallest rock faces on the island and are home to thousands of breeding guillemots, shag and kittiwake in summer.

5. Return to the lighthouse and turn left past the picnic area. There used to be two more cottages here where the lighthouse keepers and their families lived.

6. Follow the boardwalk through an area filled with puffin burrows and take a quick detour left to the Quarry Viewpoint. Bamburgh Castle is straight ahead of you on the mainland.

7. On your left is a large expanse of rocky foreshore. If there's a large sea swell, you might see the Churn blowhole spout out water up to 90ft (27.4m) in the air.

8. Return to the information centre, passing the monks' old vegetable garden on your left.

Make the Most of Your Day
The Farne Islands have strong links with Celtic Christianity and St Cuthbert who lived there; visit the church and find out more. Many of the islands hide underwater at high tide. Take a boat trip to these inaccessible islets – a short journey to a different world. Bring a picnic, relax, and enjoy the views.

Food and Facilities
There are toilets and a small shop on Inner Farne.

71. Newton Pool Coastal Walk

Low Newton
Northumberland
NE66 3EH
northumberlandcoast@
nationaltrust.org.uk

About this walk
Magnificent views

Birdwatching

Marine life

Rock pooling

Dogs welcome, please keep
them on leads near to bird
hide at point 4

Distance 1 mile (1.6km)

Time 30–40 mins

Enjoy a gentle stroll beside the Northumberland coast with plenty of wildlife-spotting opportunities along the way. In spring, thousands of birds arrive for the start of the breeding season.

Things to see

Dunstanburgh Castle
Savour the breathtaking views of the magnificent ruin of Dunstanburgh Castle to the south and, on a clear day, the distant Farne Islands to the north.

Birdlife
Stop off at the wildlife hides at point 4 to enjoy the view and to see how many different birds you can recognise using the visual guides and your binoculars. One hide is fully accessible for wheelchairs; the other has steps to climb to enter. Look out for oystercatchers and other shore birds around the Emblestones, an outcrop of hard volcanic rock protecting Newton Haven from the main ravages of the North Sea. Sometimes seals can be spotted basking at the far end of the rocks.

Above: Distant view of Dunstanburgh Castle from Low Newton, across Embleton Bay, Northumberland.

Below: Seaweed and lichen in the rock pools at Low Newton.

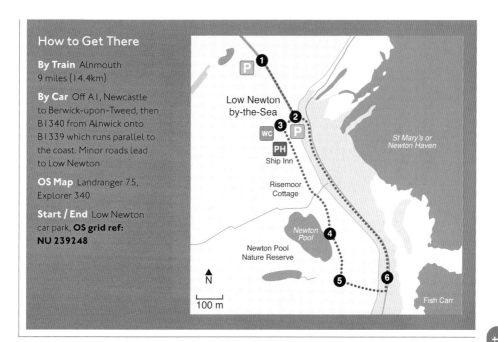

How to Get There

By Train Alnmouth 9 miles (14.4km)

By Car Off A1, Newcastle to Berwick-upon-Tweed, then B1340 from Alnwick onto B1339 which runs parallel to the coast. Minor roads lead to Low Newton

OS Map Landranger 75, Explorer 340

Start / End Low Newton car park, **OS grid ref: NU 239248**

Low Newton by-the-Sea

St Mary's or Newton Haven

Ship Inn

Risemoor Cottage

Newton Pool

Newton Pool Nature Reserve

N

100 m

Fish Carr

---

1. Start at the public car park above Low Newton. Head down the hill to the village square, the road is quite steep. Low Newton is an eighteenth-century fishing hamlet, with white-washed cottages and a historic pub set around a pretty village green.

2. As you arrive at the square in the village take the right-hand turn, following the road behind the square by the National Trust information board. The first ⅓ mile (500m) to Newton Pool bird hides has a surfaced track suitable for wheelchair access.

3. Turn left behind the Ship Inn and follow the road south past the back of the cottages, parallel with the seashore. Continue past the Boat Park, checking the field to your right for visiting wetland and coastal birds on the muddy scrape.

4. Continue on the track past Risemoor Cottage, a former fisherman's pub, through a small woodland path until you see the two wildlife hides on your right facing into the waters at Newton Pool. You can now reverse your route back to Low Newton or continue on to point 5.

5. Continue southward from the bird hide, and after about 33 yards (30m) the path forks. Take the left track past some beach bungalows in the dunes. Head for the centre of the green space where a waymarker shows the path through bracken leading to wooden steps to the beach.

6. Take in the spectacular views of Dunstanburgh Castle across Embleton Bay before turning left on the beach and heading back towards the village.

Make the Most of Your Day

As you arrive back in the village square of Low-Newton-by-the-Sea take time to relax on the beach, picnic on the village green or explore the shoreline and rock pools.

Food and Facilities

Food and drink are available at the Ship Inn during opening times. There are toilets at Low Newton beach.

72. Craster to Low Newton Coastal Walk

Craster
Northumberland
NE66 3TT
northumberlandcoast@
nationaltrust.org.uk

About this walk
Superb views

Birdwatching

Geological interest

Dogs welcome under close
control near livestock or on
the beach

Distance 6 miles (9.7km)

Time 2 hours

This route begins at the fishing village of Craster, passing the mighty ruins of Dunstanburgh Castle and the long sweep of Embleton Sands, before reaching Low Newton-by-the-Sea. With a combination of habitats attracting a huge variety of birdlife, this is the perfect destination for bird lovers.

Things to see

Above: Boats in Craster Harbour.

Below: View of Dunstanburgh Castle taken from the south (Craster) side in the morning.

Birdlife

Spot eider ducks bobbing around in the sea, known locally as Cuddy's duck after St Cuthbert; he's said to have cared for them on the nearby Farne Islands where he lived as a recluse in the seventh century. Waders like oystercatcher, dunlin, ringed plover, turnstone and redshank can be found on the shoreline in large numbers, and you might spot linnet or yellowhammer in the scrub and grassland behind the dunes and castle. Geese, swans and ducks, like pochard, teal and goldeneye, visit Newton Pool in winter. The best place to watch them is at the wildlife hide overlooking the water (see point 7).

Dunstanburgh Castle

Just 1 mile (1.6km) north of Craster, the fourteenth-century ruins of Dunstanburgh Castle stand on a rocky headland. The castle fell into disrepair after the Wars of the Roses. The outcrop on which Dunstanburgh Castle sits is called the Great Whin Sill, a stripe of hard volcanic rock that passes from the Pennines north to the Northumberland coast. It emerges above the surface here, at the castle, and at the Farne Islands.

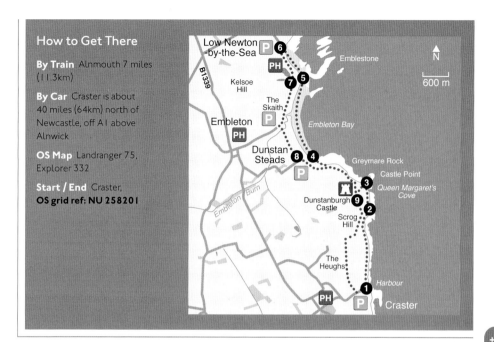

How to Get There

By Train Alnmouth 7 miles (11.3km)

By Car Craster is about 40 miles (64km) north of Newcastle, off A1 above Alnwick

OS Map Landranger 75, Explorer 332

Start / End Craster, **OS grid ref: NU 258201**

1. Start in Craster and walk towards Dunstanburgh Castle, passing Craster Harbour. Craster used to be a busy fishing village, but now only a few boats moor in the harbour. The path takes you through farmland with the rocky shoreline and birdlife to your right.

2. Pass the castle (or pop in – National Trust members can visit the castle for free).

3. Edge around the base of the castle. The Greymare Rock to your right was formed by volcanic pressure that folded the limestone.

4. Pass a golf course on your left and walk down onto the beach. The concrete bunkers on the sand were built during the Second World War. Stroll to the far end of Embleton Bay and cross Embleton Burn.

5. Look out for oystercatchers and other shore birds around the Emblestones as you approach the harbour at Newton Haven. Search for marine creatures, such as sea anemones, limpets, crabs and starfish in the rock pools, and various types of seaweed.

6. Climb up from the beach to Low Newton's picturesque three-sided square. Like Craster, Low Newton has a strong fishing heritage. The little square of cottages was built in the nineteenth century for

local fishermen. The former Coastguard Station on top of the hill is now a National Trust holiday cottage. Continue inland via a track that starts behind the village square, cottages and boat park.

7. After ¼ mile (400m) walking next to sand dunes and through a little woodland, you reach a wildlife hide that faces out over the waters at Newton Pool Nature Reserve. Newton Pool attracts a variety of wildlife to its scrub woodland, fen and open water habitats.

8. Continue on this path towards Dunstan Steads. Dunstanburgh's precipitous cliffs loom large again as you pass the golf course.

9. After the castle, climb up to your right on a higher level track back to Craster.

Make the Most of Your Day
Dunstanburgh Castle is open Saturdays and Sundays only 10am–4pm from November until the end of March (check for school holiday opening times).

Food and Facilities
There are pubs in Craster, Low Newton and Embleton. Toilets can be found in Craster, next to the Tourist Information Centre and behind Newton Square.

73. Allen Banks Morralee Tarn Walk

Allen Banks
Northumberland
NE47 7BP
01434 32188
allenbanks@nationaltrust.org.uk

About this walk

Ancient woodland

Fungi

Superb views

Some short, sharp climbs

Dogs welcome on leads

Distance 2½ miles (4km)

Time 50 mins

With over 100 acres (41ha), and lots of hiding holes on offer, it's no surprise that there's an abundance of wildlife at Allen Banks – from birds and insects to bats and rare species such as the red squirrel and the elusive dormouse.

Things to see

Wildlife

This ancient woodland is host to an array of wildlife ranging from common birds to the elusive and rare, but extremely cute, dormouse. More than 70 species of bird have been recorded on the estate, including species in decline, such as wood warbler and pied flycatcher. The River Allen provides a great feeding ground for heron, goosander and dippers and plays host to rare visits by the kingfisher and otter. Other animals to keep you company are red squirrels, roe deer, bats, badgers and foxes – plus a whole world of bugs and insects.

Fungi

Allen Banks is one of the best places in the north-east for fungi, with over 500 species recorded here. Autumn is the best time to see mushrooms and toadstools, as this is when most fungi develop a fruitbody to distribute their spores and reproduce. Deathcap, destroying angel and panthercap fungi are deadly poisonous with no known antidote; all can be found in the woodland here, so to be safe, look but don't touch.

Above: View of the River Allen with thickly wooded banks by Morales Wood, Northumberland.

Above: Fly agaric fungi growing on the woodland floor.

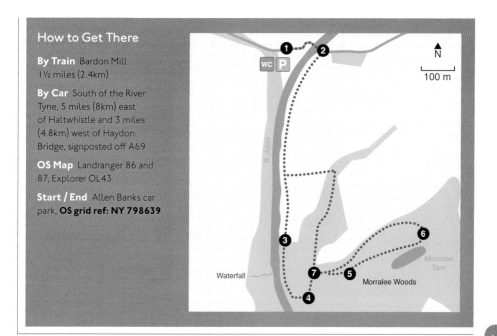

How to Get There

By Train Bardon Mill
1½ miles (2.4km)

By Car South of the River
Tyne, 5 miles (8km) east
of Haltwhistle and 3 miles
(4.8km) west of Haydon
Bridge, signposted off A69

OS Map Landranger 86 and
87, Explorer OL43

Start / End Allen Banks car
park, **OS grid ref: NY 798639**

---

1. Starting at the car park, exit the main gate (where you came in) and turn right following the road over the bridge.

2. As you leave the bridge, take a tight left and go through the gate, merging onto a footpath that takes you through a couple of fields beside the river. The River Allen is rocky and fast flowing here, a prime spot for birds like dipper and grey wagtail.

3. Venture into the woods where you'll start following the purple waymarkers up to Morralee Tarn. Keep on the path straight ahead, past the site of the wobbly bridge and up the steps until you meet the main path through Morralee Woods.

4. Follow this path left, take the next right and go right again. At the fork keep right, following the purple waymarkers up the hill, there are some steep sections here and the terrain varies so please take care.

5. As you reach the top of the hill, take the steps on the left and follow this path to Morralee Tarn. The tarn itself is a historic feature in the landscape, originally dug out as a boating lake by the Victorians. It is now a real oasis and a great place to spot some wildlife, with superb views of the Tyne Valley and Hadrian's Wall in the distance.

6. Once you're ready to make your way back, continue to walk with the tarn on your right, then take the path heading left away from the end of the tarn. This will take you on a loop until you reach the path you originally started on.

7. As you come down the little slope by the big fallen tree stump, rejoin the main path through Morralee Woods, turn right and follow the waymarkers to a gate out of the woods and into the field. Go straight towards the river and then retrace your steps back to the car park.

Make the Most of Your Day

Storm damage and a landslide in 2016 destroyed some footpaths in Walks Wood on the west side of Allen Banks, but rangers and volunteers have worked together to reinstate access through this side of the valley. Opening paths through Walks Wood offers the chance to discover some more of the fantastic features created by Susan Davidson during the 1800s, when she lived at Ridley Hall, and Allen Banks was her 'wilderness' garden.

Food and Facilities

There is a picnic area and toilets at Allen Banks.

74. Gibside Liberty Trail

Gibside
Near Burnopfield
Newcastle upon Tyne
NE16 6BG
01207 541820
gibside@nationaltrust.
org.uk

About this walk
Wildlife interest

Countryside views

Georgian architecture

Dogs welcome on leads

Distance 2⅓ miles (3.8km)

Time 1–2 hours

Gibside's 600 acres (243ha) of woodland and parkland is home to a
variety of wildlife. There is a great emphasis on conservation here, and
rangers monitor nesting birds including buzzards, kestrels and tawny
owls, as well as pipistrelle bats that roost near the stables. Keep an
eye out too for red kites and the roe deer that live at Gibside.

Things to see

Green Close Field
The mound in the middle of Green
Close Field is likely to have been a
water feature or fountain forming
part of the original garden design.
Now the field is used mostly for
events, picnics and sport activities.
The next field along lies in front
of the Hall. This field is classed
as a SSSI (Site of Special Scientific
Interest), indicating its importance
for wildlife.

Octagon Pond and Banqueting House
The Octagon Pond was part of
the garden design, creating a
regimented eight-sided water
feature. Now the pond edges are
hidden behind the reeds and rushes
that provide a home to a wide
range of aquatic species, including
great crested newts. There was
once a fountain, and the slopes
leading up to the Banqueting
House were terraced with statues,
while the Gothic-style house
would have been the venue of
many a Georgian feast or party. It is
now a holiday cottage managed by
the Landmark Trust.

Column to Liberty
This was commissioned by George
Bowes as part of the garden
design to show his support for the
political Whig party. In its time it
was the second tallest monument
in the country, pipped only by
Nelson's Column in London.
Gibside's Column to Liberty is a
prominent feature in the Derwent
Valley today, visible from many
miles around.

Above: The Orangery at dawn at
Gibside, Tyne & Wear.

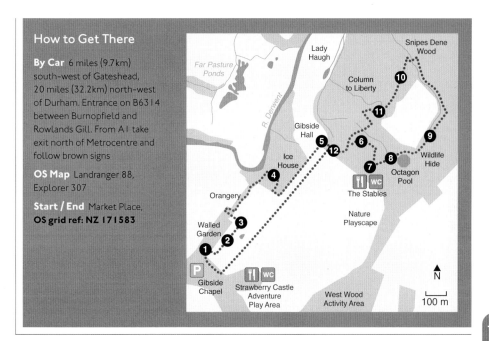

1. Find the start of the trail after crossing the road from the raised wooden walkway beside the estate map. Go straight ahead with the Walled Garden wall on your left and the play castle on your right.

2. At the doorway to the walled garden, take a left turn and head through the door. The path leads you straight through the middle of the garden, passing apple trees and allotment plots. The end of the path leads to large wooden gates.

3. Once outside the walled garden turn left, and just outside the small garden door, follow the path to the right, carefully crossing the road, and head into the shrubbery. Follow the grassy path as it leads you to the Orangery, with a field on your right. Continue straight ahead and walk down the flight of steps. (If you struggle with stairs or have a wheelchair or pushchair, you can take the level grassy path through Orangery Field – the gate is in front of the ruin. This will miss out point 4 of this walk.)

4. At the bottom of the steps head straight across the path and up the steps on the other slope, leading you into Ice House Dene. The path bears to the right through the woodland, and out of the woods at the corner of the Orangery Field and the Avenue Road. Turn left out of the woods and left again along the road.

5. Before heading up the Avenue Road, glance to your left to see the Column to Liberty above the treetops. Continue along the Avenue Road with the Avenue on your right and passing the field with the mound on your left (known as Green Close Field). Head straight on to the Hall Field which is on your left and lies in front of the ruin of Gibside Hall. Turn right at the end of the Avenue, following the road.

6. Continue up the road that winds its way between historic yew trees, until it emerges at the top with a grassy lawn on your right in front of the Stables. At the top of the hill at the T-junction, turn right towards the stables.

7. Follow the road towards the stables and take the opportunity for a welcome break if needed. When you are ready to continue, head up the hill away from the stables, back into the woodland. After about 110 yards (100m), take the path into the woods on the left, just after passing the Woodland Bothy (on your right).

8. Follow this roughly surfaced track through the woods, where it will emerge beside the Octagon Pond. The path becomes grass as you venture around the pond (on your right). Continue on with the pond to your right, passing under the cypress tree, towards the road. Turn right and then immediately left, back into the woodland.

9. As you wander through the woodland, notice the bird hide on your left. The path follows the boundary of the field also on your left (Brick Kiln Field). Walk straight ahead, then at the next path junction turn left, and after a few hundred yards of weaving through the trees and passing the edge of the field, take another left.

10. Emerge from the woods to see the Column to Liberty (194ft/59.1m) sitting in a clearing. Take time to walk around it and then return to the side of the column with the grassy glade towards the field and find the path entering the woods again on your right. Continue down through the woodland until it emerges out of the wood onto the road.

11. The trail takes a left turn as you come out of the woods. Start to walk up the hill, but before reaching the slope, take the path on the right that cuts across the Hollow Walk. This path rejoins the road below the yew trees. At this point, turn right and walk back to the end of the Avenue.

12. Head up the grassy slope to wander along the grassed Avenue under the trees. (If you need a surfaced route, then you can always stick to the road.) You will see the Hall ruins, Green Close Field this time on your right, and Park Fields, usually full of sheep and cows, on your left. Head straight on towards the Chapel, and to keep to the trail walk on the left-hand side down the gravel path, turn right behind the chapel and finish your walk as the path re-enters Market Place.

Make the Most of Your Day
One of the few surviving eighteenth-century designed landscapes, Gibside was fashioned with two things in mind: spectacular views and 'wow' moments. The estate, commissioned by coal baron George Bowes, offers a glimpse into the past. Escape the hustle and bustle of modern life here in this 600-acre (243ha) wildlife haven on the edge of urban Tyneside.

Food and Facilities
There is a range of facilities at Market Place. There is also the family-friendly Gibside Pub (open late Fridays and Saturdays).

Left: Visitors by the log braziers at Gibside Pub.

75. Souter Lighthouse Nature Trail

North East

Souter Lighthouse
Coast Road
Whitburn
Sunderland
Tyne & Wear
SR6 7NH
0191 529 3161
souter@nationaltrust.org.uk

About this walk
Rare flora

Coastal views

Industrial history

Be aware of cliff edges

Dogs welcome under close control

Distance 1⅔ miles (2.7km)

Time 30 mins–1 hour

This is an easy route for all ages, taking in ponds and a bird hide as well as plenty of coastal views. There is an exciting assortment of maritime plants and wildflowers, as well as seabirds, wildfowl and birds of prey.

Things to see

Whitburn Nature Reserve
Whitburn Nature Reserve is reclaimed colliery land and includes a bird observatory, viewing screens and wetland habitats. It was designated a Local Nature Reserve in 2003.

Whitburn Coastal Park
Whitburn Coastal Park used to be the site of Whitburn Colliery. Opened in the late 1870s, it closed in 1968 and at its height produced 2,600 tons of coal a day. Children as young as 13 worked down the pit

which stretched out for many miles under the North Sea.

Rocket Green
Rocket Green has the richest variety of rare wildflowers on this coast. The cliff-top meadow is home to autumn gentian, bee orchid and dropwort. Small scabious even grow in the shallow, lime-rich soils.

Above: Souter Lighthouse, Tyne & Wear. This was the first purpose-built lighthouse in the world powered by electricity; it was opened in 1871 and decommissioned in 1988.

Left: Kestrel, perched on rocks in Trow Quarry. Kestrels are residents at Souter Lighthouse.

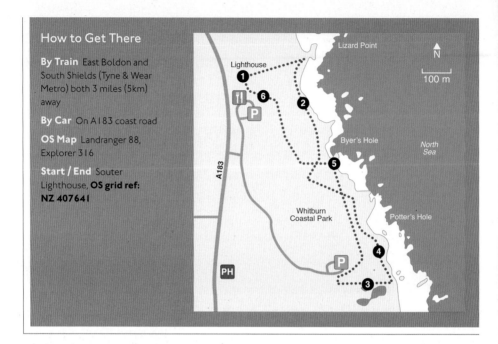

1. Start at the lighthouse itself and make your way towards the foghorn at the bottom of Foghorn Field. Exit through the green gate behind the foghorn.

2. Make your way to the coastal path nearest to the cliffs. Start making your way south to point 3.

3. Walk past the pond and make your way to point 4. Here you will find a birdwatching hut. Feel free to use the hut to gaze at the many species of birds we have on our land at this time of year.

4. Walk back along the other coastal path as marked on the map.

5. Go down to the wherry. Here you can take a look at our stunning sea views and maybe skim a few stones.

6. Go back to the coastal path and walk north to the lighthouse. Walk up the bank and to the green gate at the south of the lighthouse. Turn left and make your way to the front of the lighthouse.

Make the Most of Your Day

Built in 1871, Souter was the first lighthouse in the world purpose built to use electricity. Learn more about it and the area's treacherous seas in the Compass Room at ground level. Make time to see how many different types of bird you can spot, go rock pooling down on the shore or dipping in the ponds. There is also a wildlife garden at Souter. The project was undertaken by local charity the Coastal Conservation Group and includes ponds, wildflowers, trees, berry-bearing shrubs, bog garden, hibernation areas and much more – the perfect haven for wildlife. You can also run in the Leas – the finishing stretch of the Great North Run.

Food and Facilities

There is a café, picnic area and toilets at Souter Lighthouse.

76. Yockenthwaite to Cray Wildlife Walk

Upper Wharfedale
Yockenthwaite
North Yorkshire
BD23 5JH
01729 830416
upperwharfedale@
nationaltrust.org.uk

About this walk
Flora and fauna

Breathtaking views

One steep climb

Dogs welcome but must be
kept on a lead

Distance 6 miles (9.7km)

Time 2 hours

Discover a landscape of limestone pavement, glaciated valleys and flower-rich hay meadows in the glorious setting of the Yorkshire Dales. There is much to see in Upper Wharfedale: abundant birdlife, butterflies and some of the best wildflower meadows in the country.

Things to see

Wildflowers
The first signs of spring arrive with wood anemones, primroses, lesser celandines and the smell of wild garlic; later in the spring cowslips, mountain pansies and early purple orchids appear. These flowers then start to support the dormant insect population. Bees that have spent the winter hibernating in holes in trees and the gaps in drystone walls emerge looking for some sweet early nectar.

Birdlife
There is a strong bird population in Upper Wharfedale – you will begin to hear and see oystercatchers, lapwing and curlew in March with the wintering blackhead gulls beginning to show their distinctive (black head) breeding summer plumage. From April onwards, you start to notice the golden plover and skylarks on the fell tops on Buckden Pike.

Butterflies
The common blue butterfly starts to fly in May and is often seen over grassland. It's particularly associated with the plant bird's-foot trefoil, which provides food for the caterpillars. Also look out for tiny craven door snails on old walls and in moist, shaded rocks, and butterflies, such as the northern brown argus (associated with common rock rose) and the green-veined white.

Above: Cowslips.

Above left: Yockenthwaite, Upper Wharfedale, Yorkshire Dales.

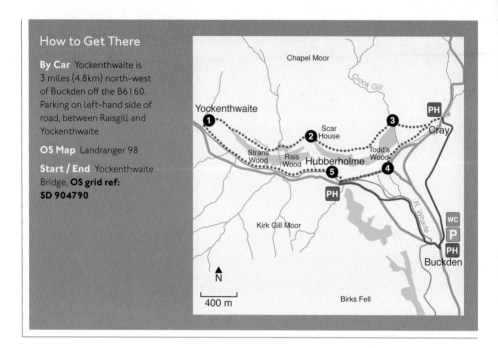

How to Get There

By Car Yockenthwaite is 3 miles (4.8km) north-west of Buckden off the B6160. Parking on left-hand side of road, between Raisgill and Yockenthwaite

OS Map Landranger 98

Start / End Yockenthwaite Bridge, **OS grid ref: SD 904790**

1. Start at Yockenthwaite (meaning 'Eoghans clearing in a wood') Bridge and follow the footpath signposted to Scar House. Turn right off the farm track at another footpath sign, going through Strans Wood and emerge onto the open hillside.

2. In 1652, George Fox, the founder of the Quakers, stayed at Scar House and 'converted the farmer to the Quaker Truth'. The house later became a Quaker meeting place. A small enclosure with five trees marks an old burial ground. Continue towards Cray, keeping the woodland boundary on your right. (For a shorter walk, turn right at Scar House and follow the track into Hubberholme.) Enjoy the view down Wharfedale's glaciated valley with its wide floor and ice-carved steep sides.

3. Cross Crook Gill and carry on through hay meadows to Cray. Hay is a valuable crop to farmers and it can suffer if trampled by too many feet, so please walk in single file.

4. Drop down to your right when entering Cray and follow a footpath along Cray Gill to a road. Turn right and walk along it for ¼ mile (400m) until you reach Hubberholme.

5. Return to Yockenthwaite via a footpath behind Hubberholme Church and follow this route beside the River Wharfe all the way back.

6. There are lots of other interesting places to discover around here. If you have time 3 miles (4.8km) extra will take you to Buckden, which has an exhibition of the area's history at Townhead Barn. Take the fellside path across the stepping stones from Cray to get there. Take the riverside path from Buckden to Hubberholme to rejoin this walk.

Make the Most of Your Day
Upper Wharfedale is full of spots to enjoy the stunning scenery or picnic by the river. If you are feeling energetic you can jump on your bike and follow in the tracks of the Tour de France that came to the area in 2014.

Food and Facilities
The nearest cafés, pubs and toilets are in the village of Buckden.

77. Roseberry Topping Woodland Wildlife Walk

Roseberry Topping
Newton-under-Roseberry
North Yorkshire
TS9 6QR
01723 870423
roseberrytopping@
nationaltrust.org.uk

About this walk
Spectacular views

Birdwatching

Fungi

Tracks and paths can be
muddy

Dogs welcome

Distance 3⅓ miles (5.4km)

Time 1 hour 30 mins

The woods that surround Roseberry's lower slopes are a great place to enjoy a quiet stroll in a beautiful setting. Oak and ash trees – some of which are several hundred years old – tower over the network of paths that thread their way through the understorey. Newton Wood is renowned for having the best displays of bluebells in the area, while in Cliff Ridge Wood there are signs of the area's industrial past.

Things to see

Roseberry Topping

As soon as the distinctive profile of Roseberry Topping appears on the horizon, your eye can't help but be drawn to it. This unique hill has become an important landmark and countless numbers climb its slopes every year. Despite cutting an imposing figure on the skyline, Roseberry is tiny compared to the great mountains of Britain. At 1,050ft (320m) it is less than a third of the size of Scafell Pike – England's highest peak.

Above: Roseberry
Topping in autumn.

Left: Blue tit on branch.

Woodland Birds

There are many species of bird that can be spotted around the woods. Listen out for the call of the green woodpecker. It's quite distinctive, and sounds like hoarse laughter.

Fantastic Fungi

You can spot fungi all year around, but autumn, just before the trees start to drop their leaves, is the best time to find them. Fungi come in a huge variety of shapes and sizes, including the brightly coloured waxcap.

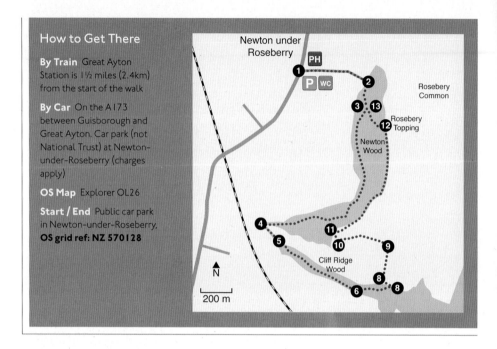

How to Get There

By Train Great Ayton Station is 1½ miles (2.4km) from the start of the walk

By Car On the A173 between Guisborough and Great Ayton. Car park (not National Trust) at Newton-under-Roseberry (charges apply)

OS Map Explorer OL26

Start / End Public car park in Newton-under-Roseberry, **OS grid ref: NZ 570128**

1. Turn right at the end of the path out of the car park and follow the wide track.

2. At the end of the lane go up the steps and through the kissing gate to enter Newton Wood. Turn right and follow the path along the bottom edge of the wood.

3. Stay right where the path forks and keep on the bottom path all the way through Newton Wood.

4. As the path leaves the wood, turn left onto a wide track and continue for 55 yards (50m).

5. Take the left-hand fork at the National Trust sign. Continue straight into Cliff Ridge Wood, staying right where the path forks again.

6. Upon reaching an old metal gate and another National Trust sign, turn left and follow the path uphill.

7. Cross the stile to leave the wood and turn left.

8. Go over another stile back into the wood and turn right. Leave the wood again through a kissing gate and continue straight on towards the cottage.

9. At the cottage, bear left and follow the path along the edge of the field.

10. Go through the kissing gate back into Newton Wood and turn immediately right through a sharp dip.

11. Turn right at the end of the path and follow the path at the top of the wood.

12. After climbing some log steps continue straight on for 220 yards (200m). Bear left onto the path that descends down through the wood.

13. Rejoin the bottom path and retrace your steps back to the car park.

Make the Most of Your Day

As well as a whole range of walks around Roseberry Topping there is plenty for the more adventurous, including geocaching, climbing, abseiling and even fell racing. The landscape is also the perfect inspiration for landscape artists of all levels – come and give it a try!

Food and Facilities

Toilet facilities in car park at Newton-under-Roseberry.

78. Malham Tarn and Great Close Walk

Malham Tarn is an area of impressive uplands that boasts England's highest lime-rich lake. With peat bogs and open moorland, it is home to a unique community of rare plants and animals.

Malham Tarn Estate Office
Settle
North Yorkshire
BD24 9PT
01729 830416
malhamtarn@nationaltrust.org.uk

About this walk

Superb views

Wildflower meadows

Rare flora

Rugged sections can be muddy after wet weather

Dogs welcome under close control; they must be kept on leads at certain times of the year

Distance 3¾ miles (6km)

Time 2 hours

North East

Things to see

Water Voles
National Trust rangers are working hard to help wildlife thrive in Malham Tarn. One project has been the reintroduction of the water vole, one of Britain's most endangered mammals. Their numbers were wiped out by mink from local farms in the 1960s. The voles are now back where they belong.

Flora and Fauna
Roe deer live in the woodlands around Tarn House, and if you are quiet you will often spot them – you'll probably find they are already watching you! Notable birds include curlew and lapwing, and, depending on the time of year, you may see early purple orchids, wild thyme and harebells in the meadows.

Above: Walking on the Malham Tarn Estate, Yorkshire Dales.

Below: Malham Tarn.

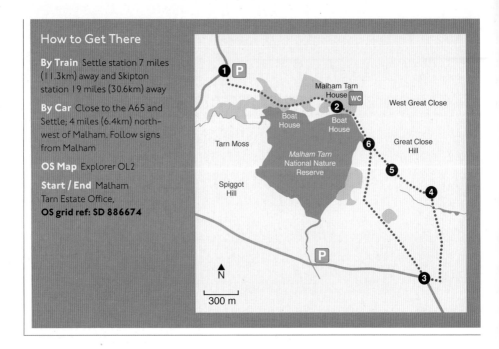

How to Get There

By Train Settle station 7 miles
(11.3km) away and Skipton
station 19 miles (30.6km) away

By Car Close to the A65 and
Settle; 4 miles (6.4km) north-
west of Malham. Follow signs
from Malham

OS Map Explorer OL2

Start / End Malham
Tarn Estate Office,
OS grid ref: SD 886674

1. Turn left from the estate office and follow the track through the woodland, catching glimpses of Malham Tarn as you go.

2. Pass Tarn House and continue on the track down through the woodland and to the shore of the tarn. Follow the stone track around the shore and go through the gate. Continue on the stone track, slowing down and taking extra care as you go over the speed bumps.

3. On reaching the road, turn left and head towards the gate in front of you. Turn left just before you get to the gate and follow the stone track towards Middle House Farm.

4. Pass over the cattle grid and through the gate. Do not take the short cut across the grass, but continue on and turn left after approximately 110 yards (100m) and follow the grassy track, which goes behind the woodland.

5. Continue on this track and enjoy the majestic views of Malham Tarn as it appears in front of you. This is a particularly rough and uneven section of track, which can be particularly wet after heavy rain;

please go slowly, picking your best route, and take extra care over the uneven sections.

6. Rejoin the stone track and retrace your path around the shores of the tarn, through the woodland and back to your starting point.

Make the Most of Your Day
There is an exhibition about the nature reserve at the learning centre at Orchid House next to Tarn House. The beautiful waterfall at Janet's Foss is a magical place to visit, and is only a short walk from Malham village. Activities held at Malham Tarn include pond dipping, den building, guided walks and star gazing evenings.

Food and Facilities
Café and pub available in Malham village. Toilet at Orchid House, behind Tarn House.

79. Moorland and Meadows Walk at Brimham Rocks

Brimham Rocks
Summerbridge
Harrogate
North Yorkshire
HG3 4DW
01423 780688
brimhamrocks@
nationaltrust.org.uk

About this walk
Panoramic views

Geological interest

Pondlife

Some paths can be muddy during prolonged wet weather

Dogs welcome under close supervision

Distance 5 miles (8km)

Time 3 hours

North East

You can see for miles at Brimham Rocks. Admire the magnificent, long-distance views, and if you pick a clear day you may even see York Minster. Stumble upon fantastic pondlife, tree stumps of all shapes and sizes, cotton grass growing wild and waist-high bracken in the Yorkshire Dales.

Things to see

Ponds in the Pasture
Look to your right at point 5 for the interestingly shaped ponds. In springtime you can see lambs enjoying the fresh air in the surrounding pasture.

Cotton Grass
In summer months, the fields at point 7 are abundant with wild-growing cotton grass. They make for a great landscape scene with the giant balls of Menwith Hill in the background.

Bracken
During the summer at point 9, search for the hidden path amongst the lush green bracken, which can reach waist height.

Above: Visitors at Brimham Rocks, North Yorkshire.

Below: Cotton grass grows wild in the Dales around Brimham Rocks.

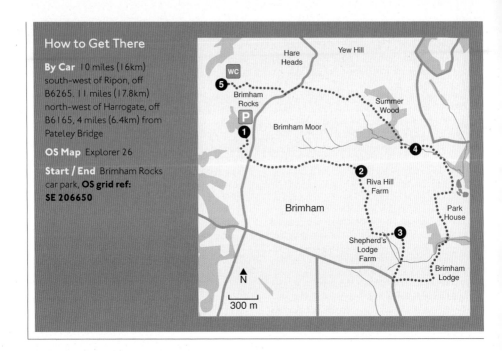

How to Get There

By Car 10 miles (16km) south-west of Ripon, off B6265. 11 miles (17.8km) north-west of Harrogate, off B6165, 4 miles (6.4km) from Pateley Bridge

OS Map Explorer 26

Start / End Brimham Rocks car park, **OS grid ref: SE 206650**

(Map labels: Hare Heads, Yew Hill, WC, 5, Brimham Rocks, P, 1, Brimham Moor, Summer Wood, 4, 2, Riva Hill Farm, Brimham, Park House, 3, Shepherd's Lodge Farm, Brimham Lodge, N, 300 m)

1. From the Brimham Rocks car park, go down the road you came in on, but before reaching the public road, turn right down the track marked 'Private Road to Druids Cave Farm'. After about 80 yards (75m) – and just before the track passes between a gap in a wall with a National Trust boundary marker – there's a footpath to your left. Take this path, and then immediately the left fork, to continue to the road. Cross the road and take the footpath signposted 'Nidderdale Way'. Follow this path for about ⅔ mile (1km) to a stile at the boundary of Brimham Rocks. Go over the stile and continue straight on, then through a gate passing the track to Riva Hill Farm on the left. About 30 paces further on, look out for a rusty brown gate on the right.

2. Go through the gate, heading upwards through ferns – bear left at the gate – until you reach the elderflower tree on the crest of the hill. After admiring the view, head for the green barns you can see pretty much straight on by skirting to the left of the gorse patch and towards the corner of the field. You will reach a stone wall with a stile; go over this and then over two wooden stiles into the pasture. Follow the path, staying beside the fence on your right to reach a stile straight ahead. Cross over the stile to the concrete path and go left towards a barn.

Shortly before reaching the barn look for the path on your left through the fields towards the gate and stile. Go over the stile and follow the path across the field beside the hedgerow on your left. Head for the stile in the top corner of the field.

3. Cross the stile and turn right along the bridleway (Nidderdale Way). Continue until you reach the road. Turn left, then immediately left again onto the farm track signposted Public Bridleway/Nidderdale Way/ Shaw Mills. Follow the track through Brimham Lodge Farm, then through a wooded area and continuing straight on uphill signposted Park House/Warsill. After passing Park House Farm continue up the slope and just before the brow of the hill take the footpath on the right through a gate. Follow the footpath, passing first some small lakes on your right and then 220 yards (200m) or so further on, past houses on your left. After another 110 yards (100m) and immediately after a landscaped lake on your left, take the left fork Public Bridleway between some houses up to the road at Warsill Parish Hall.

Opposite: Walking at Brimham Rocks, North Yorkshire. These weird and wonderful rock formations have been sculpted over centuries by ice, wind and rain.

4. Turn left on the road. Shortly after entering a wooded area and crossing the beck onto the concrete track, take the path to the right and follow it for about 200 paces until you reach a stream. Cross the stream via stepping stones (with care). There is now a steady climb onwards and upwards until you reach a wooden gate which leads you into a meadow. Take the path straight ahead through the meadow, following the tree line on your left to a wooden gate leading to the drive of the house on the left. Follow the drive as it bends left and over a cattle grid, then further on you'll cross another cattle grid at the National Trust boundary. Continue to the road and turn left. After about 150 paces along the road – opposite a rough lay-by – look for a path on the right leading up through the bracken. Follow whichever path you like the look of and, bearing slightly left as you go, you'll soon see the main cluster of rock formations ahead. The Visitor Centre and refreshment kiosk are at the highest point and so will be easy to find.

5. Head towards the very large rocks and bear left along the ridge. Head right from the moor towards a large outcrop of rocks; then bear left and then right. Beware of cliff edges and follow the undulating path taking in the magnificent views over Nidderdale. Stop and be amazed by Idol Rock. You will approach a wooded area and emerge to redeem Brimham Rocks in all its wonderful splendour. You can now return down one of the many paths that meander through the rock formations to the car park at your leisure.

Make the Most of Your Day

The natural spectacle of Brimham Rocks, with its giant rock formations, was created by an immense river 100 million years before the first dinosaurs walked the Earth; a visit to this amazing landscape is truly a journey into prehistory. As well as a gentle stroll taking in the views, you can climb, cycle and explore to your heart's content.

Food and Facilities

A refreshment kiosk is available at the Visitor Centre. Toilets 600 yards (550m) from the car park.

80. Boots, Gaiters and Vistas Walk at Fountains Abbey

Fountains Abbey and
Studley Royal Water Garden
Ripon
HG4 3DY
North Yorkshire
01765 608888
fountainsabbey@
nationaltrust.org.uk

About this walk
Glorious views

Farmyard and tracks can be
muddy and slippery

Strong shoes or boots
recommended

Dogs welcome; please keep
them on a short lead

Distance 5 miles (8km)

Time 2 hours 30 mins

Take in the fresh air and open vistas on this circular route around the estate. You can look over the valley to St Mary's Church and Ripon in the distance. It's an easy-going walk that'll take you over rustic bridges and through this secluded valley. Wildlife is a huge part of the estate, from birds to deer, and butterflies to hedgehogs.

Things to see

Fountains Hall
Sir Stephen Proctor built this elegant mansion as his country home in the early seventeenth century. He reused sandstone blocks and a stone staircase from the Abbey but had fresh limestone cut for the windows and main façade. Since then, several families have called the Hall their home, including five generations of the Messengers. The Vyner family were the last to reside in the Hall before it was sold to the West Riding County Council.

Above: Picturesque view along the walking trail at Fountains Abbey and Studley Royal Water Garden, Yorkshire.

Birdlife at Fountains Abbey
The monitoring and conservation of birds is an important part of the work the National Trust does at the Abbey. Nest box checking and bird ringing is undertaken to contribute to an overall understanding of population numbers across the country. Birds you can expect to see are goldfinches, blue tits, jackdaws, great spotted woodpecker, green woodpecker (Studley Royal deer park), song thrush, geese and swans. A protected species, the marsh tit, has also nested at the Abbey.

Studley Royal Deer Park
Studley Royal Deer Park is a much-loved part of the estate, and home to over 500 wild red, fallow and sika deer. The deer park once contained the Tudor manor house known as Studley Royal House – but this was largely destroyed by fire in 1716. Its Palladian successor was also damaged by fire in 1946 and was demolished shortly afterwards. The deer park also contains a large variety of ancient trees – many are over 300 years old. The lime tree avenue leads the eye down through the deer park to the original entrance to the estate and all the way to Ripon Cathedral.

How to Get There

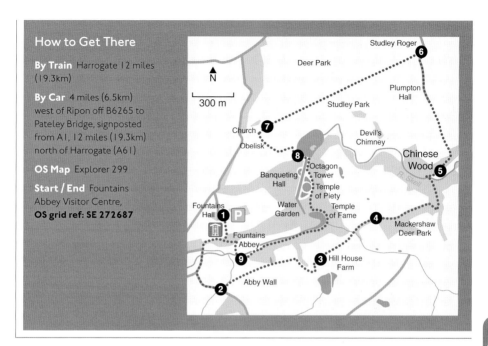

By Train Harrogate 12 miles (19.3km)

By Car 4 miles (6.5km) west of Ripon off B6265 to Pateley Bridge, signposted from A1, 12 miles (19.3km) north of Harrogate (A61)

OS Map Explorer 299

Start / End Fountains Abbey Visitor Centre, **OS grid ref: SE 272687**

1. Leave the Visitor Centre on the main (right-hand) access path to the Abbey. Pass Swanley Grange, following signs to Fountains Hall. Pass the Hall on the right and go through the West Gate exit, turning left onto the road to Harrogate. Follow the road uphill for ¼ mile (400m), turning left at a gate by a bridleway sign.

2. Go through the gate and follow the clear path ahead – initially with a hedge on the right and then the Abbey wall. On reaching the end of the wall, go through a gate and cross a field, by a fenced path. Take the last gate on the right to follow a clear farm track to Hill House Farm.

3. Initially turn right past farm buildings – watch out for waymarkers taking you first left and then right past the final farm buildings and through a gate into a field. Continue ahead on a clear track until the hedge on your right ends. Then veer slightly left and go through a gate into the corner of the wood ahead of you.

4. Follow the well-marked path ahead, along the left-hand edge of the wood, passing the impressive estate gate, ruined Mackershaw Lodges and the Mackershaw Deer Park beyond. Continue along the woodland path with a wall to your left, eventually

Above: The Temple of Piety.

bearing right downhill to a junction of paths. Take the left-hand path, continuing downhill to reach the River Skell.

5. Ignore the ford and take the footbridge river crossing to your left. Turn right at the end of the footbridge and follow a clear track uphill to emerge from the woodland through a gate at the top. Continue to follow the clear track ahead, with a hedge on the left. Take in the glorious views to your right over Ripon and in the distance the edge of the North Yorkshire Moors, Sutton Bank and the White Horse.

6. Pass the medieval Plumpton Hall farmhouse on your left and continue until you reach the Studley Royal driveway. Walk up the driveway, through the impressive East Gateway and Lodges, towards St Mary's Church spire ahead of you. Just before you reach the church, turn round and take in the magnificent view down the tree-lined driveway to Ripon Cathedral and the North Yorkshire Moors beyond.

7. From the church, turn left off the driveway and take the grass path downhill, past a rustic seat, to

the lakeside car park. Continue downhill to the lake itself, the Victorian tea-rooms and the impressive lakeside gateway to the formal water gardens and Fountains Abbey.

8. Go through the gate and take the first left turn, which takes you over the canal by the cascade waterfall. Follow the clear path, passing the Moon Pond and the Temple of Piety. Continue along the path, turning left at the next junction to pass the half moon pond and along the left bank of the River Skell. Revel in the views of the Abbey ruins ahead.

9. Continue along the path to eventually reach the Abbey. Take time to explore the ruins and then return to the Visitor Centre via the clearly waymarked path uphill from the Abbey.

Make the Most of Your Day
There is much to explore at this World Heritage Site and events take place throughout the year.

Food and Facilities
There is a restaurant and tea-room at Fountains Abbey. Toilets can be found at the main car park and Fountains Hall.

Above: Spring at Fountains Abbey and Studley Royal Water Garden, Yorkshire.

81. Nunnington Hall up Bank and Round Rye Walk

Enjoy this walk around historic Nunnington Hall, taking in the views from Caulkleys Bank followed by a peaceful stroll along the River Rye. This beautiful spot on the North York Moors is home to a wealth of plants and wildlife.

Nunnington
Near York
North Yorkshire
YO62 5UY
01439 748283
nunningtonhall@
nationaltrust.org.uk

About this walk
Panoramic views

Peaceful river walk

Dogs welcome, but keep under close control around livestock

Distance 4½ miles (7.2km)

Time 2–2 hours 30 mins

North East

Things to see

Nunnington Hall
A dwelling of status has been recorded on this site from 1249, but the existing house has grown out of a Tudor hall. Over the past 450 years, the house and estate have been altered to suit a succession of owners and tenants. The house you see today is a fascinating combination of renovation and re-purpose, creating an atmospheric and comfortable home.

Caulkelys Bank
Enjoy the panoramic views from Caulkleys Bank. A trig point marks the highest point.

River Rye
This is the main river of the western moors and drains much of the higher ground in the area. In its lower reaches the Rye is a gentle, meandering river and supports a variety of wildlife.

Above: Roses in the garden at Nunnington Hall, North Yorkshire.

Below: The south front of Nunnington Hall seen from the gardens in June.

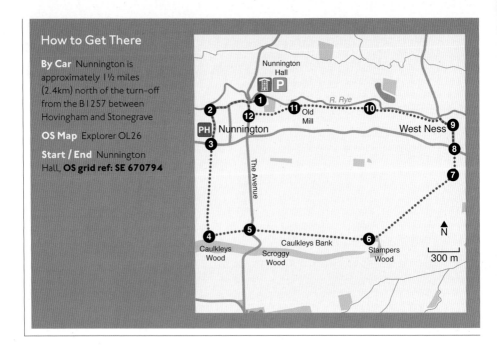

How to Get There

By Car Nunnington is approximately 1½ miles (2.4km) north of the turn-off from the B1257 between Hovingham and Stonegrave

OS Map Explorer OL26

Start / End Nunnington Hall, **OS grid ref: SE 670794**

1. Leave Nunnington Hall through the main gates, don't go over the bridge. Cross the road with care and bear right onto Low Street.

2. Continue along Low Street, turn left at the end into Church Street and proceed uphill past the Church.

3. At the junction, carry straight onto a rough track following a finger post towards 'Stonegrave 1 mile'.

4. At the top of the bank, you reach a three-way finger post; turn left at this point towards the Avenue.

5. On reaching the road, cross over to the wide verge and enjoy the stunning views. Follow the finger post to West Ness along the crest of Caulkleys Bank.

6. Cross the stone track above Stampers Wood and follow the public bridleway, which is flanked by hedgerows.

7. After passing farm buildings the bridleway sinks into a stone-bottomed track as it descends towards the lane near West Ness.

8. On meeting the tarmac lane, bear left towards Kirkbymoorside rather than turning left to Nunnington.

9. After 275 yards (250m), the road bends sharply left, then passes farm buildings, a disused chapel and a phone box. Do not cross the bridge over the River Rye, turn left on the footpath.

10. The path follows the river upstream back to Nunnington. You'll pass the Old Mill with its nearby weir.

11. Follow waymarkers away from the river to skirt around the boundary of Nunnington Hall.

12. Turn right at the road and head back towards the Hall.

Make the Most of Your Day

Nunnington Hall is a picturesque Yorkshire manor house on the banks of the River Rye. You can explore the period rooms and the organic walled garden with its flamboyant resident peacocks. The house also hosts exciting exhibitions and is home to the Baby House, one of the world's finest collections of miniature rooms.

Food and Facilities

The tea-room is located in the historic house and there is a tea-garden outside for dog owners. Toilets are located in the house.

82. Nostell Menagerie Garden Walk

This walk takes in the peace and tranquillity of the lakes, pleasure grounds and gardens at Nostell. Listen out for woodpeckers (green lesser spotted and great spotted) in the woodlands, and look for herons, swans and ducks as you walk along the lakeside paths.

Nostell
Doncaster Road
Wakefield
West Yorkshire
WF4 1QE
01924 863892
nostellpriory@nationaltrust.org.uk

About this walk
Peace and quiet

Historic garden features

Lovely views

No dogs allowed in the garden

Distance 1⅓ miles (2.2km)

Time 45 mins

Things to see

The Lakes
The Winn family kept a small boat in the boathouse and would have enjoyed boating on the Lower Lake. There are lovely views across the tree-lined lake from here. From the Swiss Bridge you can see both the Middle and Lower Lake divided by a cascade; the small stone bridge is the restored Druids Bridge.

Gothic Arch
The Gothic Arch was built along with the development of the Menagerie Garden between 1759 and 1761 on the site of a medieval quarry. If you take a closer look you will notice evidence of pebble dashing both inside and out; this is original and would have once covered the entire building. Bats roost in the crevices of the arch today.

The Menagerie Garden
Did you notice the cock-fighting pit, now a pond and home to both smooth and great crested newts? Beneath the large holm oak tree there are the remnants of a stone lion. The garden was once home to a large black-eyed lioness which was once reported as lost in 1882. This and other animals were kept in cages along the quarry wall.

Above: Cattle in the parkland at Nostell, West Yorkshire.

Below: A lake in the grounds of Nostell Priory and Parkland.

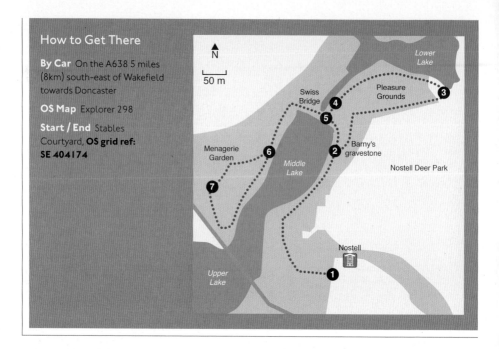

Map labels: N, 50 m, Lower Lake, Swiss Bridge, Pleasure Grounds, Menagerie Garden, Barny's gravestone, Middle Lake, Nostell Deer Park, Nostell, Upper Lake

1. Follow the footpath opposite the garden entrance signposted 'Lakeside Walks'. This path will lead towards the back of the house and you will have glimpses over the lake towards the Menagerie Garden.

2. Go through the small gateway and follow the footpath on the right. Look out for Barny's gravestone, one of the Winn's dogs. At the bottom of the slope follow the path to the right.

3. You are now in the area of the gardens known as the Pleasure Grounds. At the bottom of the slope you can see the Boat House and Lower Lake.

4. Continue along the footpath where you will pass Druids Bridge. Glance back for a view of the Obelisk then scale the steps. To avoid the steps, branch left away from the lake, then keep right until you see the Middle Lake.

5. Turn right and go over Swiss Bridge to continue your lakeside walk.

6. At the fork in the path, take the route that branches out left along the lake to the large cedar tree with views to the bridge. You will then come to the Gothic Arch, the entrance to the Menagerie Garden.

7. Through the magnolia trees and beyond the acers there is the Menagerie House, built as a keeper's house with garden room. Hidden in the trees behind is the ice house where ice was stored, once collected from the lake. The structure is now unstable and is not safe to enter. Leaving the Menagerie Garden you will pass by the dell. From here, return to the lakeside path and the route back. Retrace your steps over the Swiss Bridge, then turn right up the hill and back to the courtyard.

Make the Most of Your Day

The decorative interiors at Nostell were designed by Robert Adam and the ornate rooms are home to a world-class collection of Chippendale furniture and one of the first long-case clocks made by inventor John Harrison. As well as the wonderful gardens, outside there is an adventure play area and woodland cycle trails. There are also regular tours, talks and events and special activities throughout the year. Although dogs are not allowed in the garden, they are welcome in the parkland.

Food and Facilities

A café, shop and toilets are located in the Courtyard.

83. Longshaw Estate Woodland Walk

The wetlands, meadows and woodlands of Longshaw play host to a range of wildlife, including many species of birds, dragonflies, damselflies, butterflies, wood ants, badgers and red deer.

Longshaw
Near Sheffield
Derbyshire
S11 7TZ
01433 637904
peakdistrict@nationaltrust.org.uk

About this walk
Birdlife
Ancient woodland
Wildlife interest
Dogs welcome on leads
Distance 2¼ miles (3.6km)
Time 1 hour

Things to see

Birdlife
The Longshaw Estate provides a home for many birds, either as residents or visitors, such as the great spotted and green woodpecker, pied flycatcher, redstart, swallow, dipper and nuthatch.

Padley Wood
The ancient woodland of Padley Wood is the most important on the estate. It is one of the best examples of the old oak-birch woodland that once covered much of the Peak District.

Longshaw Lodge
The lodge was built around 1827 as a shooting retreat for the Duke of Rutland and his guests, amongst whom were King George V and the Duke of Wellington. In 1927 the Longshaw Estate was put up for sale and in 1931, after a fund-raising campaign to save the estate, it was handed to the National Trust. For a while the lodge was let to the Holiday Fellowship as a guesthouse, but in 1969 it was converted into private flats.

Left: Cobweb with dew drops on an autumn morning at Longshaw, Burbage and the Eastern Moors, Derbyshire.

Above: Winter evening sunshine filters through the trees at Padley Gorge on the Longshaw Estate.

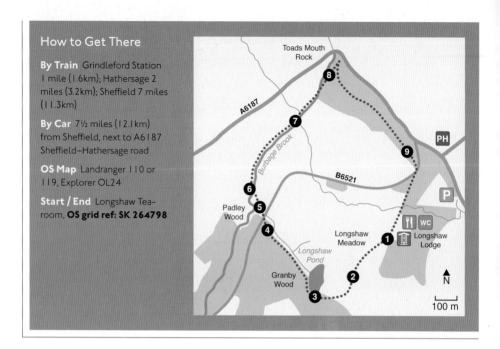

How to Get There

By Train Grindleford Station
1 mile (1.6km); Hathersage 2
miles (3.2km); Sheffield 7 miles
(11.3km)

By Car 7½ miles (12.1km)
from Sheffield, next to A6187
Sheffield–Hathersage road

OS Map Landranger 110 or
119, Explorer OL24

Start / End Longshaw Tea-
room, **OS grid ref: SK 264798**

1. From the tea-room, cross the drive and turn left along the path by the fence. Go through a small gate. Turn right and go downhill to, and through, the next gate.

2. Follow the path downhill, through a corridor of rhododendron bushes, to Longshaw Pond. Longshaw Meadow will be on your right as you walk.

3. Follow the path round the pond, then downhill through Granby Wood, named after the Marquis of Granby, the Duke of Rutland's son. It was replanted with Scots pine in 1990.

4. Go past the small barn and through a small gate before crossing the road, then go through another gate a little further down the road.

5. Cross the bridge over Burbage Brook. To the left is Padley Wood. The sunken track leading away from the bridge is Hollowgate. It was once a busy route for packhorses, carrying goods across the Peak District.

6. Walk upstream along the side of the brook. The alder trees on the banks of the brook need wet or damp ground to survive.

7. Continue up to the next bridge and cross over it to the path on the other side. This path was repaired by our wardens using an old technique known as stone pitching, which is embedding small stones into the ground like cobblestones.

8. Walk up the path, looking out for Toad's Mouth Rock on the roadside to the left. At the junction, near a small stream, turn right to a gate. Continue through the wood to a white gate.

9. Cross the road to the entrance of Longshaw Lodge and return to the tea-room along the drive.

Make the Most of Your Day
It's all about the outdoors at Longshaw, with its natural play trail and waymarked walks, organised runs and a range of other activities for all the family.

Food and Facilities
Refreshments and toilets are available in the tea-room.

84. A Bracing Walk at Derwent Valley

Near Derwent Dam
Peak District
Derbyshire
S33 0AQ
01433 670368
peakdistrict@nationaltrust.org.uk

About this walk
Wonderful views

Military history

Wildlife interest

Rough walking on varied terrain

Dogs welcome

Distance 4 miles (6.4km)

Time 1 hour 20 mins

Wonderful for taking in the many Peak District habitats, this walk takes you alongside the Ladybower Reservoir, through farmland, and emerges high on the moors with fantastic views of the Derwent Valley and opportunities to spot local wildlife.

Above: A mountain hare in its winter coat.

North East

Things to see

Derwent Valley and Dam
This area is good for certain types of bats. If you are walking at dusk, look out for noctule, pipistrelle and Daubenton's bats. The brown long-eared bat is also present in this area, although sightings are rare. Derwent Dam and its twin, Howden Dam, were built at the beginning of the century and became famous for being used for RAF flying practice for the Barnes Wallis bouncing bomb in 1943. It subsequently featured in the acclaimed Second World War film, *The Dam Busters* (1955).

Pike Low
This Bronze Age barrow, or burial mound, can be found at the highest point on the moor. The moors provide habitat for a variety of birds, including birds of prey. You may be lucky enough to spot some of England's only mountain hare population. In winter, their fur turns white, acting as camouflage.

Right: The shore of Derwent Reservoir in the Peak District.

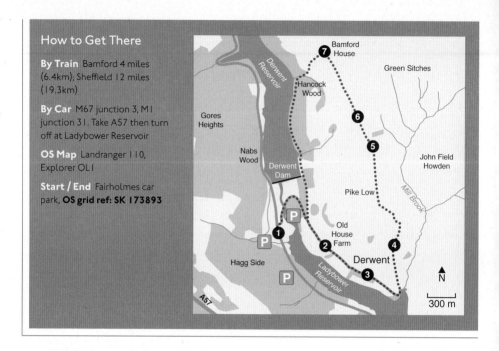

How to Get There

By Train Bamford 4 miles (6.4km); Sheffield 12 miles (19.3km)

By Car M67 junction 3, M1 junction 31. Take A57 then turn off at Ladybower Reservoir

OS Map Landranger 110, Explorer OL1

Start / End Fairholmes car park, **OS grid ref: SK 173893**

Bamford House
Green Sitches
Hancock Wood
Derwent Reservoir
Gores Heights
Nabs Wood
Derwent Dam
John Field Howden
Pike Low
Mill Brook
Old House Farm
Hagg Side
Derwent
Ladybower Reservoir
A57
N
300 m

1. Turn right out of Fairholmes car park and follow the road towards Derwent Dam.

2. Walk past the Dam and follow the road uphill, walking alongside Ladybower Reservoir on the right and Old House Farm on the left, towards the site of the old Derwent village.

3. The village was flooded when the Dam was built in the Second World War. Only two buildings remain: the Lodge and the schoolroom. To view the site of the village and an information panel, continue down the slope and across a bridge. Retrace your route back up the short slope and at the top, turn sharp right at the end of a high wall onto a track, over a stile and past the ruins of a farm.

4. Continue uphill until just after a cottage where the path divides. Keep left and climb through open fields and over a stile onto moorland. After about ½ mile (800m) and a right turn by a wall corner, as the track levels, you will pass Pike Low 100 yards (90m) on your left.

5. Continue along this track above Mill Brook, below on your right. Follow the track to the Scots pine shelter belt ahead, the site of a substantial shooting cabin,

with two lines of grouse butts running towards Green Sitches. Keep left at a fork just before the pines.

6. Follow the track until it turns right at a fence. Cross the fence by the stile and continue to the derelict farmstead of Bamford House along the edge of the moor, with Derwent Reservoir below on your left.

7. On reaching Bamford House, turn left and take the steep path downhill towards the reservoir. Turn left again once you reach Derwent Reservoir and follow this track alongside the reservoir and back towards Derwent Dam and Fairholmes car park.

Make the Most of Your Day

There is so much to explore at many different locations across the Dark Peak, including Mam Tor, Kinder Scout, Snake Pass, Alport Castle and the reservoirs. It doesn't all have to be on foot – you can hire bikes from a number of locations in the Peak District National Park, including Derwent.

Food and Facilities

There is a refreshment kiosk and toilets at Fairholmes car park. The Penny Pot Café in Edale is an ideal place to warm up, with its log-burner and hearty food.

Opposite: Murlough National Nature Reserve (walk 93)

Northern Ireland

85. Castle Coole Lake Walk

This pleasant, gentle walk takes you around the tranquil Lough Coole, providing opportunities for wildlife spotting and glimpses of the magnificent mansion house along the way.

Castle Coole
Enniskillen
County Fermanagh
BT74 6JY
028 6632 269
castlecoole@nationaltrust.org.uk

About this walk
A gentle, peaceful walk
Wonderful views
Wildlife interest
Dogs welcome on leads

Distance Just over 1 mile (1.8km)

Time 30 mins

Things to see

Queen Anne House
To the south of Lough Coole is the site of the Queen Anne house, which was destroyed by fire in 1789. In the mid-eighteenth century between the house and the lough, a formal garden was laid out which comprised raised parterres and a sunken bowling green; a water garden was also added with a canal stretching 275 yards (250m) to the north-east known as the Banjo Lake. Traces of some of these features can still be seen.

Area of Special Scientific Interest
Castle Coole has been designated an Area of Special Scientific Interest (ASSI) by the Northern Ireland Environment Agency due to its rich parkland habitat and associated species. In places where the tree canopy is denser, a woodland flora has developed, with typical species such as wood anemone, bluebell, pignut, primrose, lords-and-ladies and the notable bird's nest orchid. The wetland vegetation fringing Lough Coole provides even more diversity with species such as common reed and water horsetail, and the wet grassland supports a range of plants including quaking grass, carnation sedge, devil's-bit scabious and meadow vetchling.

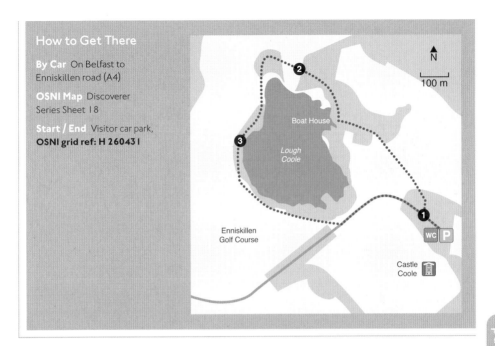

How to Get There

By Car On Belfast to Enniskillen road (A4)

OSNI Map Discoverer Series Sheet 18

Start / End Visitor car park, **OSNI grid ref: H 260431**

Boat House

Lough Coole

Enniskillen Golf Course

Castle Coole

N

100 m

Above: The south façade of Castle Coole seen from across Lough Coole.

Opposite above: Wildflower meadow and Castle Coole, County Fermanagh.

1. Starting from the visitor car park, take the path on the right past the play park. This path passes the site of the original Queen Anne house. At the boat house, turn right and follow the path around the lake.

2. Shortly after the boat house, a gravel path to your left reaches the shore of the Lough. Take a stroll down, see if you can spot our resident swans before returning to the path and continuing your walk.

3. At this point, catch glimpses of views of the house across the lake. Continue on the path, taking a left at the main exit road and another once that reaches the drive. Continue on up the hill to return to the visitor car park.

Make the Most of Your Day

Built in the eighteenth century, Castle Coole is one of Ireland's finest Neo-classical houses. Here you can discover the story of the people who lived and worked below stairs as you explore the suite of servants rooms and service quarters of this magnificent property.

Food and Facilities

The Tallow House Tea-room provides meals and snacks. Toilets available during estate opening hours.

86. Nature Walk at Crom

Upper Lough Erne
Newtownbutler
County Fermanagh
BT92 8AP
028 6773 8118
crom@nationaltrust.org.uk

About this walk
Autumn fruit and berries

Wildlife interest

Crom is open until the end of October

Dogs welcome on leads

Distance 3½ miles (5.6km)

Time 1 hour 10 mins

The mature oak woodland, meadows, parkland and snaking waterways of Upper Lough Erne mean Crom is a haven for wildlife. The estate is home to a vast array of rare species like otters, red squirrels and pine martens, as well as some of the UK's scarcest butterflies and moths. The lough also attracts many wetland bird species.

Things to see

Boathouse and Orchard

Enjoy the view of the boathouse from point 3 on the map, after you cross over White Bridge. To the north of the walled garden is Crom's orchard, which was planted some time in the late nineteenth century and flourished until the 1960s. The orchard has been re-established by restoring the existing trees and planting saplings of traditional varieties.

Butterflies

Crom is a hotspot for butterflies in Northern Ireland, who appreciate the flower-rich meadows and hedgerows. The woodland glades and mature oaks provide a home for rare species like the silver washed fritillary and the purple hairstreak butterflies as well as the dark umber moth.

Above: Fallow deer grazing peacefully at Crom Estate, County Fermanagh.

Below: Long grass at Crom being mown in September.

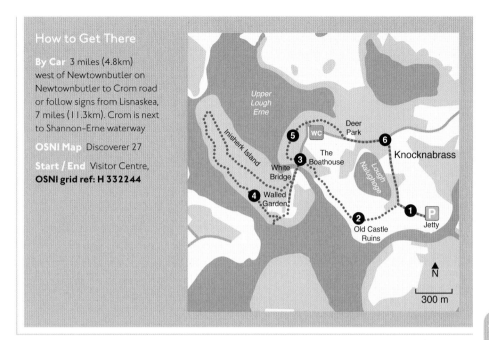

N. Ireland

How to Get There

By Car 3 miles (4.8km) west of Newtownbutler on Newtownbutler to Crom road or follow signs from Lisnaskea, 7 miles (11.3km). Crom is next to Shannon-Erne waterway

OSNI Map Discoverer 27

Start / End Visitor Centre, **OSNI grid ref: H 332244**

Upper Lough Erne

Inisherk Island

Deer Park

The Boathouse

Knocknabrass

White Bridge

Lough Nalughoge

Walled Garden

Old Castle Ruins

Jetty

N

300 m

1. Start at the Visitor Centre; its barns are a roosting site for bats, with seven different species inhabiting this area. Turn left as you leave the yard and walk along the old carriageway towards Crom Castle for a short while before turning left again through a gate into the parkland.

2. Follow the path to the Old Castle. Here you'll encounter one of the oldest yew trees in Ireland. Estimates of its age vary between 400 and 1,000 years. Be careful not to damage its roots or branches.

3. Continue along the loughside, past the pretty boathouse, before crossing the White Bridge onto Inisherk Island. Around here, and around points 4 and 5, you can harvest fruits and berries from the hedgerows and bushes. Be careful to only pick berries that you know are safe, such as blackberries and raspberries.

4. Make a little loop of the island, passing the Walled Garden. Here, and at point 5, you should keep a look out for rare red squirrels, which you may see foraging for nuts to store for winter.

5. Cross back over the bridge and turn left, taking a path through trees with Upper Lough Erne on your left and the grounds of Crom Castle to your right.

6. Reach the castle's main drive and continue walking until a path breaks off to your right near the small inland Lough Nalughoge. Continue on to return to the Visitor Centre and the car park.

Make the Most of Your Day
Located on the shores of Upper Lough Erne, Crom is one of the most romantic and peaceful places in Northern Ireland. After your walk you can visit the castle ruins, hire a boat, go fishing or spend time birdwatching. The grounds are open all year round.

Food and Facilities
Refreshments and toilets are available at the Visitor Centre, which is open until the end of October (weekends only).

87. Sand Dune and Estuary Walk

Portstewart Strand
118 Strand Road
Portstewart
County Londonderry
BT55 7PG
028 7083 6396
portstewart@nationaltrust.org.uk

About this walk
Sandy beach

Birdlife

Historic ruins

Some steep paths

Dogs welcome on leads until the lifebuoy stations

Distance 3½ miles (5.6km)

Time 2 hours

The coast at Portstewart Strand provides the perfect backdrop for a walk. Enjoy the long stretch of magnificent golden sand and the 6,000-year-old dunes that line the river edge at the Bann estuary, a favourite haven for birds.

Things to see

Saltmarsh
The dunes are home to robins, goldfinches, dunnocks, goldcrest, bullfinch and blackcaps. The Bann estuary usually supports about 4,000 birds each winter, including oystercatchers, black-headed gulls and several species of duck.

Sand Dunes
The spectacular sand dune system at Portstewart Strand has been declared an Area of Special Scientific Interest due to the rare and fragile habitats and wildlife that it supports. The National Trust is working in partnership with the

Northern Ireland Environment Agency to maintain and protect the site. Cattle graze the dunes during winter, allowing wildflowers like bird's-foot trefoil, wild thyme, pyramidal orchid and the northern marsh orchid to flourish the following spring and summer.

Above: A family on the dunes at Portstewart Strand, County Londonderry.

Right: Misty beach at Portstewart Strand.

How to Get There

By Car Take A2 to Portstewart and follow signs to The Strand

OSNI Map Discoverer 4

Start / End Entrance to the Strand, **OSNI grid ref: C 813368**

Atlantic Ocean

Strand entrance

LBS 14   LBS 10   LBS 8

Crab Bay

Dunes

Dunes

R. Bann

N

400 m

1. Start your walk at the entrance to the Strand and make your way to lifebuoy station 8 or 10, approximately 1 mile (1.6km) from the entrance.

2. Climb the steps at these stations and soon you will enjoy the tranquillity of the dunes.

3. There are three ways you can reach the Bann estuary. From station 8, proceed into the dunes, keeping the fence on your right. At the bottom of the hill, go through the kissing gate, climb the hill and keep the fence on your left until you reach the Bann estuary, exiting through the kissing gate onto the saltmarsh. Alternatively, at station 10, enter through the left kissing gate and proceed directly along the path, exiting a kissing gate to the Bann estuary. Or, once again from station 10, enter through the right kissing gate and follow the small waymarker posts to the Bann estuary, exiting the kissing gate onto the saltmarsh. Be aware that cattle graze within all fenced areas and on the saltmarsh from October to April.

4. On arrival at the Bann estuary by any of the above three routes, turn right along the saltmarsh.

5. Follow the paths through the saltmarsh and you will arrive at a kissing gate onto a small beach and bay. At the end of the beach ascend back into the dunes and follow the path along the edge of the river.

6. This will bring you back onto the beach at lifebuoy station 14 from where it is approximately 2 miles (3.2km) back along the beach to the Strand entrance.

Make the Most of Your Day
Across the river estuary, Downhill Demesne is a striking eighteenth-century mansion that was owned by the eccentric Earl Bishop and now lies in ruin. Mussenden Temple, that once held the Bishop's library, is perched on the cliff edge.

Food and Facilities
Refreshments are available in Harry's Shack and toilet facilities are available during National Trust staff working hours. Additional refreshments and public toilets can be found in Portstewart.

88. Giant's Causeway Trail

This is a bracing cliff-top walk with spectacular views of the world-famous Causeway Coast and North Channel. The prime habitats in this area are home to a huge range of different species of plants, fungi, lichen, birds, spiders, beetles, butterflies and moths.

Giant's Causeway
60 Causeway Road
Bushmills
County Antrim
BT57 8SU
028 2073 1855
giantscausewaytic@gmail.com

About this walk

Breathtaking views

Wildlife interest

162 stone steps with handrail

Please be aware of unfenced cliff edges, high winds, steep steps and rock falls

Dogs welcome on leads

Distance ⁴/₅–2 miles (1.3–3.2km)

Time 30 mins–1 hour 30 mins

Things to see

Grand Causeway
Get a bird's-eye view of the causeway bays from the Red Trail that runs along the cliff-top. The rock outcrop stretching into the sea is the Grand Causeway.

Stonechats
In the fields opposite the Aird, you may hear the call of the stonechat. It's similar to the sound of two stones being hit together. They're small birds, with distinctive black heads and white necks. There's lots of other wildlife to spot in the surrounding heath and grasses, which are full of insects.

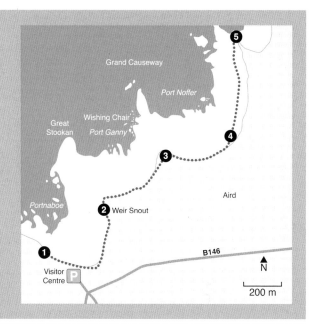

How to Get There

By Train Regular train services operate from Belfast or Londonderry to Coleraine, then by bus

By Car On the B147 Causeway road, 2 miles (3.2km) from Bushmills village, 11 miles (17.7km) from Coleraine and 13 miles (20.9km) from Ballycastle

OSNI Map Discoverer Series 4 and 5

Start / End Car park 1, **OSNI grid ref: C 946438**

Map labels: Grand Causeway; Port Noffer; Wishing Chair; Great Stookan; Port Ganny; Portnaboe; Weir Snout; Aird; B146; Visitor Centre; N; 200 m

---

1. Assume your starting point in front of the Causeway Hotel. Facing the hotel entrance, turn right and walk in the direction of the Visitor Centre. You'll see the sloping grass roof of the Visitor Centre; providing no conservation work is in progress, you can cut across the roof and pick up signs for the Red Trail from the rear. There's a wooden plinth with a map and directions.

2. Continue along the visible path and up a steep hill leading to Weir Snout. Look for the viewfinder to get more information on the views from this point.

3. Following the visible trail from the Weir Snout Viewpoint (away from the Visitor Centre) you'll arrive on top, but inland from, the headland known as the Aird. You'll see boulders that act as a deterrent to people walking out onto this headland. This area is spectacular but extremely dangerous, particularly in high winds. It's not fenced off and we urge visitors to exercise due caution.

Opposite above: Waves crash against the Giant's Causeway, County Antrim.

Opposite below: Visitors perch on the Giant's Organ, long trunk-like rocks.

4. At this point along the path, you'll come to the top of the Shepherd's Steps. Onwards, the path becomes the Yellow Trail and leads to the Hamilton's Seat, taking in an aerial view of the Amphitheatre. To follow the Red Trail, descend the steps from the cliff-top. When you get to the bottom of the steps, you can choose to follow the trail towards the Organ (point 5 on the map), or turn left and head towards the Grand Causeway, linking to the Blue Trail.

Make the Most of Your Day

The Visitor Centre at Giant's Causeway includes interactive exhibits of science and stories. You can also find out about guided or independent walks. Proceeds help the National Trust look after and protect this unique landscape.

Food and Facilities

Refreshments available at the Nook Bar and Restaurant and the Causeway Hotel. Toilets at 'groups' entrance during Visitor Centre opening hours.

89. Springhill Beech Walk

The Beech Walk at Springhill leads you through an avenue of beech trees that was replanted in 1984; only one of the original trees remains at the beginning of the walk. The trees provide stunning colour throughout the year, from vivid green in the spring to rich reds in the autumn.

20 Springhill Road
Moneymore
County Londonderry
BT45 7NQ
028 8674 8210
springhill@nationaltrust.
org.uk

About this walk
Wildflower displays

Ancient trees

Lovely views

Dogs are welcome but must be kept on a lead

Distance ⅓ mile (0.5km)

Time 15 mins

N. Ireland

Things to see

Wildflowers and Fungi

In spring bluebells appear at Springhill and the air is scented with wild garlic. Snowdrops can be seen elsewhere on the estate. As summer comes so do more wildflowers, like the broad-leaved helleborine and the pig nut. In autumn there is a fantastic display of fungi, of all different shapes and colours, such as the beech milkcap and the grey coral.

The Tower

The Tower at Springhill has had many uses since it was built in 1731. It was originally a corn mill powered by the wind.

Above: The garden at Springhill, County Londonderry.

Opposite: Small tortoiseshell butterfly in the garden at Springhill.

Above: The rear of the seventeenth-century 'Planter' house, Springhill, taken from the Beech Walk, with the Sperrin Mountains beyond.

How to Get There

By Car On Moneymore to Coagh road, B18. 1 mile (1.6km) from Moneymore village

OSNI Map Sheet 14

Start / End Springhill House, **OSNI grid ref: H 866828**

1. Begin at the back of the house, at the crossroads of the gravelled paths.

2. With your back to the house, you will see the gravel track that leads to the beech avenue. The avenue stretches out in front of you with a clear vista straight up to the Tower.

3. The trees that line the route are beech, which were replanted in 1984. The fourth tree on your left as you begin your walk is the last remaining beech of the original planting. It is a huge specimen that is approximately 300 years old.

4. The gravel path turns to grass as you pass over the ha-ha ditch. The ha-ha is a landscape design feature dug into the ground to prevent access to livestock without interrupting the view from the house with an unsightly fence or wall.

5. As you continue up the beech avenue, on closer inspection you will notice a wide variety of flora beneath the trees.

6. When you reach the tower, you will see a stone at the front depicting the date it was built – 1731. From the tower on a clear day there are wonderful views of the Sperrin Mountains. Return via the same route you came.

Make the Most of Your Day

Springhill is a seventeenth-century home with ten generations of Lenox-Conyngham family tales to enthral you, as well as numerous portraits and much furniture to admire. The old laundry houses the celebrated Costume Collection, which features some fine pieces from the eighteenth to the twentieth century.

Food and Facilities

Picnics are welcome in the garden. A café and toilets can be found at Springhill House.

90. Lime Tree Walk

The Lime Tree Walk at the Argory is an avenue of pollarded limes underplanted with wildflowers. This walk passes the oak plantation and follows a section of the River Blackwater before returning to the house.

The Argory
144 Derrycaw Road
Moy
Dungannon
County Armagh
BT71 6NA
028 8778 4753
argory@nationaltrust.org.uk

About this walk
Wildflower displays

River views

Dogs are welcome at The Argory but must be kept on a lead

Distance 2 miles (3.2km)

Time 40 mins

Above: The Lime Avenue in the garden at The Argory, County Armagh.

Right: The south and east fronts of The Argory.

Things to see

The Argory
Built in the 1820s, this handsome Irish gentry house is surrounded by its 320 acre (130ha) wooded riverside estate. This Neo-classical masterpiece is the former home of the MacGeough Bond family; its interior has remained unchanged since 1900 and still evokes the family's tastes and interests.

River Blackwater
The River Blackwater that flows past The Argory is a haven for kingfishers. This famously colourful bird of rivers and streams is surprisingly small, only about 7in (18cm) in length, with a long straight bill. They sit quietly on low-hanging branches over the water, diving in to spear fish with their sharp beaks.

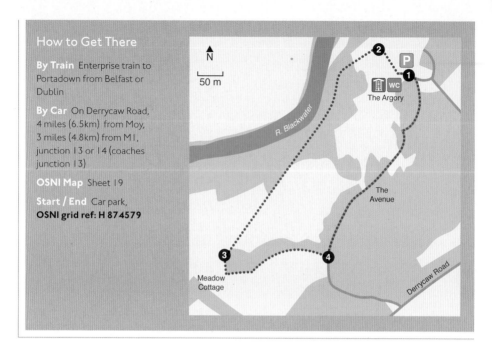

1. From the car park near reception and The Argory Courtyard, follow the path towards the Pavilion, the stone building with narrow windows.

2. Join the path at the pavilion with the river on your right and the ha-ha wall on your left. Stay on this path and within five minutes you will be under the canopy of lime trees. In spring you will also be surrounded by a carpet of snowdrops.

3. At the end of the lime trees you can go past Meadow Cottage on the right and see the wildflower meadow throughout the season.

4. At this point you can either walk up the avenue and see The Argory in all its glory or else join Lady Bond's Walk, which is to the right.

Make the Most of Your Day

The house and gardens are well worth a visit. Highlights include the cantilevered staircase in the West Hall, the elegant Drawing Room with its rosewood Steinway grand piano (you can even have a go!). During February there are self-guided snowdrop walks where you can see the wonderful varieties of snowdrops planted over the years by our estate staff and volunteers. Visit the rose garden and see the octagonal brass sundial. You can let the kids run wild in the adventure play park, where they can test their balancing and climbing skills or dare to zip the zip line. Enjoy all these activities at your leisure and then visit the Courtyard coffee shop for a drink or a tasty bite to eat. Plants are also available to buy.

Food and Facilities

There is a café, tea-room and toilets at The Argory, as well as a gift shop and second-hand bookshop.

91. Divis and the Black Mountain Ridge Trail

This walk offers exhilarating views across Northern Ireland: on a clear day you can see as far as Scotland, the Isle of Man and Cumbria. The upland bog was once a great place for extracting turf, and the thin peat and acid soils support plants such as sphagnum, bog cotton and bog asphodel, which are specially adapted to surviving in these harsh habitats.

Divis and the Black Mountain
Hannahstown
Belfast
County Antrim
BT17 0NG
028 9082 5434
divis@nationaltrust.org.uk

About this walk
Exhilarating views

Important habitat

Cartographic interest

Gravel and stone trail with some steep sections

Dogs welcome under close control

Distance 4⅕ miles (6.8km)

Time 3 hours

Things to see

Flora and Fauna

The mountains comprise a mosaic of grassland heath and bog and are home to a host of wildlife, plants and archaeological remains. The site is significant for biodiversity with red grouse, stonechats, skylark, snipe and other upland breeding birds. Peregrine falcons and ravens also feed in the area. The heath is home to some interesting flora, including purple devil's-bit scabious in autumn. Along the short grasses on the riverbanks you may discover the many colours of waxcaps during the colder months.

Trigonometry Point

A pillar marks the summit of the Black Mountain at a height of 1,275ft (389m), and was used in the mapping of Ireland in 1825. Triangulation from trig pillars is a mathematical process that made accurate map-making possible. Angles were measured from the pillar to other surrounding trig points and, for greatest accuracy, many rounds of angles would have been measured with the observations taking several hours.

Above: Divis and the Black Mountain in the snow.

Left: Walk to the summit of the Black Mountain to enjoy stunning views.

How to Get There

By Car Leave M1 motorway at junction 2 (Stockman's Lane). Take the A55 (Outer Ring), signposted Falls. Access from Divis Road, off Upper Springfield Road. Signposted from Monagh Road

OSNI Map Discovery 15

Start / End Divis Ranger Office, **OSNI grid ref: J 272744**

N

300 m

Black Mountain Trigonometry Point

Divis Transmitter Mast

The Barn and rnager office

Collin River Bridge

P

WC

Black Mountain

Glencolin Ward

Upper Springfield Ward

B38

B38

R. Collin

1. Follow the trail from the Divis Ranger Office towards the Divis transmitter masts. Bear right onto a section of wooden boardwalk, shortly before reaching the mast. The two masts relay TV, radio and digital signals covering Northern Ireland.

2. At the end of the boardwalk, turn right onto the gravel path leading towards the summit of Black Mountain, passing the Bobby Stone. The summit is marked by a trigonometry pillar. From here you can experience exhilarating views across the city and beyond.

3. Continue to follow the gravel path as it winds its way along the ridge towards Black Hill, crossing the first stile.

4. The path leaves the ridge before reaching Black Hill and continues to weave its way back towards the ranger office, crossing another stile and the Collin River along the way.

5. Turn left when you reach the access road to return to the start.

Make the Most of Your Day

Enjoy the many other walks and trails in the area and then afterwards be sure to visit the most famous pub in Belfast. The Crown Bar can be found on Great Victoria Street and is full of original Victorian features that have been carefully restored by the National Trust since it took over ownership in 1978.

Food and Facilities

The café barn at Divis and the Black Mountain is open from 10am until 5pm (weather permitting). There are toilets near the start of the walk.

92. Terrace Hill Trail at Minnowburn

A wander up Terrace Hill from the River Lagan takes you round Minnowburn pond, through beech woodland to a low-walled garden with a view over the Lagan valley to the hills beyond. As you walk along the river, look out for wetland birds, such as little grebes, moorhens and tufted ducks.

Minnowburn car park
Edenderry Road
Belfast
County Down
BT8 8LD
02890 647787
minnowburn@nationaltrust.org.uk

About this walk
Woodland
Wetland wildlife
Great views
Dogs welcome on leads

Distance Nearly 1 mile (1.4km)

Time 40 mins

N. Ireland

Things to see

Minnowburn Pond
The pond area was a rarely visited part of Minnowburn until a few years ago, when restoration began with dredging out the pond; there is now an accessible path around it together with a dipping platform. Keep an eye out and you might see ducks nesting in the reeds, frogs or a common newt feeding on the many insects that inhabit the pond.

Terrace Hill Garden
Constructed in the 1930s as the garden for Terrace Hill House, the garden is Art Deco-inspired but also shows influences of the Arts and Crafts style. Over the years it became increasingly shaded and overgrown until the Minnowburn staff started renewal work with the help of volunteers. Trees have been removed, paths added, planting done and now three sculptures are in place. Work continues to sympathetically restore the garden and it has become one of the most popular viewpoints in the Lagan Valley.

Above: A young visitor looks out at the River Lagan, Minnowburn, County Down.

Right: Rustic stone bridge over the river at Minnowburn.

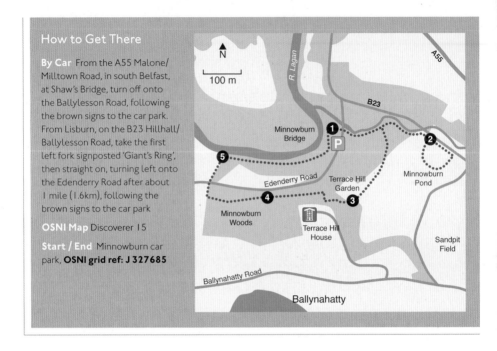

How to Get There

By Car From the A55 Malone/ Milltown Road, in south Belfast, at Shaw's Bridge, turn off onto the Ballylesson Road, following the brown signs to the car park. From Lisburn, on the B23 Hillhall/ Ballylesson Road, take the first left fork signposted 'Giant's Ring', then straight on, turning left onto the Edenderry Road after about 1 mile (1.6km), following the brown signs to the car park

OSNI Map Discoverer 15

Start / End Minnowburn car park, **OSNI grid ref: J 327685**

1. From the car park, follow the path from beside Minnowburn Bridge upstream, along the bank of the Minnowburn itself, with young broad-leaved woodland on your right.

2. After about 110 yards (100m), you'll come to a fork in the path with a wooden finger post. Take the left-hand fork to Minnowburn Pond and make your way around it, where you will see the first of a number of wooden sculptures.

3. Once you've completed the loop around the pond, go back to the fork in the path and take the left fork uphill. The path passes through younger woodland and climbs uphill to Terrace Hill Garden, with great views of the Lagan Valley along the way. Find more sculptures and enjoy the surroundings of the 1930s walled garden.

4. From the garden, take the steps from the west end of the garden up into the trees towards Terrace Hill House and follow the short path to Freddy's Steps. Descend the steps and halfway down, take the path to the left through the beech wood where you will find another sculpture.

5. At the end of the path, climb a couple of steps onto the Giant's Ring Path. Turn right and follow this path to the Edenderry Road. Cross the road and take the path opposite down to the Lagan River where you will find the last of the sculptures. At the river, turn right and follow the riverbank path with the carr (wet) woodland on your right, back to the car park.

Make the Most of Your Day

You can climb Terrace Hill and discover the garden built by linen merchant Ned Robinson and take in the views across the Lagan valley. On the other side is a short walk to the Giant's Ring, a huge Neolithic earth henge and tomb where you can imagine scenes of ancient gatherings and rituals. Look out for sculptures and natural art along the path.

Food and Facilities

Refreshments available from Piccolo Mondo coffee and pizza van in Minnowburn car park from Tuesday to Sunday. The nearest toilets to Minnowburn are at Malone House, across the River Lagan via Shaw's Bridge.

93. Murlough North Point Nature Trail

Murlough National Nature Reserve is a fragile, 6,000-year-old sand dune system cared for and managed by the National Trust since 1967, as Ireland's first nature reserve. It is an excellent area for walking and wildlife spotting due to its spectacular location at the edge of Dundrum Bay and the Mourne Mountains.

Murlough National Nature Reserve
Keel Point
Dundrum
County Down
BT33 0NQ
028 4375 1467
murlough@nationaltrust.org.uk

About this walk

Varied habitats

Wildlife interest

Take care on uneven ground and keep to pathways

Dogs should be kept on leads at all times

Distance 3 miles (4.8km)

Time 1 hour 15 mins

N. Ireland

Above: The Mourne Mountains rise in the distance from Murlough National Nature Reserve.

Below: Wooded cliffs, trees and deep blue sea.

Things to see

Woodland
The woodland at Murlough has a wealth of different wildlife. The main species of tree in the woodland behind Murlough House is sycamore. There are also a number of ash trees, plus an array of wildflowers and ferns. You can see many woodland birds here; keep an eye out for the sparrowhawks that are very common. As you leave the woodland, it's worth having a look at the beautiful old hazel stands.

Saltmarsh
When walking along the beach, look out for beautiful white bladder campion as well as sea beet and scurvy grass along the top of the shingle. Large beds of two fleshy saltmarsh annuals, golden samphire and sea-blite can also be spotted slightly lower on the beach.

Heathland
There are plenty of points where heathland can be seen on this walk; it looks its best during spring and summer months. The heathland at Murlough boasts not only ling and bell heather but also heath bedstraw, tormentil, eyebright, wild pansy and primrose. Look out for birds like ground-nesting meadow pipits, and kestrels hovering overhead as they hunt. See if you can spot the common lizard, which loves to bask in the summer sun, and butterflies such as the dark green fritillary and the rare marsh fritillary.

How to Get There

By Car Follow signs on A24, 2 miles (3.2km) south of Dundrum

OSNI Map Discoverer 29 Sheet 4

Start / End Keel Point, concrete standing, **OSNI grid ref: J 407351**

Murlough Farm

Boat House

Murlough House

Murlough National Nature Reserve

N

100 m

1. Follow the avenue from the concrete standing towards Murlough House. Turn right onto the boardwalk marked by the 'To Beach' sign.

2. As you follow the boardwalk path down the woodland area, be sure to stop at the gate, where you will be treated to your first glimpse of the sea.

3. Carry on until you reach the beach. Turn left and walk along the beach as far as the green marker post.

4. Turn left and take the path that climbs up steeply into marram grass and sea buckthorn and then into a sycamore wood. Turn right before reaching the garden of Murlough House.

5. Follow straight along the path into the area of woodland, ignore the turn to the left and continue on the path down the slope to emerge on the beach next to the boat house.

6. From the boat house, turn left and walk along the beach until you reach the green post. Take the path to the left, up the bank and back into the hazel path.

7. At the junction with the main track, turn right and follow the path along the edge (ignoring a turning to the left). Follow the path as it descends into high

gorse scrub and turns right onto the beach of the inner bay.

8. Turn left and walk along the beach until you reach a narrow set of steps up the bank. Go up these steps and follow the path back into the Reserve.

9. As you follow the path, you will come to a point where five paths meet. Take the first left and walk through open heathland and through a squeeze stile to join a main track.

10. Turn left and take the next path to the right. This path rises to one of the highest points in the area with great views in all directions. From this point, continue along the track downhill and to the right. When you reach the avenue turn left and follow the road.

11. Continue until you reach the starting point.

Make the Most of Your Day
As well as Murlough's nature, make time to explore the shingle beach and 4 mile (6.4km) strand with features that have been shaped over the last 12,000 years, and enjoy a day on the beach.

Food and Facilities
Amenities can be found in Dundrum.

94. Mount Stewart Red Squirrel Trail

Portaferry Road
Newtownards
County Down
BT22 2AD
028 4278 8387
mountstewart@
nationaltrust.org.uk

About this walk

Red squirrels

Lakeside views

Mixed woodland

Dogs welcome on leads

Distance 1 mile (1.6km)

Time 1 hour 30 mins

N. Ireland

Treat yourself to a gentle stroll around this beautiful lake and World Heritage Site-nominated gardens. Red squirrels are among the most well-loved mammals in the UK, and Mount Stewart is one of the best places in Northern Ireland to spot them.

Things to see

Red Squirrels
The habitat of mixed broad-leaf and conifer plantations at Mount Stewart is ideal for red squirrels. They live mostly in trees, but can sometimes be seen on the ground. They are not always red; they vary in colour and can be brown, greyish or nearly black. While we can't guarantee a sighting, you're most likely to encounter them early in the morning or late afternoon, in the Red Squirrel Hide, behind the house and to the north of the lake.

The Lake
This expansive, 4 acre (1.6ha) lake was created in the 1840s by Charles, 3rd Marquess, and later landscaped in the 1920s by Lady Londonderry, wife to the 7th Marquess. Take a closer look at the small trees and shrubs by the lakeside and you will see that they are teeming with beautiful green lichens.

Above: View of Tir N'an Òg, the family's burial ground, between the trees across the lake at Mount Stewart.

Right: The lake in autumn at Mount Stewart, County Down.

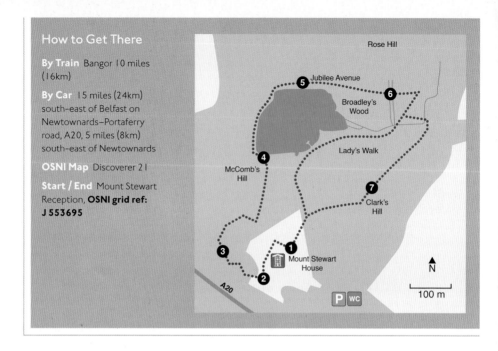

How to Get There

By Train Bangor 10 miles (16km)

By Car 15 miles (24km) south-east of Belfast on Newtownards–Portaferry road, A20, 5 miles (8km) south-east of Newtownards

OSNI Map Discoverer 21

Start / End Mount Stewart Reception, **OSNI grid ref: J 553695**

Rose Hill

Jubilee Avenue

Broadley's Wood

Lady's Walk

McComb's Hill

Clark's Hill

Mount Stewart House

N

100 m

1. Start at Mount Stewart Reception and make your way to the front of the house via the courtyard.

2. Head through the gate into the formal gardens, pass the Sunk Garden and use the stone steps to make your way down into the Italian Garden. Lady Londonderry was known as Circe, the sorceress from Greek mythology who turned some of Odysseus' crew into pigs. Their faces and Circe are depicted on the southern wall of the Italian Garden. Walk straight ahead towards the black and gold metal gate which brings you into the Lily Wood.

3. Make your way through the Lily Wood until you reach the path, then follow this towards the lake. Lord Londonderry enjoyed pigeon shooting in this wood, while Lady Londonderry indulged her passion for lilies here and planted them in large drifts along the woodland margins.

4. Follow the path around the lake.

5. Make your way towards Tir N'an Òg, the family's burial ground and the resting place of Lord and Lady Londonderry, high up on the hill.

6. Continue around the path until you reach Broadley's Wood.

7. Continue on the path around the lake towards Mount Stewart house or take an alternative route through Rhododendron Hill. Finish your walk by returning to the front of Mount Stewart house.

Make the Most of Your Day

Mount Stewart reopened in 2015 after a three-year restoration project. The National Trust has brought back the elegance and charm of the house when it was home of the 7th Marchioness – Edith, Lady Londonderry – and her family in the early twentieth century. There are events held throughout the year, including guided garden walks, wildlife hunts and music concerts.

Food and Facilities

There is a tea-room at Mount Stewart and a kiosk in the courtyard. Toilets are available in the Mount Stewart reception area.

95. Nugent's Wood Walk

Portaferry
County Down
BT22 1NZ
028 4278 7769
strangford@nationaltrust.
org.uk

About this walk
Wildflower displays
Breathtaking views
Wildlife interest
Dogs welcome

Distance 1½ miles (2.4km)

Time 1 hour

Amble through mixed woodland with a wealth of flora and wildlife at Nugent's Wood on Ards Peninsula South in County Down. Here you can spot red squirrels and see beautiful woodland flowers, especially in the spring.

N. Ireland

Things to see

Incredible Views
Look down onto beautiful vistas of Strangford Lough and The Narrows. Castle Ward and Audley's Castle can also be seen on the other side of the Lough.

Red Squirrels
Red squirrels are a regular sight around the Ards Peninsula, especially in areas where there is woodland, such as Nugent's Wood.

Above and right: Nugent's Wood, Nugent's Foreshore, County Down.

How to Get There

By Car A public car park is situated beside the Exploris Aquarium. From here, walk towards the seafront and turn right. The entrance to Nugent's Wood is behind the stone wall at the end of the row of houses

OSNI Map Discoverer 21

Start / End The gate behind the stone wall at the end of the row of houses, **OSNI grid ref: J 592509**

1. Start your walk at the gate found behind the stone wall at the end of the row of houses.

2. Walk along the grass path, enjoying the views across the lough to Castle Ward Bay, until you find the squirrel sculpture.

3. Continue along the path, passing a traditional wrought iron gate (restored by our rangers and volunteers), until you come to a set of steps on your right.

4. Take the steps up into the woodland.

5. Follow the path under oak and beech trees, keeping an eye out for some great bracket fungus growing on the trees.

6. Follow the path round continuing down the steps to a bench where you can catch your breath and enjoy the tranquil sounds of woodland birds and the water at the shore.

7. Continue along, rejoin the original path and follow back to the start point.

Make the Most of Your Day

There is much to see on Ards Peninsula South, including Kearney village and coastal path on the Outer Ards, 3 miles (4.8km) east of Portaferry. The village and coastal path has been in National Trust care since 1965. Here you can see Silurian rocks that date from 400–430 million years ago, as well as rare plants growing on the shingle. Ballyquintin Farm is about 3 miles (4.8km) to the south-east of Portaferry. This 116 acre (47ha) farm at the southern tip of the Ards Peninsula is managed using traditional mixed farming methods and was purchased by the Trust in 2000. The site also provides a valuable habitat for increasingly rare farmland wildlife. There is also Ballyhenry Island 1¼ miles (2 km) north of Portaferry. The island can be reached on foot at low tide, although there are no formal paths. As well as a rich haven for marine wildlife, here you can also see the wreck of the *Empire Tana*, a cargo liner used in the Second World War Normandy landings. The ship's remains are visible to the south of the island.

Food and Facilities

There are several popular cafés, restaurants and pubs in Portaferry. There are public toilets in the car park.

96. Castle Ward Loughside Walk

Overlooking the south shores of Strangford Lough, Castle Ward is one of Northern Ireland's finest country estates. This walk explores the waterside, a ruined castle, woodland, an ornamental lake and follies. Depending on the time of year, you may see a fantastic range of migrating birds and resident seals, or stunning wildflower meadows.

Castle Ward
Strangford
Downpatrick
County Down
BT30 7LS
028 4488 1204
castleward@nationaltrust.org.uk

About this walk
Sweeping views
Wildlife interest
Some short steep sections
Dogs welcome on leads
Distance 2½ miles (4km)
Time 50 mins

N. Ireland

Things to see

Birdlife
Around 75,000 wildfowl and waders spend the autumn and winter at Strangford Lough, including 75 per cent of the world's light-bellied Brent goose. The Ards Peninsula side of the lough is the best place to spot them. Winter is also an excellent time to watch wading birds such as oystercatcher, dunlin, curlew and knot in Castle Ward Bay. Some species perform spectacular aerial displays in the evening as they prepare to roost.

Audley's Castle and Castle Ward
Now a picturesque ruin, Audley's Castle was the home of the Audley family from the 1550s. Nearby is the site of the town that was cleared by the Wards in the Georgian era to improve the views within their new landscape park.

Viscount Bangor spent a lot of money in the eighteenth century on perfecting his country seat at Castle Ward. His family, the Wards, had lived here for several hundred years, but in order to keep up with the latest aristocratic fashions, he built a large mansion with sweeping views down to Strangford Lough.

Strangford Lough
The United Kingdom's largest sea inlet, covering 58 sq. miles (150 sq. km), Strangford Lough has more than 350 islands. Underwater reefs and kelp forests provide a habitat for 2,000 marine species like anemones, sea-squirts, starfish, sponges and urchins. Mussel beds are also an important habitat here, but in recent years trawling has done real damage to them.

Above: View down Strangford Lough from Castle Ward Bay.

Below: Flock of Brent geese flying over Strangford Lough, County Down.

How to Get There

By Car 7 miles (11.3km) north-east of Downpatrick, 1½ miles (2.4km) west of Strangford Lough, entrance by Ballyculter Lodge

OSNI Map Discoverer 21

Start / End Old Castle Ward farmyard, **OSNI grid ref: J 573498**

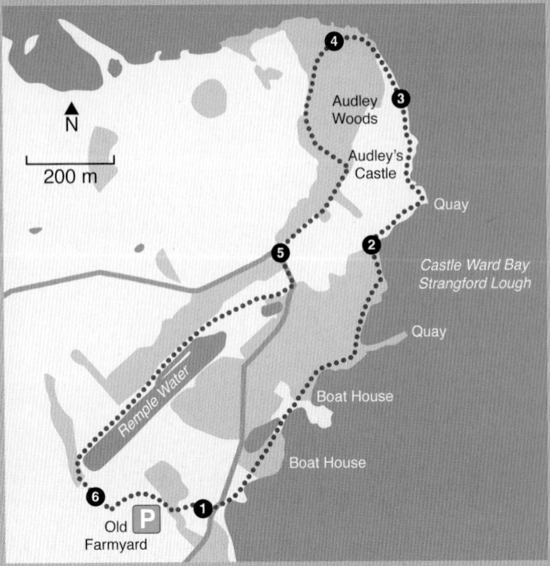

1. Start at the old farmyard. Note the tower house, a fortified home built in 1610. It was the Castle Ward estate's main residence before the mansion was built. Follow the blue trail down towards the water and boathouse through a large stone gateway. The name Strangford comes from the Old Norse for 'strong fjord' and probably describes the powerful currents where the Irish Sea enters the Lough.

2. The path leads along the water front, passing boat houses and small quays, before reaching Audley's Wood. Enjoy beautiful views across to Portaferry. You may see seals bobbing about in the water and, in autumn and winter, birds such as redshank and oystercatchers.

3. At the edge of the wood, a path on the left takes you on a short detour, up the sixteenth-century Audley's Castle. Climb to the top for a great panorama across the estate and Castle Ward Bay. Look out for pine marten and a long-eared owl that are sometimes seen here at dusk. Close to the castle is a Neolithic cairn where around 30 skeletons were found.

4. Continue walking along the loughside, then turn left away from the water and through Audley's Wood, home to badgers and lots of small birds.

5. When the gravel path exits the woodland, cross the road and enter through the gate in the stone wall ahead. Emerge through this gate into the parkland surrounding Temple Water.

6. Follow the path away from the lake along a tree-lined avenue back to the farmyard. A series of paths lead to the mansion house, woodland and playgrounds.

Make the Most of Your Day
Between March and November you can visit the house to see the Victorian laundry, dairy and corn mill. Although the mansion itself is closed during the winter, you can still take a stroll and enjoy the seasonally spectacular gardens – the Victorian Garden, the Sunken Garden and Temple Water. The farmyard at Castle Ward and the shore of Strangford Lough were used as locations for the epic TV series *Game of Thrones*.

Food and Facilities
There is a tea-room and toilets at Castle Ward.

Opposite: Castle Campbell in Dollar, Clackmannanshire (walk 99).

Scotland

97. Staffa Puffin Trail

One of Scotland's many gems, Staffa is a beautiful, uninhabited island, home to hundreds of seabirds and set within waters teeming with marine life. The island is best known for its magnificent basalt columns, especially at An Uamh Binn (Musical Cave) – more commonly known Fingal's Cave, which has enthralled and inspired travellers for hundreds of years.

Mull and Iona Ranger Service
Tigh na Rois
Millbrae Cottage
Bunessan
Isle of Mull
PA67 6DG
01681 700659
staffanationalnature
reserve@nts.org.uk

About this walk

Wildlife and geological interest

The jetty and the route to the cave are narrow and slippery. Take care near cliff edges; sturdy footwear essential

Dogs welcome on leads

Distance 1 ½ miles (2.4km)

Time Fingal's Cave 10 mins; puffin colony 20 mins; the whole island approx. 45 mins

Things to see

Wildlife
Approaching Staffa during the summer months, you will notice a variety of birds flying to and from the island. Staffa is the nesting place for a whole range of species, including fulmars, shags, puffins and gulls. The path to the north of the island is perhaps the best route to follow to see puffins (April–early August). The sea acts as a food store and below the surface there is a rich diversity of sea creatures besides fish. These include jellyfish, crustaceans, algae and a variety of marine mammals.

Geology
Staffa's amazing basalt columns formed from molten lava. As the liquid rock cooled, it hardened, shrank and fractured into a regular series of stone pillars. Because they cooled at slightly different rates, the columns vary in size and number of sides.

Above: Visitors at Fingal's Cave.

Left: The stunning coastline of Staffa.

How to Get There

By Car Staffa is 7 miles
(11.3km) west of Mull and
6 miles (9.7km) north-east
of Iona. Access to Staffa via
boat from Oban, Mull and
Iona; landing is dependent on
suitable weather conditions

OS Map Landranger 48

Start / End The jetty at
Staffa, **OS grid ref:**
NM 325355

Puffin
colony

❸

Goat Cave

Staffa

Clamshell Cave

❶ Jetty

Meall nan
Gamhna

McKinnon's cave

❷

N

Boat Cave Fingal's Cave

100 m

1. On reaching the jetty at Staffa, walk up the
short flight of stone steps. Most visitors to Staffa,
using one of the local tour boats, will have one
hour ashore.

2. To reach Fingal's Cave, turn left from the jetty and
make your way carefully along the rock surface below
the cliffs, using the handrail as required. There is a
non-slip surface painted on to some of the rocks,
which acts as a guide.

3. To reach the puffin colony, make your way directly
up from the jetty using the ladders to access the
top of the island, and then turn right, walking the
path parallel to the cliff-tops, which then takes you
down through a gully using some newly installed
stone steps, and back up the other side. Continue
walking for another 10 minutes to reach a semi-
circular bay below a small green hill, where you will
see burrows amongst the grass around the edge of
the cliffs. Sit patiently and the puffins will come to
you! The presence of humans helps scare away the
larger predatory birds, such as great skua, which might
attack the puffins.

Make the Most of Your Day
Boat tours to Staffa operate throughout the year. If
you're lucky, you might spot common and bottlenose
dolphins, basking sharks and minke whales. Guided
walks are also available throughout the summer.

Food and Facilities
There are no visitor facilities on the island – please
bring any food and drink with you, and take your litter
home again.

98. Pass of Killiecrankie

The Pass of Killiecrankie is one of the many special places the National Trust for Scotland looks after. The magnificent wooded gorge is bursting with wildlife, from red squirrels and woodpeckers in the trees, to white wood anemones on the forest floor, and leaping salmon in the river to insects buzzing among the grassland flowers. This walk showcases the very best of the heart of Scotland.

Killiecrankie
Pitlochry
Perthshire
PH16 5LG
01796 473233
killiecrankie@nts.org.uk

About this walk
Spectacular river views

Ancient woodland

Wildlife interest

Paths are generally straightforward but there are steps and steep sections at the Soldier's Leap

Dogs welcome

Distance 3 miles (4.8km)

Time 2 hours

Above: The glorious sight of Killiecrankie in autumn.

Below: Reflections in the waters of the River Garry.

Things to see

Soldier's Leap
Following the Battle of Killiecrankie between government and Jacobite troops in 1689, one government soldier – Donald McBane – made a spectacular escape. Pursued by the enemy, McBane climbed down onto the rocky riverbank and made an 18ft (5.5m) leap across the fast-flowing River Garry.

The Balfour Stone
Amongst those killed fleeing the battlefield was Brigadier Barthold Balfour of the Dutch Brigade, who commanded the left wing of the government's army. The stone, approximately two-thirds of the way down the Pass, is reputed to mark the spot where he died.

How to Get There

By Car Killiecrankie is 3 miles (4.8km) north of Pitlochry off the B8079; heading north on A9, leave at the next junction after Pitlochry; heading south on A9, leave at the junction after Blair Atholl

OS Map Landranger 52

Start / End Killiecrankie Visitor Centre, **OS grid ref: NN 917626**

1. From outside the Visitor Centre, look for the sign on the covered wooden walkway pointing the way to Soldier's Leap and woodland walks. At the end of the wooden walkway take the steps heading downhill towards the Pass of Killiecrankie. Follow the main path downhill, cross a bridge, then climb up a small number of steps, turn left and soon afterwards arrive at a viewpoint.

2. After admiring the view of the Pass of Killiecrankie, head downhill to reach a junction and turn left following the sign to Soldier's Leap. After descending some more steps, turn right to see the spot where the Redcoat soldier, fleeing after the Battle of Killiecrankie, is said to have leapt across the River Garry.

3. Leave Soldier's Leap by the way you arrived to rejoin the main footpath. Turn right downhill to reach a wooden bridge across a small burn at Trooper's Den. This is where the very first shot of all of the Jacobite uprisings was fired, and a trooper killed.

4. The footpath now runs above the River Garry through semi-ancient woodland, heading down along the Pass. After a while you will see a charcoal kiln on the right-hand side in the woods; learn all about charcoal making here.

5. Soon after passing the charcoal kiln you will reach the Balfour Stone. This marks the spot where Brigadier Barthold Balfour was killed. The footpath continues to a crossroads with a large bridge to the right.

6. The green footbridge is a prominent landmark in the Pass, and one of only two places to cross the river with dry feet. The setting is magnificent, be sure to look back up the Pass to see if you can see Carn Liath, one of the Beinn a'Ghlo Munro summits.

7. If you would like to continue to the Linn of Tummel, cross the green footbridge, turn left, and left again soon afterwards. However, if you are feeling weary or are short of time, retrace your steps back to the Visitor Centre.

8. As you walk underneath the Garry Bridge you will see the Highland Fling bungee jump. If you are lucky there may be someone jumping – it's 67½ft (42m) high! Keep going here with the River Garry on your left and a large field to your right. After climbing up a flight of metal steps, the path continues through the trees towards the River Tummel.

9. Look out for the sign for Falls of Tummel. It is down the hill and over a wooden bridge. The falls are a beautiful sight and make a wonderful place to relax before making the return journey back to the Visitor Centre.

Make the Most of Your Day
Pop into the Visitor Centre (open 10am–4pm, April–early November) where you can learn more about the fascinating geology, wildlife and history of the area. Look out for an impressive array of fungi – over 400 species have been identified. During periods of rain, enjoy the amazing sight of leaping salmon at the falls beneath the famous Soldier's Leap as well as at the Falls of Tummel.

Food and Facilities
Drinks and snacks are available at the Visitor Centre, where you will also find toilets and a picnic area.

Scotland

Left: The autumn trees in the Pass at Killiecrankie are a mesmerising blend of colours.

99. Dollar Glen and Castle Campbell Gorges Walk

Set above the picturesque town of Dollar, this circular trail leads you past waterfalls, along steep gorge edges and what has been called 'one of the most enigmatic approaches to any castle in Scotland'. Discover the layers of peace, beauty and rare ancient woodland plants that surround Castle Campbell (owned by the National Trust for Scotland and managed by Historic Environment Scotland).

Castle Road
Dollar
Clackmannanshire
FK14 7PP
0141 616 5126
www.nts.org.uk/Visit/
Dollar-Glen

About this walk
Gorge views

Ancient woodland

Much of the route has uneven surfaces, sometimes slippery open paths and some steep drops.

Wear sensible footwear and keep to the long-established path routes

Dogs welcome on leads or under close control

Distance 4 miles (6.4km)

Time 2–2 hours 30 mins

Things to see

Rocks and Rifts
The landscape has laid the base for everything else in the Glen – the natural and cultural heritage has arisen from, and been formed by, the rocks. The original high layers were hard volcanic rocks, contrasting with the sedimentary rocks in the valley below. However, as the layers folded in and a small fault line formed the Ochils, these layers became twisted around and over one another.

Above: A birds-eye view of Castle Campbell.

Woodland Wildlife
Designated a Site of Special Scientific Interest, Dollar Glen is home to over 100 species of moss and over 190 species of lichen, including some rarities not commonly found elsewhere in Scotland. The Glen is also notable for its other plants and ferns. All these species are woodland in nature, with the glen dominated by oak and ash trees. These natural shelters and food factories contain a rich array of birds and animals, including red squirrel, brown long-eared bats, ravens, nuthatch and both the green and great spotted woodpeckers.

The Stronghold
Impressively positioned above the steep gorges of the Burns of Sorrow and Care sits Castle Campbell – the chief lowland stronghold of the Earls of Argyll from the fifteenth century. It was originally called Castle Gloom or Gloume – probably after the Scots Gaelic 'glòim', meaning chasm.

How to Get There

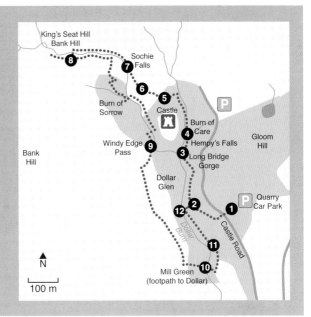

By Train Stirling 12½ miles (20.1 km) and then number 23 bus from nearby Stirling Bus Station

By Car Dollar is 14 miles (22.5km) north-east of Stirling and 42 miles (67.6km) north-west of Edinburgh (over the Clackmannanshire Bridge). We regret that, for public safety, there are no longer parking facilities at the Castle, and vehicle access is prohibited beyond the top car park

OS Map Landranger 58

Start / End Quarry car park, Dollar, **OS grid ref: NS 963989**

N
100 m

King's Seat Hill
Bank Hill
Sochie Falls
Burn of Sorrow
Castle
Burn of Care
Gloom Hill
Windy Edge Pass
Bank Hill
Hempy's Falls
Long Bridge Gorge
Dollar Glen
Quarry Car Park
Dollar Burn
Castle Road
Mill Green (footpath to Dollar)

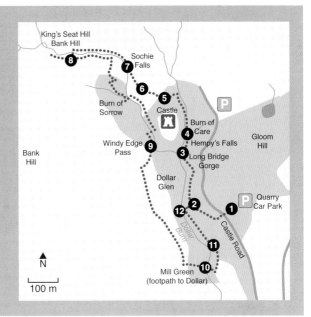

Scotland

1. On leaving the car park, carefully cross the road and go through the ornate drystone dyke, and past the first of the large ash trees. Follow the wending path to steps and downhill slopes leading you further into the wooded Glen. Enjoy the feeling of leaving the world behind you, as you stroll through mighty oaks and amongst woodland flowers.

2. At the very bottom of the sets of steps, you come to a path junction. Take the right-hand uphill trail (the East Path) and work your way carefully up, until you are looking deep down into the gorge. Here you will see the first effects of water on different rocks, constantly falling to the river below.

3. At the end of the first metal and wood stepped bridge, you'll gain views of your first waterfall. Here you should briefly turn left past the steps to a square viewpoint, which looks south down the river and west through the highest gorge walls to where there used to be a long bridge. Continue back uphill towards the waterfall and the next metal and wood stepped bridge. Enjoy the sound of the trickling water and tumbling falls as you follow the route along the Burn of Sorrow.

4. As you reach the pile of large round logs (left as food for fungi and small creatures) you will start to gain more and more views of Dollar Castle as you approach steps to it. It is around here that, in spring and early summer, you will smell wild garlic (also known as ransoms), and see Clackmannanshire's official flower, the small green-and-yellow, opposite-leaved golden saxifrage.

5. Having stormed the steps and admired the pond at the top, do take the Castle Trail to enjoy powerful history and excellent views. This will take a minimum of 40 minutes to see but well over an hour to saviour and enjoy – but it is worth it!

6. After your visit, walk down the hill onto the castle road (a good area to admire the common orchids) and turn left onto the upper path with a bench just over the bridge. This part winds and wends its way up to the great falls of Sochie on the Burn of Care, and lets you explore the faerie-like paths to the open hill. Take your time; stop and stare.

7. At the top bridge overlooking the cauldron-like pools, take the right-hand path to quickly pass through a gate. This leads onto the open hill, but by taking the steps that follow the left-hand side fence line you will quickly come to the top kissing gate leading to a bench with the most spectacular views over the castle, across to the Pentlands and the Forth Valley. Here's a good place to enjoy your elevenses, picnic, or afternoon tea!

8. Continue down the grass path towards the castle direction. At the bottom of this small hillock, join the path going to the right and wind down a wet woodland area to two bridges below the Falls – you can be amazed how high the path to the falls has taken you. The second bridge rises up slightly below the castle. Here you can follow the path back up to the East Path and the castle, but we recommend continuing to follow the burn and cross two more bridges. This leads onto the West Path.

9. Follow the path – there will soon be a gate which leads down to the Coleman Viewpoint and views from the other side of the Long Bridge Gorge. Here, you can even see the footings of the original Victorian bridge. Go back up to the main path and continue past two small benches and leave the castle behind you. Continue walking down this path, and see who finds the coin stump first!

10. Cross the bridge, over the Dollar Burn, and turn left up past the Dollar Glen information board, heading upwards – if you turn right into the recreation area, that leads you into Dollar town. At this point you will see a mauve flush of bluebells.

11. As you approach the next long wooden bridge, you will see remains of the mill lade system where water was directed and filtered for use in the milling process (Dollar Museum was one of the mills). Near here is also where you may become aware of the pale-to-white, multi-headed toothwort – it has no sun-capturing green pigment (chlorophyll) so feeds off the roots of trees, such as the hazel. Please do not pick it as it has only a short few weeks before it disappears again.

12. You capture one last view of a waterfall at the concrete horseshoe-shaped viewpoint, before meeting up with the path that you came up from Quarry car park. Go back up, claiming the prize of a good day out and stretched legs!

Make the Most of Your Day

Dating from the fifteenth century, Castle Campbell was primarily built for the Campbells to show off to the Scottish royalty at nearby Stirling. It commands great views down the Glen and over the Forth Valley, Forth Bridges and the Pentland Hills. It's a small castle packed with Scottish history – have a look out for the stone where a bored guard must have spent time sharpening his sword. National Trust for Scotland and Historic Environment Scotland members get free entry (bring your card).

Food and Facilities

There are several cafés and food sources in the pretty town of Dollar. To really enjoy the ambience of the Glen and Castle, why not bring a packed lunch and take your time exploring the area. You can then treat yourself with some well-deserved tea and cake in the town after your rambles!

Left: Lush greens of Dollar Glen looking towards Castle Campbell.

100. Alton Brae Trail at Castle Fraser

This trail takes you past a broad walk of sycamores, through coniferous woodland and beside the Flight Pond; each habitat provides the opportunity to spot a range of wildlife. There are spectacular panoramic views from the top of the round tower, revealing the courtyard, gardens and estate beyond, with the distinctive peaks of the Bennachie hills visible in the distance.

Castle Fraser
Sauchen
Inverurie
AB51 7LD
01330 833463
castlefraser@nts.org.uk

About this walk
Imposing and atmospheric castle

Woodland and freshwater wildlife

The path is unsurfaced with some slopes

Dogs welcome; please keep on leads in the courtyard and near the play area

Distance 1½ miles (2.4km)

Time 1 hour

Scotland

Things to see

Flight Pond
The Flight Pond was created in the nineteenth century in an area of low-lying bog to attract wildfowl for shooting. You can still see the remains of some shooting butts, but the area is now a peaceful haven for wildlife. Ponds are a valuable habitat for many creatures, providing a place for frogs and newts to breed, birds to drink and insect larvae to grow. Swallows, swifts and martins hunt the insects flying over the water, and in the evenings Daubenton's bats skim the surface for flies and

midges. They are able to eat up to 3,000 insects a night!

Woodland Birdlife
The woodland at Castle Fraser mainly comprises coniferous species that are home to a variety

of birds, including treecreepers, long-tailed tits and coal tits. Treecreepers move in short hops up tree trunks hunting for insects. Once they reach the top, they fly to the base of another tree and start climbing again.

Above and right: Castle Fraser in the winter – a magical place for a walk.

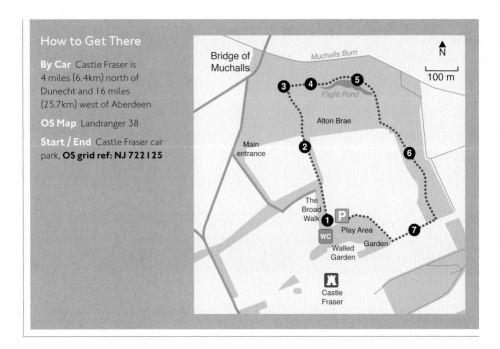

How to Get There

By Car Castle Fraser is 4 miles (6.4km) north of Dunecht and 16 miles (25.7km) west of Aberdeen

OS Map Landranger 38

Start / End Castle Fraser car park, **OS grid ref: NJ 722125**

1. Follow the Broad Walk of sycamores out of the car park on the route signposted for the Alton Brae Trail. The oldest trees here were planted over 200 years ago and connected the Castle with the old Aberdeen to Kemnay road.

2. The trail takes you downhill into coniferous woodland that is home to a variety of birds.

3. When the trail reaches a junction with a track, look into the woodland on your left. The long linear ridges you see are the remains of medieval cultivation rigs; cereal crops were grown on top of the rigs. Follow the trail around to the right and continue along past the Flight Pond.

4. The pond is now considered a Site of Special Scientific Interest because of the rare damselflies and dragonflies. Late summer is the best time to see them at their height.

5. You will also see a second pond that was created in 2015, providing a habitat for amphibians, birds and insects. After you pass the end of the ponds, follow the path uphill, and when you reach a junction with a track, turn left and continue with the trail.

6. In the late 1700s this part of the estate was divided into 'parks' for grazing the Laird's cattle, fattening them up for market. They had evocative names such as Whin Park and Clinking-style Park. When you emerge from the trees follow the path around to the right.

7. At the end of the eighteenth century, along this section of the trail, the field to your right was enclosed with stone dykes. The path then bears around to the right, past the Woodland Garden and Woodland Secrets Play Area and back to the car park.

Make the Most of Your Day
Even when the castle is closed you can admire the traditional Walled Garden with its specimen trees, herbaceous borders, medicinal border and organically grown fruit and vegetables, and explore the adventure playground.

Food and Facilities
The tea-room is not open during the winter months, but there are toilets next to the walled garden.

Index

Previous page: Puffin on the Farne Islands, Northumberland.

Picture Credits

Acknowledgements

The Publishers and the National Trust would like to thank the following:

All the National Trust rangers, volunteers and many other members of staff who kindly checked the routes and information for the properties featured in this book.

The National Trust for Scotland for their help in contributing walks and images for this book; in particular Doline Kilgour, Marcin Klimek, Callum McNeill-Ritchie, Eilidh Nicolson, Emma O'Shea and Emily Wilkins.

Project editor: Katie Hewett
Designer: Sally Bond/James Boast
Map illustrator: Mike Parsons, Barking Dog Art
Proofreader: Sarah Epton